D0988648

Yorkville
TWINS

Yorkville
TWINS

Hilarious Adventures Growing Up In New York City, 1944–1962

John F. Gindele & Joseph G. Gindele

Golden Valley Publishing, LLC
Golden Valley, Minnesota

Published by: YorkvilleTwinsBook.com
An imprint of Golden Valley Publishing, LLC
8014 Olson Memorial Highway, #243
Golden Valley, MN 55427

Email: info@YorkvilleTwinsBook.com
Website: www.YorkvilleTwinsBook.com

Order *Yorkville Twins* for gifts or your fund-raising and book club activities. Book club discussion questions are listed on our website. *Huge quantity discounts are available. Books make perfect gifts.*

Cover Photo: Twins at Carl Schurz Park (circa 1953)
Back Cover Authors' Photo: Lily French (2011)
86th Street Subway Signage: Roberto C. Tobar (adapted)
Editor: Nancy Ashmore, *Ashmore Ink*
Book Design: Dorie McClelland, *Spring Book Design*
Cover Design: Amy Kirkpatrick, *Kirkpatrick Design*

Library of Congress Control Number: 2012930698

ISBN: Hardcover, 978-0-9839337-7-9
Softcover, 978-0-9839337-5-5
E-book, 978-0-9839337-9-3

Memoir
This book is printed on acid-free paper.

Printed in the United States of America
10 9 8 7 6 5 4 3 2 1
First Edition

In memory of our parents
"Bez práce nejsou koláce." [1]

Parents are always our first and
most important teachers. It is with
great gratitude that we thank Mom
and Dad for their sacrifices and
all they have done for us and our
three siblings, especially in raising us as they did and establish-
ing that all-important foundation
that helped us achieve in later life.
Gratitude goes out to our family,
other relatives, and friends who
helped reinforce and strengthen
our value system.

Mary and Otto Gindele, Czech woods, circa 1972

This work is also dedicated to
all good, hard-working immigrant
families who desire to assimilate
into American society, who have
similar dreams and aspirations
for themselves and their children,
searching and struggling for a better life in a new land. They too
suffer and sacrifice to achieve their goals.

We also dedicate this memoir to the devoted teachers who labor
tirelessly each day to educate our children, many times teaching
under difficult conditions. They have provided us with a strong
formal education that helped us get to where we are today.

Lastly, we dedicate this publication to members of our special
"society"—twins and multiples. These folks have a distinct, personal
bond, because to understand what it is to be a twin or multiple, you
first need to be one.

---

1. "Without work there are no 'kolaches' (no rewards)." [Note: All non-English
words and phrases are defined in the glossary at the end of the book.]

Contents

List of Figures

Foreword

Anthony C. Lofaso,[2]

author of *Origins and History of the Village of Yorkville
in the City of New York* (Xlibris, 2010)

In this story, Joe and John Gindele shine a light on two threads in the fabric of New York City in the 1940s and 1950s, specifically that part of the fabric which covered Yorkville, a neighborhood on the east side of Manhattan just north of midtown.

Yorkville was, at best, an area of working class people. The people worked in jobs that kept the city running. There were no executives. No bosses, except perhaps for a few foremen who worked in some blue-collar industry and had not moved away because of the easy traveling to and from their jobs.

Most people lived in a four- or five-story, walk-up tenement building. Often their apartments had no toilet. Families would share a common toilet in the hallway. There were no showers. The only bathtub in many cases was a washtub located in the kitchen, a tub so small the best a full-grown person could do was sit on the edge and put his or her feet in the water.

The rooms were railroad style. That meant they were lined up one after the other like a train. There was little or no privacy. One could see any part of the apartment from any part of the apartment. When you stood in the living room by the window—which faced the street

---

2. Lofaso hosts the "A.C. Lowe Show," broadcasted worldwide (live from New York City) over the Centanni Broadcasting Network (www.centannibroadcasting.com).

or the back yard, depending on whether you lived in the front or the back—you could look straight through the apartment to the kitchen at the other end. It was a distance of perhaps 40 feet. You could see everyone in the apartment and they could see you.

If the building was built before 1879 the rooms between the kitchen and the front room had no windows.[3] In buildings built after 1879 when the "New Tenement Law" took effect, the middle rooms had windows facing an air shaft.

The time Joe and John Gindele reminisce about is post-war America in a large city. It was a time when news reports, politicians, and leaders were believable in the public's mind. It was a time when teachers, priests, and the police were never challenged. It was a time before TV. Some people had telephones. Most didn't. Radio programs which sparked the imagination of children and adults alike were the daily fare.

America was in a post-war leadership role. We as a people believed we had saved the world and no one could beat us. Radio shows like *Jack Armstrong, Dick Tracy, Gangbusters,* and *Superman* reinforced those ideals every day. Soap operas, programs that described the daily yearnings and dreams of ordinary people, played all day long until almost suppertime. Then the game shows would come on: *Queen for a Day, Beat the Clock,* with Bud Collier, who also played *Superman* on the radio, and the *Heart Line,* where someone would come on and tell their tale of misery and woe.

Children played in the streets. They invented a multitude of games, which kept everyone busy and happy. Kids couldn't wait to "go down." The term meant you were leaving the apartment for the street. After school, on the way home with your friend, you would say, "Are you coming down later?" If they said yes, you ran home, did your homework and all of your chores as quickly as you could, so that you could "go down" too.

---

3. Lofaso's building was built in 1876. They had four rooms: a kitchen facing the back yard, two middle rooms with no windows, and a front room facing the street.

When you got downstairs an entire world opened up to you filled with possibilities, unimaginable anywhere else in the world: parks, playgrounds, museums, elevated trains, candy stores, Broadway, Times Square, and more important and fascinating than all of that, the street itself.

This is where the story of the Gindele family in Yorkville comes into play. Joe and John make vivid the characters, personalities, and ordinary pursuits of the common people of Yorkville. Their perspective is all the more unique because they are not just brothers, they are twin brothers.

Only a few blocks away from Joe and John, on the other side of Third Avenue, lived the richest people in the world. But Joe and John's world and the world of the people who shared it with them ranged from poor to working class at best. Yet the joy and happiness in their recollections is apparent in every story, indeed in every character they describe and in almost every word.

Games such as ring-a-levio, hide and seek, kick the can, box ball, hit the stick, king-queen, and the monster of them all, stickball, were just a small sample of the possibilities available when you went "down." Joe and John experienced those games almost every day. Stickball was one of the things the police had to deal with when it came to kids like Joe and John, who were representative of most of the kids in Yorkville. The police would take your best "cat stick" and break it in two. Or they would put it in a hole in the manhole cover and drop it, never to be seen again.

In the summer the apartments were all but unbearable because of the heat. Joe and John would run downstairs to the street where it was just a little better. Some of the older kids would turn on a city fire hydrant; it would run for hours shooting out thousands of gallons of water each hour and creating a cool breeze. Or rather, it would run until the police came and shut it off. Some kids went in the water with their swimsuits. Some kids went in with all of their clothes on. Some kids (and grownups too) went in whether they liked it or not. The things the average kid did then were minor and insignificant compared to what the police deal with today.

For someone like me who grew up in Yorkville just a couple of years before Joe and John and experienced the same things and the same kinds of characters each and every day, their book is exhilarating. Nostalgia and recollection are inspired with each story.

Joe and John's stories evoked some of my own memories, such as the summer when my friend Mike and I went to the Museum of Natural History every day for a week, for free! After going through the museum all day, we would go to the Hayden Planetarium, where we would see the sky show for a quarter.

We never realized people were flying or traveling by sea thousands of miles to come and do, just one time, what we did whenever we felt like it.

When Joe and John describe the trip to Cushman's Bakery in Long Island City, I can close my eyes and smell the free jelly donuts. When they talk about swimming in John Jay Pool, I can taste the chlorinated water in my mouth. And when they talk about the Guggenheim Dental Clinic, my body grows cold with fear. I can still hear the screams of joy and feel the elation when we were "completed" on the second floor and would not have to go there for at least six months.

When Joe and John talk about getting their throats blessed at St. Monica's Catholic Church on East 79th Street, I can see the church in my mind's eye immediately. Why not? My parents were married in that church in 1932. Both my brother Joe and I were baptized there. We remember the feelings of anguish which flew through the neighborhood when on August 18, 1953, St. Monica's caught fire and was almost entirely destroyed. Hearing and seeing all of the fire engines, including fire companies not usually in our neighborhood, coming from every direction, we ran the three blocks from 76th Street where we lived. We were shocked to see the entire roof of the church on fire with flames and thick black smoke going hundreds of feet into the sky. It was the most terrible and amazing thing I had ever seen up to that point in my 11-year-old life. The fire eventually went to four alarms. Fire companies from the Bronx and the West Side had to be called in before the fire was finally brought under control. It did not matter if you were a Catholic or not; the neighborhood had suffered a catastrophe.

Joe, John, and I attended the same school, Robert F. Wagner Junior High, though at different times. I had witnessed the demolition of P.S. 70, which was torn down along with many tenements on 76th Street to make room for the new and much larger Wagner school. I remember the day when our teacher, Mrs. Schoenberg, proudly walked our class from the old J.H.S. 30 on 88th Street to the new school. We were part of the first eighth grade class the school ever had. When we arrived at the new school, the new principal, Dr. Charles Schapp, was outside to greet all of the children as classes were arriving from their old schools. Also outside were others waiting to greet us, girls from J.H.S. 96 on York Avenue and 81st Street. Both J.H.S. 30 and 96 were going to be torn down. With them an old era was ushered out and a new era ushered in. The new school would be coed.

I have never met Joe or John Gindele, but I feel as though I have known them all of my life. We shared common experiences in our daily lives growing up in Yorkville. We walked the same streets, played the same games, and shared the same values, which we all derived from immigrant and first-generation American parents.

We all had part time jobs as soon as we were old enough to work. Before we were old enough to work legally, we hustled to get money for the movies, candy, or baseball cards. We went around looking for deposit bottles that workers would leave about in the small shops, construction sites, and factories in the neighborhood. Each small bottle was worth 2¢ and each large bottle was worth 5¢. Often, we would take them without permission and run like crazy as if we had knocked over Fort Knox. It was a simple life and being led in the greatest city in the world.

In 1955 the Third Avenue elevated railway was torn down. In a way it had acted as a barrier between rich and working class in Yorkville. Its demise signaled a building boom in Yorkville. Property along Third Avenue, which had been adjacent to very expensive property for many years, increased in value once it no longer had the blight of the railroad to obstruct the view.

New buildings began to spring up everywhere. The old tenements one by one began to fall to the wrecking ball and to progress. With them disappeared the people. With the people disappeared the street games, the characters, and even the personality of the working class neighborhood as professionals and white-collar workers came into the area with the ability to pay the much higher rents in the new buildings.

Joe and John Gindele have preserved their particular recollections of that wonderful time and place in their book. Its value for those of us who shared that time, and also for those of us who would like to know what it was like, is all there in their wonderful and special story.

The Yorkville We Knew

JOE: "You guys should write a book!" We can't tell you how many times friends, relatives, and even strangers said this after hearing stories about our lives and unique experiences and reacting, usually with robust laughter. This did not start out as a public journal but as a series of private letters. It is, in part, an outcome of the Christmas letters I wrote to family and friends, describing our journeys and distinctive life events. When I intermittently stopped sending those letters, these folks protested and requested the letters continue. They had enjoyed reading about our adventures and sorely missed the narrative.

In trying to retain the interesting experiences of our 68 years, John scribbled notes on whatever was close by—envelopes, paper napkins and plates, scrap paper, index cards—and threw them into a box. Through childhood to formal education, public school teaching, business adventures, and travel, this pile of random notes grew. Finally, in the summer of 2006, John developed an outline and started to write. After seeing his material, I got excited about the project. We began bouncing ideas off one another. Our synergies work great together. John says I am skilled at embellishing narrative and "schmoozing" with the reader, adding flair with my writing style.

This memoir chronicles our first 18 years of life, plus two bonus chapters describing our undergraduate work (involving five to six additional years) in the Midwest and a twins' chapter. I originally wrote this material only for our nieces and nephews and their children, to leave a legacy—or baseline, if you will—from which they might learn and benefit. I wanted them to know what life was like for us and our parents at that time, growing up in an ethnic neighborhood of Yorkville on the Upper East Side of Manhattan, and to reflect upon how different life is today for them. John, on the other hand, thought our audience should be larger in scope, that others outside our small circle of family and friends might also enjoy our tales. In any event, we wanted to document the past and preserve our heritage and that of Yorkville by describing: (1) life in our neighborhood from 1944 to 1962, (2) struggles to improve ourselves as first-generation Americans, and (3) early lives as adventurous twins with psychic experiences, interacting, growing up, surviving, and succeeding in the urban jungle during this era.

This memoir was written to give readers insight into and a better understanding of the historical, social, and cultural perspective of the past—perhaps one of a different time and place than the reader experienced. Hopefully, it will assist you in measuring that perspective against your own life and the times of yesteryear compared to that of today. You are invited to reflect upon *your* first 18 years of life, comparing and contrasting those experiences with that of the authors. What was important in life when you grew up? What has changed since then? What has not changed? Where change occurred, was it for better or worse? What has been lost and should be brought back? What might never come back? Why? How was life for you different or similar to those the authors experienced?

This is our "Manhattan safari." This is the Yorkville we remember. Enjoy your journey with us—we hope it fosters many warm memories and nostalgia.

Joseph Gindele, D.I.T.

JOHN: This book will help readers (1) revisit childhood memories and (2) understand what it is to be an American and how the immigrant experience of the past and the present has enabled our nation to grow. It is the story of twin sons born of immigrant parents in New York City during World War II (WWII). This is not a heroic story, but one of how love, discipline, hard work and sacrifice, tenacity, and ingenuity combined to produce productive and contributing members of society. It is serious, tragic, educational, entertaining, humorous, silly, sad, and occasionally even naughty. It is about survival and a life rich in relationships and friendships that have shaped us into being who we are, the story of the successful realization of the ultimate dream that immigrant parents wanted for their children in this great country called *America*.[4]

PART I describes the early years, a general overview of life with our German father and Czech mother, our siblings, relatives, family friends, and neighbors.

PART II describes the learning years, our formal public education from kindergarten (1949) through high school (1962), various part-time work experiences, and how we spent time vacationing.

PART III is a Bonus Section that includes (a) our post-high school move to Minnesota and the completion of our undergraduate degrees and (b) a chapter about twins.

At the end you will find a helpful list of resources for those wishing to understand better the times, the places, and our family and friends. Appendix A (Figure 6) is our relationship tree of family, friends, and neighbors. The Annotated Resources section (Appendix C) offers the reader access to additional insight with Internet search terms, website addresses, organizations, and references. The Glossary defines unfamiliar words and phrases.

To assist the reader, each chapter is narrated, alternately, by only one of the authors.

John Gindele, D.I.T.

---

4. See Appendix C, Item 1e, Memories, Dances and Songs: Songs.

Joe and John Gindele, age one

The Twins

In form and feature, face and limb,
I grew so like my brother,
That folks got taking me for him,
And each for one another.
It puzzled all our kith and kin,
It reached a fearful pitch;
For one of us was born a twin,
Yet not a soul knew which.

One day, to make the matter worse,
Before our names were fixed,
As we were being washed by nurse
We got completely mixed;
And thus, you see, by fate's decree,
Or rather nurse's whim,
My brother John got christened me,
And I got christened him.

This fatal likeness ever dogged
My footsteps when at school,
And I was always getting flogged,
For John turned out a fool.
I put this question, fruitlessly,
To everyone I knew,
"What *would* you do, if you were me,
To prove that you were *you*?"

Our close resemblance turned the tide
Of my domestic life,
For somehow, my intended bride
Became my brother's wife.
In fact, year after year the same
Absurd mistakes went on,
And when I died, the neighbors came
And buried brother John.

Henry Sambrooke Leigh
(1837–1883)

PART I

The Early Years

CHAPTER 1

Our Family

The Cheesecake Phenomenon

JOHN: The long, hard rain had finally ended. It wasn't yet 5 p.m., but twilight set in quickly as we walked along the tracks 1,200 miles from home and discussed our futures. The cold stink of heavy wet barley soaked our clothes, assailed our nostrils, and permeated our lungs. Joe was insisting that one day we would earn our doctorate degrees. I didn't believe it. We had barely started our undergraduate studies. Why this thought came into his head is still a mystery, but Joe seemed to have a knack for predicting the future. But I am getting 18 years ahead of myself. I'll tell you more about our move to the "Mill City" of Minneapolis, Minnesota in Chapter 9. Let's start at the beginning and work our way there.

We were born several weeks prematurely at New York's Lenox Hill Hospital in 1944.[5] We were not expected to live and remained there in an incubator for four to five weeks. Lenox Hill, formerly known as German Hospital, is located in the Yorkville section of Manhattan, at 100 East 77th Street, between Park and Lexington

---

5. Joe remembers life before he was born: "I remember life in the womb and kicking John numerous times—no doubt he deserved it—and Mom in pain. However, John must have been fed up living with me, and with his determined kick I was first born. I was angry at birth because I was soaking wet and 'freezing,' coming into a world 30 or more degrees colder than where I came from. No handshake awaited me, only a smack on my rear end. What a welcome! I wanted to go back where it was warm and safe (sans John) and where life was simple, less complicated, and quieter."

Statue of Liberty

Avenues. At the time, the main entrance was on 76th Street. The building on 77th Street did not exist then.

Dad and Mom emigrated from Germany and Czechoslovakia, respectively. Their names are proudly inscribed on the granite "Wall of Honor" on Ellis Island, along with thousands of other immigrant names. Nearby stands the Statue of Liberty. Lady Liberty, an 1886 gift from France, stands on Bedloe's (Liberty) Island in New York Harbor welcoming freedom-seeking people from foreign lands— the lost, the needy, the rejected, the exiled. Words by Emma Lazarus on the statue's pedestal speak compassionately, "Give me your tired, your poor, your huddled masses yearning to breathe free."[6]

Dehdee: "Wie Geht Es Ihnen?"

His Family

Our dad, Otto Gindele, Sr., was born in 1908 in Ersingen, a small village near the Black Forest region of southern Germany. At one time this region was part of the Alsace-Lorraine District of northeastern France. The town is located near Pforzheim, between Stuttgart and Karlsruhe. Dad was one of 13 children, half of whom died at childbirth or shortly thereafter. He completed the eighth grade, an accepted and common practice back then. Dad's family worked in the jewelry business in Pforzheim.

To America

Prior to World War I, 33 million immigrants came to America in search of a better life.[7] In so doing, they helped our nation grow. Our family members came shortly thereafter and contributed to that growth. Dad came to America in 1926 with his brother

---

6. See Appendix C, Item 1a, New York City: Emma Lazarus's sonnet: "The New Colossus."

7. Marie Jastrow, *Looking Back: The American Dream through Immigrant Eyes, 1907–1918* (New York: W.W. Norton, 1986), 10.

Thomas. Traveling third class tourist on the SS *Belgenland,* they arrived from Amsterdam on Dad's 18th birthday. What anxiety they must have felt. Seventeen years later to the day Dad would become an American citizen.

They disembarked at Port Newark near Hoboken, New Jersey (not Ellis Island), after first going through American immigration in Bremen, Germany. The American government set up immigration offices in major European ports because it was cheaper to process those emigrating to the U.S. from outside the U.S., since our government would not have to be involved in the cost of sending back those immigrants deemed inadmissible into our country.

After clearing customs in New Jersey, Dad and Uncle Tom immediately boarded a train to Minnesota, to the Monticello/ Albertville/St. Michael area where their older brother, Hugo, was farming. Neighboring German farm families had sponsored each of the brothers, paying their passage of $250 each, so they were indentured servants for two years.

The three worked separately on different farms, 35 miles northwest of Minneapolis. As hired hands, Dad and Uncle Tom were badly mistreated, both physically and emotionally. They earned $29 per month and sometimes received $3 a day during the threshing season. They were half starved and had to work from morning to night outside in sub-freezing weather during the winter season, with almost no breaks.

Dad ate his meager meals with his farm family. Very little food was served at his meals, since the farmer claimed he was poor and could not provide much in food. After one particular meal, Dad was told to go outside and do a certain chore. About 20 or 30 minutes later, Dad came back into the house because he had a question for the farmer; he was unsure about how to do part of his newly assigned task. Can you imagine his surprise and pain when he entered the house and saw the farmer with his family still sitting at the same table, but with all kinds of dishes of food, with lots of

Dad, indentured servant, on a farm in Albertville, Minnesota, circa 1926

Left to right: Uncle Tom, farmer, Dad, and farmer at church time,
Albertville, Minnesota, circa 1926

meat and a variety of vegetables stacked high and wide? Uncle Tom wasn't treated much better.

In 1928, they worked off their passage, and Dad and Uncle Tom left the farms for a better life in New York. Good riddance, they thought. Uncle Hugo remained behind.

Baker

Dad found work in the Catskill Mountains resort of Sharon Springs, New York, as a dishwasher and porter. He also mowed lawns and swept floors. In 1929 he moved to Yonkers, New York, just north of the city, and continued work as a porter in an orphanage. He then got a job in Manhattan at Silvers Cafeteria (19th Street and 10th Avenue) as a cook. (The cafeteria was once a funeral parlor.) This is where his brother Thomas had found work when he left Minnesota. One day one of the bakers was ill, and Dad was asked to fill in. So began his true journey into the bakery business. Dad would eventually work for a number of other bakeries: his own in 1933 in

Dad working at a resort in the Catskills, 1928

Stewart Manor, Long Island (1½ years), in 1934 at Abel's Bakery on Ditmar's Boulevard, Long Island (4 years), in 1938 at Gotfried's and Hanscom Bakeries (10 years), and in 1948, Éclair (24 years).

Most of Dad's baking years would be spent as a night baker for

Éclair,[8] a commercial bakery at 812 Greenwich Street on the west side of lower Manhattan, near the Hudson River. Its specialty was making petit fours, tortes, and pastries for high-end restaurants and major airlines. The bakery also made pies, cakes, cookies, stollens, specialty breads, and theme cakes for children's birthday parties. The bakery had a few retail stores throughout the city.

Dad would wake up at 5 p.m. and have supper for his breakfast. At 6 p.m. he walked eight blocks to the 77th Street Lexington Avenue subway station to ride three trains to work. He returned home around 4 a.m., had a couple of beers as he read the *New York Daily News,* the *New York Daily Mirror,* or the *New York Post,* then went to bed. Other times he would read the *New York Herald Tribune* or the *New York Journal American.*

During one of New York's major power failures, on November 9, 1965,[9] Dad still went to work. Since there was no electricity, the subways didn't work, but the busses were still operating above ground. It took hours to get to work because it was the height of the rush hour, compounded by traffic congestion caused by inoperative traffic lights. At work, the bakers burned vats of lard, like torches in a cave, so they could see. The ovens were gas operated, so they had no problem baking.

Bakers were able to bring home freshly baked goods from work if the items were burnt or "crippled"—if they didn't come out looking just right. The bakery could not sell pies with burnt crusts or those that were damaged in some way. These products got discarded or were up for grabs at nominal cost. It is not likely that anything was wasted.

Besides apple pies, Dad also brought home empty flour sacks. These were used as diapers for us kids. Flour sacks for diapers were not the softest of materials. A liberal amount of cornstarch

---

8. Dad worked alongside a baker whose daughter was the famous 1960 Olympic champion ice figure skater, Carol Heiss.

9. See Appendix C, Item 1a, New York City.

was used to relieve the chafing. Diaper washing was no "special event" for Mom who had to clean them by hand on the small portable washboard. Our family of seven had no washing machine in the early years; disposable diapers were not yet invented, and if they had been, our family could not have afforded such an unnecessary luxury.

Dad was part of the crew that made the presidential inaugural cake for Lyndon B. Johnson. The cake was so large, it was delivered to Washington, D.C., in two trucks. The cake pieces were shaped into the contours of each of the 50 states. They were then assembled to form the shape of the United States. Hundreds of pounds of butter, flour, sugar, milk, and eggs were used. Dad was very proud of this accomplishment.

Pineapple cheesecake was one of the bakery's specialties and was expensive to produce. In the retail stores, their cheesecakes sold, but management thought they should be selling better. So someone got innovative and had the brilliant idea of *doubling* the price of the cheesecake from $3.50 to $7, to see how they would sell. The cheesecakes began "flying off the shelves." It seems customers thought they had to be something very special and out of the ordinary, with only the very best and most expensive ingredients, otherwise why would the price be so high? (We call this marketing strategy "the cheesecake phenomenon.") "I'll take two, please, and hurry before they are all gone!"

Father

As a father, Dad was a very strict disciplinarian—what German isn't? His philosophy was, "Shoot first, and ask questions later." When we got into trouble, and saw him taking off his belt, we knew we were in for it.

Joe and I remember fighting over something when we were about 10 years old. Joe chased me straight through all five rooms of our railroad flat, then into the bathroom, adjacent to the kitchen.

I slammed the bathroom door behind me, and Joe's hands crashed through the frosted glass. Mom was screaming at us; she and Dad were angry, to put it mildly. After carefully checking that neither of us was bleeding from the broken glass, had any broken bones, or were dead, Dad used his strap to wake us up. Usually the strap was preceded with a whack on the side of the head, to catch our attention and knock sense into us. We experienced similar "tough love" on numerous occasions during childhood. Ouch! Dad's actions were justified, although we didn't think so at the time.

One of Dad's favorite pastimes was going to the park. He was the happy wanderer, and the boardwalk at Carl Schurz Park was only a few blocks away.[10] The boardwalk ran along the East River starting from 81st Street up to 90th Street, where one could watch barges and other ships pass by. One day he was alone, walking along the boardwalk of John Finley Walk, just north of Gracie Mansion by the fireboat station at 90th Street, when a Puerto Rican kid chased him with

Dad on the boardwalk by the East River, circa 1930s

a knife. The guy wanted to rob Dad. Dad must have been in his 50s. Dad ran across three lanes of heavy traffic on the Franklin Delano Roosevelt (FDR) Drive, which emerged from a tunnel under the park at 90th Street, and he came very close to getting struck by speeding cars. Luck was with him. Another time a kid attempted to mug Dad by pulling a knife on him. But Dad was prepared this time

10. See Appendix C, Item 1d, Yorkville.

and had the advantage. Dad pulled a *bigger* switchblade knife from his pocket. The kid ran for his life. Boy, was *he* lucky. During a different visit to the park, Dad found a parakeet on a bush and brought it home. This became our first *real* pet; the price was right.

Another favorite pastime of Dad's was listening to the radio or watching television, especially when the Yankees played baseball from Yankee Stadium in the Bronx or the Brooklyn Dodgers played out of Ebbets Field in Brooklyn. Over the years, he enjoyed hearing and watching great ballplayers like Hank Aaron, Yogi Berra, Roy Campanella, Joe DiMaggio, Gil Hodges, Harmon Killebrew, Sandy Koufax, Mickey Mantle, Roger Maris, Willie Mays, Stan Musial, Jackie Robinson, and others play ball. I can still hear those baseball fans singing, "Take me out to the ball game, take me out with the crowd . . ."[11]

Dad also liked to read and smoke one of his many pipes or cigars, soaking up the sun near the window and drinking beer in his tank-style tee shirt. There was always a tin of Prince Albert tobacco nearby. Unfortunately for us, his smoking also took place in the sealed confines of our car.

Once a week, a short, muscular, stocky German man drove his truck to our apartment building and delivered a 24-bottle case of Old Brau beer. This continued for decades. After we moved, the case of beer had to be carried up to our fifth floor apartment. There was no elevator.

Joe and I used to walk around the apartment puffing on some of Dad's unlit pipes or used cigar stubs. Once, when we were 11 or 12 years old, we asked him if we could smoke a real cigar. Dad said, "You vhant shmok?" We replied, "Sure." He gave us each a cigar and lit them. We thought we had entered adulthood. Mom was yelling in both English and Czech for Dad not to light up. She said, "Who is ghoink to clean up dha 'kutz' (all the mess, the vomit) vhen dey get shick?" Joe and I inhaled and after a few puffs turned six shades

---

11. See Appendix C, Item 1e, Memories, Dances, and Songs: Songs.

of green. On cue, we both threw up as we ran to the bathroom. Dad was laughing. For a long, long time, smoking was the farthest thing from our minds.

Later on, when we were older and went to visit relatives in Germany, Dad told us to never talk about WWII with them. The war had only been over less than 30 years. During the war, in the early 1940s, while he was going to work, some people called him a Nazi, only because of his German heritage. The ethnic neighborhood we lived in experienced street battles between pro- and anti-Nazi Germans and German-Americans. More about this later. Dad did his civic duty and served in the New York National Guard and took training one weekend each month. What must have gone through Dad's mind if he thought he might one day find himself in a position of fighting his own people in a war?

Hitler invaded the Sudetenland in the late 1930s, capturing and occupying parts of Czechoslovakia, suppressing Mom's countrymen.

Dad marching in National Guard Reserves,
left outside column, fourth back, circa 1950

What must have gone through *her* mind about German people? After all, she was married to one and we were at war with Germany. What inner conflicts did she have? Were they ever resolved, and if so, to what extent? Did she ever harbor any internal bitterness against Dad, because of his nationality, or against the German people? She knew the destruction and atrocities the German military were engaged in. She read the newspapers and listened to the radio. But she also had common sense and knew that there were good and bad people all over the world. It was governments and their war-causing policies that were bad. The war with Germany gave rise to nationalism here in America. Many things with a German name or reference were changed during WWI and WWII. Frankfurters became hot dogs; German Hospital became Lenox Hill Hospital, etc.

New York courts did not like to have Dad serve on jury duty. Why? Because he told the lawyers and judge, in front of other jurors being selected, that if the cops brought in the [alleged] offender, the offender *was* guilty, otherwise the cops would not have arrested him or her in the first place. He truly believed this. Juror dismissed!

"Ouch time" occurred regularly a few times each year when Dad gave us haircuts using his mechanical clippers. We thought he got his training shearing sheep. We sat in the kitchen with a bed sheet or towel around our necks, sitting on two hard-covered 5-inch thick encyclopedias on top of a wooden kitchen chair—there were no telephones or telephone books in our home at that time. Oh, the clippers grabbed and pinched. And having them banged on the back of our heads to make us sit still was no picnic, either.

"Ouch time" came once again when we came home from elementary school scratching our heads. Somehow we caught head lice from a classmate. Mom took kerosene and dabbed it liberally on our heads. It did the trick, but our scalp burned and we smelled. It was a good thing we were not near any open flames.

Even though Dad was strict with us kids, he and Mom knew

the importance of discipline and getting a good education. Education was their children's key to a brighter future. We heard so many times Dad's remark, "Opin a book und schtick your noss in it." This was his gentle way of saying, "*Learn!* Don't be idle! Idleness will get you into trouble." Idleness, however, seemed to be a lot more fun than learning.

Dad was thrifty and didn't like to go to doctors or dentists. When he developed a tooth problem and couldn't stand the pain any longer, he had little choice and finally went to see the dentist. After treatment, the dentist gave Dad a bill for $80. Dad went berserk and yelled, "Vhat? $80 for vhat?" At which time he took out a $20 bill and slammed it on the counter, saying, "Dhat's all yous ghetin!" Then he stormed out of the office. Trust us, you don't want to mess with a stubborn and especially an angry German. We had enough welts to attest to that.

He also didn't spend much money on shoes. For over 20 years he got his shoes from dead people—friends or relatives who died. (Well, they didn't need them anymore, did they?) Some of the shoes were a little large, so Dad stuffed cardboard or paper into them, always achieving a perfect fit. When Dad had shoes with holes in the sole, he placed cardboard or a piece of leather inside the shoe and wore them. We did the same. Of course, when it rained, they didn't help much in keeping socks and feet dry. When the shoe separated from the sole, Dad tied string or a rubber band over the shoe to hold the flaps together. Shoe retailers rarely made money off of him.

We remember Dad making a salary of $10,000 in 1968. We said we would live like kings if we ever made so much money or even came close to it. Of course, we had little realization of the costs involved in maintaining a residence, buying food and clothing, paying for utilities, and the concept of inflation.

Neighbors from across the street had a farm in upstate New York. It was at that farm where Joe first learned to use a shotgun. However, no one told him about recoil, the "kick" against the shoulder that occurs when firing a shotgun. His right shoulder is *still* hurting. Uff da! Joe quickly learned not to like high-powered guns.

BB guns were a different matter. When I was much younger, I asked Dad if I could have a BB gun for Christmas, while Joe asked for a pony—in a New York City apartment? Dad's usual safe reply to the vast majority of our requests was, "Vhee'll zee." This remark pretty much kept us content and happy, at least for a while, since he hadn't actually said, "No!" which we were on high alert for. Our requests never materialized. We finally figured out after many years that "Vhee'll zee" meant, "Forget about it! Never in your life if you live to be 100 will your parents *ever* buy this for you." I did get a cork-pop gun and made my own rubber-band gun. Joe got his pony in the form of a hamster. Kind of like a miniature pony—don't you think?

Mumma: "Jak Se Mate?"

Her Family

Mom (Marie), whom everyone called Mary, was born on a farm in 1906 in the small village of Pole. This village was part of the Austro-Hungarian Empire, which in 1918 became Czechoslovakia.[12] There were nine children in her family. When she was young, her mother tried to drown her and her siblings. No one knew why, but Mom thought it was because of very bad economic times. Her family was very poor. Some of her siblings died young or in the Great War, WWI, among them her brother Willy, a teenage soldier.[13] Her brothers were stonecutters, later building stone monuments in

---

12. Mom's mother also came from this part of Eastern Europe. Mom's relatives and friends, the Chaloupkas, Novaceks, and Solars, also came from the Austro-Hungarian area before it became Czechoslovakia.

13. After Willy died, his parents received word from another soldier the weather and battle conditions were so severe, in order to survive, Willy had to shoot a horse, gut it, and crawl into its now opened cavity and cover himself up with the horse's intestines for heat. The body heat of the horse kept him from freezing to death overnight, and it hid him from the enemy for a brief period of time. Rest in peace, Uncle Willy.

Joe, Mom, Elizabeth, William, Bohus, Grandma, and Grandpa on the farm in
Pole, Austro-Hungarian Empire (later to become Czechoslovakia), 1908

Paris where there was more opportunity for work. Mom completed
a sixth grade education, which was standard for girls living in the
country at that time.

Mom said this about her early life and school in Czechoslovakia
in 1977 when her granddaughter, Julie Sullivan, a 3rd grader, inter-
viewed her for a class assignment:

> Dear Julie,
>   When I was a little girl on a farm in Czechoslovakia, I wore
> wooden shoes. When I got to school, I had to take my shoes
> off and leave them in the hall and go upstairs with my stock-
> ing feet.
>   Every class had a big coal-burning stove. We put in coal and
> wood in the fire to keep us warm.
>   Our principal lived in a few rooms on the ground floor of the
> school.
>   We had about 30 children in each class.
> Once a week for one hour, a priest would come to teach us
> religion.

Before I went to school in the morning, I had to do some kind of work. It was my job to take the geese out to pasture.

For lunch we would eat a piece of dried bread and drink water in the hall. Some children had butter on their bread.

School started at 9 o'clock. We left the house between 8 and 8:30 and walked three kilometers [1.8 miles] to school and back at 4:00.

On Wednesday and Saturday, we had a half-day of school. The other days, we went the whole day. On Sunday, we had no school.

If we did wrong things in school, we would get spanked by the teacher and then by our parents at home.

When we got home from school, my mother had dinner in the oven for us. We would eat, and then there was a long list of chores to do. Bring in water, feed the geese, chickens, and pigs, collect the eggs, and milk the cows.

Love,

Oma

P.S. Every Saturday night, we had to shine all the shoes and line them up in a row by the door. You couldn't go to church unless your shoes were shiny.[14]

---

14. Mom told us chilling stories about the "old country," stories about hearing screams coming from the nearby cemetery. Once, townspeople dug up a recently buried coffin and found the body with scratch marks inside the coffin lid. Apparently in those days, people who "died" were not embalmed and perhaps some presumed to be dead were actually alive but in a coma when buried. These were the "un-dead." When they awoke, they found themselves in a cold, damp, dark box underground with no escape.

As children, we were brought occasionally to the funerals of family friends. It scared the hell out of us to see a dead person sleeping in a coffin in a suit or dress in a dimly lit parlor full of people wearing black, the overpowering sweet smell of buckets of fresh flowers accompanied by sobbing and wailing widows, widowers, other family members, and friends. Who sleeps in a suit or dress—with a tie, glasses, and pearls—anyway? It didn't make any sense. We were certain the person was going to wake up, open his or her eyes, and snatch us quickly and assuredly into the dark casket with them and slam the lid shut, entombing us forever. We hated to go to funerals and had nightmares for years because of it.

To America

Mom came to America on September 22, 1922, with her friend Frances Vibiryl, sailing from Holland on the *Rotterdam*. She was almost 16 years old. She had an Aunt Josephine here who sponsored her and who owned a clothes factory in Brooklyn. Her Aunt Chadda had sent her $300 for the second-class passage ocean voyage. What must have gone through her mind crossing the ocean at such a young age? What were living conditions aboard ship? How long was the journey?

She landed on Ellis Island—from 1892 to 1954 Ellis Island was the usual but not exclusive entry point for European immigrants coming into the U.S.—a place where she would unexpectedly stay for three weeks because Aunt Josephine died at age 33 before Mom arrived. With no one to claim her, they wouldn't let her enter the country, so the waiting began. She had other relatives in New York who intervened, which allowed her entry. A friend or relative, someone who was known to us as "Fat Mary," got Mom a second sponsor—Dr. Goldberg—thereby allowing her to remain in America.

As a house maker, working for $25 a month, Mom cooked, cleaned, and cared for children of the Goldberg family and learned to eat and prepare corn on the cob, matzo ball soup, and gefilte fish. In Europe, corn was for animals and definitely not for human consumption. She didn't understand why the corn stalk didn't get soft when cooked. She also shoveled coal, took away the ashes, made a fire to boil the laundry, sewed socks and did embroidery, shined a brass bed every week, and washed 15 windows every two weeks. She worked there for two to three years. Then she got a job with a Russian family who was nicer to her. The Finkels had a business making dill pickles and ketchup. They had two children and a big German shepherd dog. Mom's wages were now $60 a month.

Speaking no words of English, she was told that if any boys tried to bother her, she should keep repeating to them in English, "Shut up! Shut up!" She worked most of her life as a domestic, cleaning apartments, doing laundry, and ironing clothes for the same few people in Manhattan.

After Mom worked off her passage to America, she went up to the Catskill Mountains and worked as a chambermaid in one of the resorts. While there, she met a baker, Peter. Her friends urged her to say "yes" when he asked her to marry him. Mom did marry Peter. After all, he was older and somewhat established. In 1930, they left the Catskills and opened a bakery/lunch room in Stewart Manor, a village in Nassau County on Long Island. That's where Mom and Dad met in 1932. Dad was a hired hand who soon became their partner. The Manor Bakery, which specialized in French-American pastry *par excellence*, was located at 78 Covert Avenue. Their telephone number was "Floral Park 6695."

Mom in her Chevy coupe, circa 1930

When Peter's daughter, who was about the same age as Mom, came to visit her father, Mom discovered that he had a wife back in Europe and she filed for divorce. Soon after, Mom and Dad married in a civil ceremony in a court of law. The marriage fee was $2. She was 27, he was 25. The year was 1933, and Peter bought out their part of the business.

Dad and Mom at their bakery in Stewart Manor
(Long Island), New York, circa 1933

Owning and working in a combination bakery/lunchroom café made Mom nervous, especially when the high school kids came in for cookies. They were mischievous and mixed the salt with sugar or loosened the caps of the salt and pepper shakers so the contents spilled out when shaken. The local police came by and hung their guns and holsters on the coat rack. Mom never did like guns. Some of them actually expected free meals, taking advantage of these new immigrant "greenhorns" in America.

Domestic

After Mom and Dad sold the bakery to Peter, they moved to New York City, to an area on the Upper East Side of Manhattan. Yorkville was a predominantly German-Bohemian (thought to be Czechs, Slovaks, and Poles) ethnic neighborhood, although Irish, Italians, Hungarians, and Jews also lived here.

Mom worked odd jobs cleaning other people's apartments and taking in their laundry. She worked for people in pre-war elevator apartments—the elevator was hand-operated by an attendant—on 73rd Street. Mom washed and ironed their shirts, blouses, and underwear at home. This was in the 1950s before permanent press clothes were available, so it was more time-consuming and more difficult to do. Our cousin Carl relates,

> Your mother worked so hard and I always remembered her walking down the block with a full shopping bag of wash in each hand. Note: Women at that time carried a cloth shopping bag with them. Food purchases were usually picked up on a daily basis when passing neighborhood stores.

Mom did not have a steam iron. So when she ironed clothes, she put water into an empty beer bottle and inserted in it a mushroom-shaped stopper with holes in it so she could "spritz" water drops on the clothes and then apply the hot iron to "steam iron" them. Sometimes she used a baby bottle nipple and poked larger holes in it. She worked domestically for decades at two residences cleaning for five people in two high-rise apartment buildings.

Mom did all this work besides raising five kids in our small apartment. She liked the flexibility of the job, because she could schedule her work around her children and generally be home before we returned from school. In the early years, she got paid 15¢ for each shirt she picked up, washed, hung to dry, retrieved, ironed, buttoned, folded, and delivered. Mom first had a washboard, then a washing machine with a wringer, but never a clothes dryer. When the clothesline outside our kitchen window was full of clothes hanging out to dry, additional ropes were strung in the kitchen and three bedrooms to air-dry other laundry. There were times when we ate breakfast or dinner sitting under damp bras or bloomers. It was usually humid on the East Coast, and wet laundry drying in the apartment made it even more so. It was like living in a Chinese laundry. On a hot summer day, it could be very uncomfortable. We are sure it must have been even more uncomfortable for her.

One perk of Mom's domestic work was that before she came home she was able to look through the newspaper/magazine trashcan bins in the basement of the 15-story apartment buildings on East 73rd Street. This is where the "really rich" people lived, at least that's what we thought. Mom brought home newspapers, magazines, books, etc., that others discarded. An entertainer or his children may have lived in one of these buildings, since some of the magazines had the family name of a famous entertainer on them. These magazines supplemented her and her children's learning. Mom believed that things other people discarded might still be of value and could benefit others.

Mother

Mom kept an exceptionally clean house; you could literally eat off her floor. She was proud of this and in keeping us all healthy. Once a week she got down on her hands and knees and scrubbed the floors of each room with soap and water. After rinsing and drying, she liquid-waxed it. Sometimes we helped her with this chore. Her floors shone. To save money, she even made her own soap from lye. (It was strong soap as Joe and I can attest, having had the pleasure of tasting it—not by choice—on more than one occasion.)

Joe and I helped Mom dust our linoleum floors with a dust mop and then shook it clean in an outside open window through the kitchen or air shaft. Sometimes the wind blew the dust balls right back into our face. Other times the debris was directed into the open window of the apartment next door; we believed in sharing.

We didn't have carpeting. Carpeting—as opposed to an area rug—was for rich people, especially wall-to-wall carpeting. When we needed to paint, we purchased our supplies from Martin's Hardware Store on First Avenue and 80th Street. Our walls were a rainbow of colors, not white (i.e., pink with gray trim in the kitchen). Other bedroom and front room walls were painted aqua or green or yellow with flat paint, sometimes with white semi-gloss trim. Rich people had white walls.

We used oil-based paint with lead, as latex was unknown or not widely used in America. The walls in the kitchen were painted with *glossy* pink enamel paint—Mom liked pink—for wearability, so we could wash the walls down a few times each year, removing the cooking grease and soot that accumulated on it. We sometimes washed only one half the wall from floor to ceiling. When Dad got up, we showed him the before and after result, before we cleaned the last half. He saw a dramatic difference. Our kitchen didn't have a fan over the stove to remove exhaust fumes or splattering grease. However, some kitchens had small exhaust fans placed in the window that helped in this regard, especially exhausting heat generated in the kitchen.

We never ate out at restaurants unless there was a funeral gathering and not always then. Mom was an excellent cook and baker, and she loved to cook for her family and friends, with potato pancakes being one of her favorites. She enjoyed having visitors. In fact, on numerous occasions she had us deliver potato pancakes to a few special neighborhood storeowners.

Mom's chicken soup was the best because it contained fat from the chicken and chicken skin, which added to the flavor. She said you needed to have some fat in your system, to "ghrease your bhones." Mom cooked chicken feet to make inexpensive stock for the soup.[15,16]

---

15. Just before the feet were to be boiled, Joe and I each grabbed a foot, chasing each other, pretending we were fighting. We terrorized each other by sticking the claws of chicken feet in each other's faces. We were especially successful and thrilled doing this to our little sister, who couldn't run as fast.

16. We bought food at John's or Mellian's, our small local grocery store down the middle of the block. Supermarkets did not exist in our area in the early 1950s.

Mom prepared a meal for granddaughter Debbie, 1961

Teta Chaloupka, Tante Ida, Mrs. V., Mrs. H. (neighbors) and Mom,
seated Eileen with Debbie and Tommy (410 East 81st Street), 1959

Mom cooking soup (420 East 81st Street), 1979

Eastern Europeans eat lots of pork, dumplings, sauerkraut, red cabbage, and noodles. We grew up on this. Mom made her own noodles from scratch, with flour and eggs. These tasted better and were always less expensive than those in the store. Remember, she had to feed five children, Dad, and herself; she learned to stretch the food dollar as far as it would go. On Saturday mornings, upon awakening, we found 16-inch diameter rounds of flat noodle dough, like very thin rolled-out pizza crusts, drying on linen towels, positioned all over the apartment on the backs and arms of sofas and chairs. When they dried, Mom cut them into strips for soup.

Freshly made noodles have a remarkable flavor. Mom made chicken *paprikasch* with *vomacka* spooned over noodles and chicken. To die for! (We didn't realize how good we had it then.) Sometimes we enjoyed eating cooked noodles fried in butter with bits of smoked ham or dried mushrooms. Mom called this *sunka fleki* and *houby fleki*, respectively. Mom made *livance* (crepe suzettes) which we especially enjoyed. Our Hungarian next-door neighbors, the Kovos, had their pancake version, which was called *palacsinta*. Mom also made bread-based and non-bread-based versions of *knedliky* and *holubky*. For desert she made apple or peach tarts or *kolache* filled with prunes, apricots, other cooked fruits, cheese, or poppy seeds. On Friday evenings the family dinner always included cod fish cakes, extended with lots of breading, of course, and spaghetti. The spaghetti *had* to be LaRosa Spaghetti #9. She also insisted on using Del Monte tomato sauce—for her, no other brand would do. We almost never ate meat on Fridays, not that we were particularly religious. Mom bought cod or meat, and we clamped a hand grinder to the tabletop or chair seat to grate it up. Then other ingredients were added and they were made into fish patties or meatballs.

When we had dinner we had to sit and eat everything on the plate. We were not allowed to leave the table until we finished all of it. Dad was especially strict with us on this.

"We know, Mom and Dad, people are starving in Europe."

"*Já vím,*" Mom would say. "I know."

There was a time when Mom did not cook for us for over a week. The year was 1948. She was in the hospital giving birth to our sister. Dad was the cook. He was not a great cook, nor did he have the patience that Mom had. Oh, how we missed her. It seemed to take forever for her to come home. However, we were fortunate that Dad was a great baker—after all, that was his profession.

For our birthdays, Mom made sure that we, along with each of our siblings and friends, had a birthday party. She never failed at this. Mom usually made homemade strawberry shortcake for us, with real whipped cream. This was our favorite dessert. The second was ice cream cake made with vanilla ice cream and dark chocolate cake rolled around it, and our third favorite was coffee ice cream. Sometimes we helped Mom beat the whipped cream. (A couple of times we overdid it, producing butter instead.) Then we took turns

Birthday party—Mary Ann, left, and John, middle,
with friends, circa 1950

licking the spoon or beater blades. Mom always made sure she left plenty of whipped cream on them. Then our friends were invited over to celebrate and play Pin the Tail on the Donkey. We even got to drink a delicious Yoo-Hoo chocolate drink and eat a small bag of potato chips. Adult relatives and friends were also invited to the festivity, and we all sang "Happy Birthday." This was Mom's celebration of love to each of her children, and she wanted to share that love. So many people loved Mom. You would too.

Even though the Gindele family was poor, we kids didn't know it. At one time Joe asked Mom, "Are we rich or are we poor?" She answered, "Vhee nut rhich, but vhee nut poor, needa." That answer seemed to satisfy Joe. She further said, "Rheememba, vhatever you do, vhat goes rhound comes rhound," and, "No madder vhat you do, you mhust dhink of oders foist." Mom was like that. She liked people and people liked her.

Well, we children might have been poor in *things,* but we were rich in *love* and *values.* Our parents' work ethics were strong. It meant working hard at your job and always doing the best you can for the boss. After all, our parents were very grateful to have the opportunity to live and work in America, truly a land of opportunity for them. It meant telling the truth and treating others as you wanted to be treated. These values were instilled within us from an early age.

When Mom was in her 50s she decided to become a U.S. citizen. She studied the materials intently and when she went before the judge, one of the questions he asked her was, "What flies over the White House?" She thought and thought silently to herself, got nervous and frustrated, and thought silently some more, thinking, "Vhat dha hell, vhat flies ova Vhite House?" Then she firmly proclaimed, "Pigeons!" The judge laughed, hit the gavel, and granted her full citizenship. He had expected her answer to be "the American flag." In fact, Mom *had* a large wooden placard of the American flag at home. It hung for decades on the wall next to her bed. She was very proud of it; it was an inspiration to her.

In 1958 Mom and Dad had their 25th wedding anniversary. Joe contacted one of the major NYC radio shows and had them announce the anniversary over the air. They did so, but he had to call them a few times to convince them to schedule the announcement around 5:30 p.m. so that our parents could listen to it before Dad went to work. It worked perfectly, and they were surprised and happy. Now tens if not hundreds of thousands of people could celebrate with them.

As we grew up and began walking to school, Mom always reminded us to regularly change our underwear, "in case you ghet rhunn ova by thruck on Second Avenue." She didn't say, "in case you ghet hid by *car.*" Would First Avenue or a car have been safer? Could we have worn the same underwear longer by walking a different route to school? Joe, did we miss an opportunity here?

Later in life Mom had to go to New York Hospital to have kidney cancer surgery. At the same time, a former U.S. president, now a private citizen, was having some issues taken care of down the hall. Joe rode the elevator with one of his bodyguards. At about the same time that Mom was hospitalized, the president of a national labor union was also being evaluated on that floor. This entire floor was devoted to urology.

While walking to the hospital to see Mom, we passed through John Jay Park by the FDR Drive overlooking the East River between 76th and 78th Streets. Next to the park were the Cherokee Apartments, a complex that initially housed mostly Czech immigrants. We played in this park and went swimming there at two huge outside community pools. We met comedian Rodney Dangerfield there. He lived nearby and came prepared to play handball with the locals.

Children

All five Gindele children were first-generation Americans. Through our parents' hard work, values, and guidance, each of us graduated from college. This was unheard of and atypical of families in our neighborhood at the time. Many families on our block had children who never graduated from high school. We knew families who had children in jail or who "graduated" into the state penitentiary system for murder and other serious crimes.

John Jay Park, FDR Drive overpass, looking north

Thomas

Tommy, the oldest child in the family, was born in 1934 in New York Hospital. Being 10 years older than us, he was our big brother and mentor, although we didn't remember much about him in those early years, since our ages and interests were so widespread. He attended elementary school at P.S. 158 on York Avenue and 78th Street, P.S. 30, an all-boys junior high school at 88th Street (between Second and Third Avenues), and Seward Park High School on the Lower East Side of Manhattan.[17] Tom completed a two-year A.A. degree in air conditioning, heating, and refrigeration from SUNY, then a junior college in Farmingdale, New York. He worked himself up from mechanic to vice president of a commercial air conditioning company in New York City.

---

17. Frank McCourt, the late Irish-American author of *'Tis, Angela's Ashes,* and *Teacher Man,* taught at Seward, but at a different time. He won the Pulitzer Prize for *Angela's Ashes.* Joe and I had the pleasure of meeting him in Chester, Mass., on October 5, 2008, when he spoke about teaching. He also autographed books for us.

Tom, Joe, Otto, John, Dad, and Mrs. Novacek in Carl Schurz Park, 1946

Dad, Mary Ann, Mom, Otto, John and Joe (410 East 81st Street), 1948

Tom once was called to a company whose manager complained that their air conditioner wasn't working—they were not getting cooling. The company was located by the Hudson River and used cold river water as part of their air conditioning system. Tom asked to be shown the water intake for the air conditioning unit. Upon checking it in the sub-sub basement, he discovered a corpse stuck against the outside grating of the water intake, severely restricting inflow water supply and preventing it from doing its job. Tom said, "Call the police, have them remove the body, and your system should work. Oh, and here's our bill."

Mom, Dad, and baby Tommy on roof, 1934

Cousin Carl was about the same age as Tommy. They were also best friends. Carl was generous in commentary about their lives growing up in Yorkville during WWII and the 1940s. Carl wrote,

> Your brother Tom and I hung out together during the war years on 81st Street. Games like tag, hide and seek (hangleseek), Johnny on the pony, ring a lareo, box ball, stoopball, stickball, handball, and basketball (using a 14-pound fruit basket with the bottom removed and hung on the wall of the bank post office building) kept us busy. There were always kids around. We would get Pepsi or Mission soda (orange or cream) because they were 12 oz. bottles.
>
> Kids in the block were tough and very concerned about nationality during this time. Calling people: German (Krauts, Nazis, Heines), Blacks (Niggers, Shines, Moolars, Jigs), Jews (Kikes, Sheenies), Irish (Micks, Potato Heads), Hungarians (Bo Hunks), Czechs (Gypsies, Slavs), Italians (Ginnies, Wops, Greaseballs), Hispanic (Spics, Puerto Ricans).[18] Living was rough and friendships were often strained because of this. So Tom and I stuck together mostly during this time. We would go downtown to 42nd Street, check out Broadway, and go to Central Park, museums, art, and history. In October of each year they drained Sail Boat Lake in Central Park and during the war years the soldiers and sailors when on leave would throw coins into the lake when it was full to impress the girls. We would get up early on Saturday and pick up these coins. WOW! Did we do *good!* Five to ten dollars each. Reading comics and listening to stories on the radio was a great pastime. Tommy liked the classics. We got these used in a junk shop on York Avenue and 81st Street for 2¢. We could also trade for new used ones or sell back at 1¢ each. Things settled down after the war and we mingled and played with all the kids on 81st Street's upper block. Girls were a no/no until 12 or 13 years old. Teenage years we got jobs part-time and slowly drifted apart. Tom was a good boy, friend, and man.

---

18. Note: Joe and I would be lying if we said we never said these words. We used some of them until Mom and Dad set us straight.

Cousin Carl B. and Tom in Connecticut, 1949

Strange as it seems, this was our vocabulary in the 40s and I think it was a result of the Irish. The Irish established Franks'Tavern and most of the beer joints in the neighborhood. New York City was corrupt as a result of Tammany Hall. The political machine at the turn of the century with total power consisted of Irish politicians and their henchmen. After this political machine was disbanded in the 1920s and 30s, the Irish were still in control of the city as leaders in government and held all of the good jobs. They ran the cops, firemen, and transit positions along with union bosses.

The beat cops were tough on us kids and would often take our Spalding balls (cost 15¢) and break our broomstick. If we would balk, it was not unusual to be hit on the back of our legs with the nightstick. Tommy did not care much for sports either, preferring to read his classic comics or play with his A.C. Gilbert Erector Set. (Each December we would visit their science center and look at their new toys.) The 2002 film *Gangs of New York* gives you an idea of NYC corruption. The 1940s were a grim time for us kids on the street, but we had each other for support and friendship. After the war there was a resurgence of growth in the city and most of us kids took delivery boy jobs in the neighborhood. Tommy worked for a messenger service downtown and started saving his money (again, following your dad's good advice). We kids just blew it on movies, clothes, and dates to impress the girls. Boy, was I dumb! Yorkville stayed the same in the 1940s but then migration from the south and from Puerto Rico and Europe rose sharply in the 1950s. The neighbors changed, locals moved away, we all grew up, we moved to the suburbs, and the brownstones made room for high-rise unaffordable apartment buildings.

Tom developed colon cancer, and during his treatment he received care at the Memorial Sloan-Kettering Cancer Center, along with the Shah of Iran who was also being treated there at the same time. Tom died at the age of 45, leaving his 44-year-old wife, Eileen, and three children: Tom, Jr., 22, Debbie, 21, and Dennis, 16. His family lost a breadwinner. We remember meeting lots of mourners and seeing and smelling the myriad of flowers that filled the air with aromatic fragrances. Tom was laid to rest at St. Charles cemetery in Farmingdale, New York. Mom is also buried with him. Dad's ashes are in the woods in Massachusetts. It is always difficult when one passes and is especially difficult on younger children—and older parents who they believe should be the first ones to predecease their children. Sadly, Tom never got to walk his daughter down the aisle or meet any of his children's spouses or any of his seven grandchildren. It was a loss for his wife and children who never got to know and grow up with their granddad. He is sorely missed.

Otto, Jr.

Brother Otto, born in 1940 at Lenox Hill Hospital, was the second child. He attended P.S. 190 for elementary school and P.S. 30 for junior high (like Tommy). He graduated from the High School of Commerce on West 65th Street. In college, Otto received his A.A. degree, majoring in automotive technology at SUNY Farmingdale, where Tommy graduated from.

Tommy and Otto
in Carl Schurz Park, circa 1943

When he was a teenager Otto worked part-time delivering groceries and telegrams. One day he delivered a telegram to former First Lady Eleanor Roosevelt. She gave him a 25¢ tip.

Most of his life's work was with a telecommunication company, first as an installer, then in management. He had some interesting early work-related stories. He had to "ride shotgun" in his utility truck while working in Harlem, in order to protect his partner who fixed equipment while working in apartments, basements, roofs, and on poles in backyards. Sometimes debris and even appliances were thrown down on them from apartments above. Sometimes when they got a repair call to fix or install equipment in people's apartments, they organized their daily schedules so they went to women's apartments first, early in the morning, especially women they determined were single. Sometimes two installers were sent, one to install the unit, the other to make conversation with the lady, so the installation indeed would get completed in a timely manner. Also, if only one installer appeared, sometimes the female customer had another not-so-technical agenda on her mind.

Otto had an office in the Wall Street area and in one of the World Trade Towers. Four days before the 9/11 events, he walked around the grounds of the Twin Towers, showing the sites to some friends from Denmark.

He liked hunting and the outdoors. When he was younger he found a man's wallet in the woods. He found the man's address and mailed the wallet to him, along with the money and everything else that was in there. We found out the man lost his wallet two years earlier; he was thankful enough to send Otto a reward. This is how our brother operates—"he would give you the shirt off his back." This was part of the values Mom instilled within us, to always think of others first.

Joseph and John

Joe was born about 15 minutes ahead of me. Perhaps this is why Joe keeps reminding me to "have respect for your elders"—especially meaning him. Since this book is about *our* growth, we will continue to describe how our lives evolved.

Mary Ann

Our only sister, the baby of the family, Mary Ann, was also born at Lenox Hill Hospital, in 1948. She, and later her daughter Julie, was in an accelerated academic program at Wagner Junior High School and skipped eighth grade. They both graduated from the prestigious, elite, and nationally known Bronx High School of Science. At the time, Bronx Science had a high Asian and Jewish population of students and faculty and many staff members had Ph.D's. Mary Ann and Julie didn't like it there. They thought the kids were too pushy, aggressive, and fiercely competitive. They were!

Mary Ann married Joe Sullivan, a civil engineer, licensed to practice in New Jersey and New York. Joe grew up at 445 East 68th Street. He later became director of sewers for Orangetown, New York. While they lived in Yorkville, first at 420 East 81st Street, then at 320 East 83rd Street, Mary Ann graduated from City College of New York (CCNY) with an M.A. in early childhood development and her husband obtained his master's degree in sanitary engineering at Manhattan College. Mary Ann held a 16-year position as director of a private school, the William Woodward, Jr. Nursery School, located on East 69th Street between First and York Avenues. She and her staff taught the children of medical personnel affiliated with The New York Hospital/Cornell University Medical Center, Hospital for Special Surgery, and Memorial Sloan Kettering Institute, all located in the vicinity of the school. She got to know many doctors whose children attended her school. (While teaching at a previous nursery, Mary Ann had the granddaughter of a cosmetic queen in her class. At Christmas time, their chauffer drove to the school bringing bags of cosmetic gifts to the staff.)

After a number of years, the Sullivans got tired of the hustle and bustle of city life and yearned to live in the country. One of their favorite pastimes had been making wine in their small fifth-floor kitchen apartment. They, along with Julie and her husband Scott, now live in the Berkshire Mountains of western Massachusetts, where for 10 years they owned and operated Chester Hill Winery, specializing in various kinds of blueberry wine, as well as other wines.

Tommy and Otto married Irish and Italian girls, respectively. Mary Ann chose an Irishman. The growth of our blended family continued.

A Slice of Daily Life

Our parents lived in various apartments in Yorkville from 1928 to the 1970s. In 1928 Dad lived at 301 East 82nd Street and then on 84th Street, paying $8 per week rent. After he and Mom got married, they first lived at 243 East 78th Street and paid $25/month;

they had no heat, but they had a coal stove in the kitchen. After our oldest brother Tom was born, they moved to 418 East 78th Street and then to 425 East 79th Street, between First and York Avenues, where brother Otto was born. Dad was working for 29¢ per hour at a bakery—top wages—and he worked 72-hour weeks. To supplement their income, they also took in two renters—Uncle Tom and another man named Robert, who each paid them $7/week—in one of their 78th Street apartments.[19]

Then they moved to a ground floor apartment at 410 East 81st Street, between First and York Avenues. (The width of the apartment was about 10–12 feet. However, the room with the air shaft was much smaller—probably 6 to 8 feet—and the width of the building was about 25 feet.) That was the first apartment that Joe and I lived in.[20] In 1960 our family moved to a fifth floor walk-up apartment at 420 East 81st Street, five narrow apartment buildings away—just down the block. Our family was finally "moving up on the East Side."[21] After brother Otto got married, he lived briefly at 422 East 73rd Street in a three-room apartment.

Mom says she remembers the streets were paved with wood blocks and cobblestone. Dad burned wood in a stove that he had stored in the cellar. This was probably damaged wood that was taken out by the city and replaced with new wood. It was full of tar and smelled horribly. They remember the milkman and iceman delivering their goods

19. Renovated or new high-rise buildings have since replaced some of these buildings.

20. York Avenue was originally known as Avenue "A." East of York Avenue is East End Avenue, once known as Avenue "B." East End Avenue is near the East River and extends from 79th to 90th Street.

21. East End Avenue had coal yards. Ships would bring coal there to 81st or 82nd Street. There was also a big ice house there. Coal and ice were delivered by the same man. There was a farmers field across from John Jay Park. Spent malt was brought there from the breweries for fertilizer (there was Ruperts and seven or eight others). In 1903, 125th Street was all farms. It was the last stop for the trolley (pulled by horses). Goats grazed on a farm in what is now Carl Schurz Park. There was a ferry on 86th Street—before WWII—that went to Welfare Island and Queens, for 5¢ up to 25¢. The ferry landing was then moved to where the 78th Street overpass was built by John Jay Park.

on wagons pulled by horses along Second Avenue. Pushcarts with vegetables were covered with cloth—probably to keep coal dust off them and to secure the vegetables so they wouldn't fall off the push-cart when it was moved. There was also a stream on Second Avenue that caused a lot of trouble.

When we were little, Mom dressed Joe and me alike, and she pushed us in our doublewide baby carriage to the park. When we were a few years older, we went for walks to the park or down the street. Our clothes were spotless. Many people stopped to talk to Mom, inquiring about us. They thought Mom was a nanny taking care of twins from a rich family. "Já vím," Mom exclaimed, because she heard this from many people. We don't remember how many new clothes we got, but we do remember accompanying Mom many times to the thrift or second-hand store to buy clothes for different members of the family. I don't think it was easy for Mom to find identical outfits in the thrift store for us.

When we were small and in the park or outside, got dirt on our faces, and were not near a water fountain, Mom took out her handkerchief, moistened it liberally with her saliva, and rubbed the dirt off our faces. We hated this, since the saliva was sometimes odorous and Mom was rubbing us raw. Every morning we lined up in the kitchen like soldiers and were forced to down a teaspoon of cod liver oil or castor oil and other "special" drops. Ish! Cod liver oil was for vitamin A or D, and castor oil was to stimulate our bow-els. (It actually stimulated our *vowels;* we became very vocal and protested, because we disliked the taste so much.) Mom and Dad believed the worse a "medicine" tasted, the better it must be for you. "Dhat vhill teach yous to ghet shick on us!" When we did get sick with a cold, Mom would rub vaporizing ointments on our chest. We loved breathing in those aromatic vapors of Vicks VapoRub and Mentholatum.

Each of us had to take a bath once a week, usually on Saturday nights. The kids went first, then the parents last. When we were very little, John and I and our sister shared baths to save water. We were instructed not to waste water. Our bathtub had lion-claw feet and the porcelain glaze had been worn off long ago. Some of us thought bathing weekly was too frequent and a waste of good water. Later we protested over our mother's exclamation that we had enough dirt in our ears to grow potatoes and if we didn't clean ourselves up, she was going to come in and take care of the job herself. Being 12 years old at the time, we were mortified at the prospect. We quickly got religion and dug out those potatoes ourselves. At least we got most of them out. We think.

Joe and John in Carl Schurz Park, wading pool with sprinklers in background, 1945

Joe, Otto, and John in Carl Schurz Park, 1945

Joe, Otto, and John
in Carl Schurz Park, circa 1947

Joe and John
in front of Irving Savings Bank, circa 1948

Joe and John
on telephones, circa 1949

Joe and John
by Irving Savings Bank, circa 1948

Joe and John (wearing pea coats) with Otto and Mary Ann, circa 1950

Speaking of religion, Saturday nights were the times when we cleaned and polished our shoes for church the next day. We went to mass at St. Monica's Catholic Church (413 East 79th Street, between York and First Avenues). Built in 1881–83, it is still in operation. The mass was in Latin and we didn't understand anything the priest said. It seemed very mysterious to us. We hated kneeling on the unpadded wooden kneeler; it was so painful on our skinny, bony knees. Sometimes I brought a small towel to kneel on. Mom and Dad didn't have any of these problems, since they didn't attend church.

When the priest learned, through our sister, that Mom and Dad had been married in City Hall, he wanted to get them married "for real" in the eyes of God—in the Catholic Church. So one day Mom came home and told Dad to put on his shoes, they were going to church to get remarried. Dad said, "Nutting doink! I'm ahlready married to you mit five kids."

Our parents were our guardian angels, although we kids didn't always recognize or appreciate it. At times when I did something bad, Joe got punished for it. That was fine with me. The opposite

St. Monica's Catholic Church, 2009

also occurred. At one time, we got Mom so angry that she threw
Joe's guitar through two bedrooms, smashing it into smithereens on
his shoulder. She should have pitched for the Yankees. Thus, Joe was
doomed from the start not to become the next international record-
ing star. No doubt, he deserved it.

At times, Joe and I hid under our high-standing iron-framed
beds to escape from being punished. Mom flushed us out by pok-
ing us with the end of a long broom handle or dust mop. At one
time she went on strike. She had had it and was totally annoyed
with us. Sometimes she got so mad that she swore in both English
and Czech. "*Jezis Kristus, Maria a Josef* (Jesus Christ, Mary and
Joseph)," she said in Czech. Between the ages of 8 and 9, I thought,

by deductive reasoning—although I didn't know what "deductive reasoning" meant until years later—that I must be Jesus, because sister Mary was Mary and brother Joe was Joseph.

After the scolding, Mom continued her excellent parenting. When we did something wrong, and for us twins this seemed often, we got punished. Yes, we did find coal in our Christmas stockings more than once. This broke our hearts, but more than that, it scared the hell out of us. (Could we have been *that* bad? No way!) Terror set in. Was Santa not going to come this year? We better shape up.

Mom always took the time to sit us down and explain why our actions were wrong, why we were being punished, and how we should behave correctly in the future. We pouted, made contorted faces for her to see, then twisted and stretched our heads and faces as far away from hers as possible, "staring 100 miles away." But we *listened* very intently to every word Mom said. We were not happy at the moment, but internally we agreed with her and respected Mom's decisions. After all, she had proven herself right on many previous occasions. She was teaching us. Teaching was love. Teaching was hard work. We were learning. She took the time and effort to educate us. She was honest, she was right, and we trusted her. Even though our parents had minimal formal education, we saw them later in life as having Ph.D. skills in parenting. They got their degrees from C.S.U. ("Common Sense University").

Other adults in the community also disciplined us as we played outside our apartment. If someone saw us doing something wrong, they got involved. They would tell us to stop, that they knew our mother and would tell her. (Everyone seemed to know each other on the block.) This always worked; we didn't know that sometimes they used this as an idle threat and didn't actually know Mom. It was a cultural thing, an educational thing, and a loving thing—a good thing—and we got the message.

CHAPTER 2

Relatives, Friends, and Neighbors

Sasha, Where Are Your Shoes?

JOE: Although we have seen pictures of our grandparents, none of us five siblings ever met them. Our grandparents all lived and died in Europe. However, we do wonder about them. What were they like? What could we have learned from them? What loss did we incur by not knowing them?

Mom's mother, also Marie, was born in 1876 in the same village of Pole in the Austro-Hungarian Empire—part of which later would be called Czechoslovakia. On October 4, 1900, she came on the ship *Lahn* to New York City (via Bremen, Germany), to earn enough money so she could get married back home. It seems that Grandma had a boyfriend in the "old country" who had land, but she had nothing. She traveled in steerage, which was the least expensive way to travel, and returned to Europe in 1902 with her dowry and married Josef. Later, Grandma told Mom that there were farms north of 86th Street. I wonder where Grandma lived in New York when she was here? What type of work did she do, what were her living conditions, and how much of a dowry did she bring back?

Well, we may not have known our grandparents, but relations, near-relations, and close family friends provided us with lots of guidance . . . and colorful stories.

Relatives

Uncle Tom and Peggy

Uncle Tom, who left Minnesota with Dad, was married to Feeny, but she died of cancer in 1948. We remember meeting her when we were 4 years old. They never had any children. He then met and lived with Peggy, who eventually became his common-law wife. They lived at 1374 York Avenue, about eight blocks from us, in a small three-room apartment, three flights up, facing the avenue. Their apartment building is still standing.

Peggy always told us that she was born in a coal mine in Pennsylvania and that she was dumb. She was. Uncle Tom and Peggy were well known in Yorkville, especially in the bars. When our parents needed to get in touch with them, John and I would run out of our apartment and "hit" all the bars on York and First Avenues, between

Joe, Uncle Tom, and Peggy (420 East 81st Street), 1962

72nd and 79th Streets, looking for them, since no one in our family had a telephone. We were usually successful. Dad said over the years Tom and Peggy spent about $30,000 in the saloons. They had lots of like-minded friends there. With a cigarette in one hand and glass of whiskey in the other, Peggy loved listening to and singing along with the jukebox tune, "Anytime you're feeling lonely, that's the time . . ."[22]

Their apartment building, built in the late 1800s, was made of brownstone, and at the time it still operated with direct current (D.C.) electricity. This was to their advantage when the big power failure of 1965 blackened New York City.

Their bathtub was in the kitchen. Both the tub and sink had a spring-rope around them with a curtain to hide the tub and cleaning supplies under the sink. The cover over the bathtub was made of white porcelain over a steel plate; you could cut bread and meat on it. (If someone wanted to take a bath, he/she chased everyone out of the kitchen, removed food and other kitchen items from the top cover, and raised and tied the steel cover tightly so it wouldn't fall on their head, injuring and entombing them. Then the person turned on the water and bathed. Not much privacy.) Their toilet used to be in the hall; other tenants on the floor shared its use along with cleaning duties. Later on, the landlord modernized the building by removing the toilet from each hallway and installing one inside each apartment. Such progress was welcomed.

When we were kids, Uncle Tom and "Aunt" Peggy would come to visit. Peggy chain-smoked her Lucky Strike cigarettes and drank. She came into our bedrooms half-boozed up and slobber-kissed us goodnight in our beds. The heavy smell of alcohol on her breath helped put us to sleep. It acted like chloroform. Her burning cigarette wasn't a lucky strike for us, however. On many occasions, we were left with cigarette burns on our arms. Thinking about it later in life, we were surprised that the mattress, bedding, or either of us never caught fire.

---

22. See Appendix C, Item 1e, Memories, Dances and Songs: Songs.

Nana Juba

Nana Juba was Mom's aunt. Her husband Walter was a warden at the Bronx House of Detention in New York. We children heard stories that after he transferred prisoners to Sing Sing prison in Ossining, New York, he would sit in the electric chair between formal uses and eat his lunch. (We thought he didn't have to go far to get a "grilled cheese" sandwich.) It was quiet there and he could think in solitude.

Nana and Walter had two sons, Joe and Willy. One day Joe died. Right after the funeral Nana Juba and Walter came home to their apartment. She dropped dead in the vestibule; she never did make it to her flat. She was a kind and gentle person who we will always fondly remember.

Mom had another friend or relative that we called "Nana from the Bronx." She occasionally went to Florida for the winter. One time she brought us back two 6 oz. glasses for drinking orange juice. Each glass had a different picture of an animal on it. I still have mine. John accidentally broke his decades ago. What a *dummkopf!*

Drunken Willy

Drunken Willy was Nana Juba's other son. He was in the U.S. Navy, and when his ship pulled into port in New York in the 1950s, Willy would make a beeline to our apartment so that he could bum a free home-cooked meal from Mom. (He may also have had other intentions on his mind. I think he had the hots for Mom, since when he visited, she didn't want to be alone with him and kept us nearby.) He knew where delicious food came from. He was usually drunk when he got there. After a few of these visits, he seems to have disappeared. We never saw him again and have no idea what happened to him.

Mrs. Chaloupka

Mrs. Chaloupka, or Teta, was actually Mom's first cousin from Kadov, a neighboring village. She and her husband John lived down the block at 424 East 81st Street. They got together with our folks and their friends, Frantisek and Josephine Smrcka[23] from Long Island City, to play cards. All families took turns hosting these events. They tapped a wooden keg of beer and enjoyed eating head-cheese sandwiches or *jaternice* on seeded-rye bread. The more seeds the better. They always made their own headcheese and *jaternice*. It was less expensive to make meals at home versus paying unnecessary "good money" in a store or restaurant, and you controlled the ingredients. These were all thrifty people. They had to be. They lived through the Great Depression and learned to get the most value out of their money.[24]

Teta was superstitious, like Mom, and they occasionally visited their friend Lola to have their fortunes read. When Teta played cards with us, after losing a few poker hands, she always insisted on changing her seat, hoping her luck would improve with every move.[25] While they partied on Friday night, we kids were four rooms away watching *I Remember Mama* and *Boston Blackie* on our black and white television, filling our bellies with chocolate milk or soda, pretzels or potato chips, or toasted heavily seeded rye bread with butter and garlic slathered and floating high on top.

When we were very young, we observed Teta dressing up to go out on special occasions. She wore a fox stole around her shoulders, with full body fur, tail, feet, and head with mouth sewn shut, and glass eyes clearly visible. This frightened us at first. We thought the fox might not be dead and its eyes were following us. She later gave Mom the stole and eventually, when styles changed, it found a new home in the thrift shop.

---

23. The Smrckas had one child, a daughter who became a Ph.D. professor of anthropology in Colorado.

24. In fact, when Mom and Dad came to visit us decades later in our Minnesota home, they washed and dried the used coffee paper filter for reuse the next day. Using it twice resulted in a 50% savings. Sometimes it was recycled a third time.

25. She was constantly rubbing her rabbit's foot to gain additional advantage for winning. It certainly brought no luck to the rabbit. The gaming authorities should have been alerted, because of her unfair advantage.

After her husband died, Teta's apartment building was scheduled for demolition, so she moved to 73rd Street, between First and York Avenue. Her new apartment now had three railroad-style rooms, as opposed to the five-room railroad flat she previously lived in.

Tante Ida and Uncle Otto

We called her Tante, even though she was Dad's cousin. Most every adult was either "aunt" or "uncle" to us. When family and friends got together, and she or they didn't want us kids or sometimes even Dad to know what they were talking about, Mom spoke in Czech with her friends and relatives. Dad didn't understand much Czech, just a little. Likewise, Dad spoke in German to Tante Ida and her husband. Mom understood some German. We kids learned what some of the words meant and were especially delighted in knowing and being able to correctly pronounce each of the naughty words. The naughtier the words, the better educated we thought we were.

Tante Ida and Uncle Otto had a son named Carl. On numerous occasions when young Carl played with brother Tommy, he too recalled our Mom yelling out to us in the Czech language, saying, "*Jezis Kristus, Maria a Josef*," because John and I were always getting into trouble at ages 2, 3, and 4. This always made Carl and Tommy laugh. Our father was so cool, sitting at the table, relaxed, smoking his pipe. However, Mom was *not* so cool or relaxed. Dad's favorite phrase was, "*Que sera, sera*. (Whatever will be, will be)." He usually hung loose and didn't get too uptight about things—unless the German in him was provoked. (Who would have been capable of doing that?)

A very young Carl describes his first encounter with our dad in Carl's parents' front room on East 77th Street:

> I first remember seeing your father in 1939. We were sitting in the front room and my father and your father [two Ottos] were talking and from under the couch ran a mouse and in a split second your father stepped on it and killed it. My sister and I

were so impressed. The conversation at the time in the room was always remembered because of the event [to wit, that]: Construction crews at the time were taking down the Second Avenue El (Elevated Railroad, above-ground "subway") and your father said they (the U.S.) were sending the steel to Japan and a war was coming!

Incidentally, I went to elementary school at P.S. 70 on 76th Street. I only spoke German and was transferred to P.S. 158 on York Avenue because there were more krauts attending there. Things were tough on us kids and when the war broke out, I and the family lived on 77th Street. We were the building superintendents and the owners were Jewish. We were told to move out. It was then that we moved to 65 East End Avenue where there were more Germans living, and my sister and I went to St. Joseph's school on 87th Street. Once in awhile I would go to John Jay Pool or the East Side Settlement house and meet Joan there. [Joan would later become his wife.]

We ate at 5 p.m. since Dad had to leave for work by 6 p.m. Numerous times per week, for years and almost to the minute, our apartment bell rang at 5 p.m. We all knew who was coming—it was Tante Ida. Occasionally she would bring a homemade apple strudel. It was always mouth watering and special. Although she would say, "Oh, I didn't come here to eat," Mom would always say, "Sit, sthay, vhisit un essen." Mom always invited folks to join our family for a meal. Carl especially loved Mom's dumplings and French toast. The food was always good and plentiful, and we all enjoyed Tante Ida's company.

At one time Tante Ida was visiting Mom and they were talking in the kitchen. I was 6 or 7 years old. I was on a scavenger hunt and found a treasure. Holding it up in the air, I ran into the kitchen with glee happily sharing my new find with them, exclaiming, "Look, I found a balloon!" Upon seeing it, Tante Ida let out a loud shriek while quickly covering her mouth. Mom also saw it, but she appeared to have fire shooting out of her ears, eyes, nose,

Left to right, clockwise: Mom, Dad, Uncle Tom, Peggy,
Teta Chaloupka, and Tante Ida (420 East 81st Street), 1962

and mouth and loudly ordered me to, "Drhrow it in dha gharbage, NOW!" "Why?" I inquired. "It's nhot vhat you dhink," she said. I asked her, then, what was it? Mom, being the teacher that she was, was brutally honest and quickly explained it all to me in perfectly clear detail. She said, "If you have sore fhinger, you vhould put it in dare un it vhould get bedder."[26]

Tragedy #1: We witnessed a number of tragedies in our lives. One of them involved Doris, the daughter of Tante Ida and her husband Otto. One day Doris went to Central Park. She met a man there whom she soon married. John and I were first introduced to her husband, Kip, at their wedding. As we shook hands with him at St. Stephens of Hungary Catholic Church at 414 East 82nd Street (between First and York Avenues), John's silent question to the

26. Boy, was I learning good and useful stuff! I was being educated. I'll try to remember that next time I hurt my finger. Thanks, Mom. Come to think of it, maybe I shouldn't have thrown it out. Maybe I should have brought it to school for show-and-tell. Maybe some of my classmates were suffering with sore fingers, too. I'm sure some of them were.

man was, "Have you ever been arrested?" The vibes I received at that same time, shaking hands with him and looking into his eyes, was, "That man is going to kill Doris." John and I never discussed these thoughts with each other or our parents or anyone else, not until many years later. Who would believe two 8-year-olds anyway? Based on what? Carl later told us his wife Joan's twin sisters, Carol and Patty, have this same psychic ability to think and predict alike.

Well, it turned out that Kip had mental problems. He was shell-shocked from the Korean War. Soon after they were married, Doris became pregnant. Kip was drinking a lot and abused her physically many times at their 86th Street apartment. The last time was so bad that she went back with her parents and brother. Seven months after the marriage, Doris was getting more fearful of his behavior, and because of his abuse he was placed in a mental hospital. Less than a week later he escaped. Two days after that, on the evening of February 22, 1953, on George Washington's birthday, Doris and Tante Ida were at home alone watching *I Love Lucy* on television in their fifth floor apartment at 65 East End Avenue between 82nd and 83rd Streets. Kip climbed onto their apartment roof using the fire escape, dropped down onto a 6-inch brick ledge, side-stepped many feet along the narrow ledge to their kitchen window, opened the window, entered the room, got a bunch of kitchen knives, and went into the front room to do harm. Tante Ida was stabbed several times. Doris, who was 21 years old, was killed, along with her unborn baby.

They could not use the telephone to call the police because it had a lock on it, since Uncle Otto, who was usually drunk, had a propensity to call relatives in Germany, thereby running up bills in excess of $100 each. Others in the apartment building heard the screams and called the police, although not many residents had telephones at that time. Soon the police arrived and took Kip into custody.[27]

---

27. Months earlier, Uncle Otto had come home, unlocked the door to his apartment, and pulled Kip away from the oven. Kip had turned on all the unlit oven gas jets, had his head in the oven, and was trying to commit suicide by gassing himself. Had he succeeded, Doris, her fetus, and her mother would not have been attacked.

Dad was at work when the police called him. He came home right away. Mom was surprised and asked, "Vhy ahre you home so oily?" Never one for beating around the bush, Dad blurted out, "Dohriss is ded und Ida is in hoshpitel."

Doris's brother Carl, 17 years old at the time, was not in the apartment during the attack. Carl was coming home that night after playing pool at Santos, a local pool house on 81st Street, between First and Second Avenues. Upon arriving at the scene, realizing something horrible had happened, his heart just sank. He was met on the stairs by the famous syndicated newspaper and radio commentator Walter Winchell, who had been attending a party nearby at Gracie Square (84th Street and East End Avenue) that night. This is one reason for all the media attention at the time regarding the tragedy. Carl was told they took his mother to Misericordia Hospital at 531 East 86th Street. He went to the hospital and met our dad and came home to our apartment to stay for a while. The next day our parents and their friends went to Carl's apartment to clean it up.[28]

This story made the front page of the *New York Daily News, Daily Mirror,* and *Post* newspapers as well as national TV news. Our family watched it being broadcast on television by news anchor Walter Cronkite, who, incidentally, lived a few blocks away. We saw Tante Ida being wheeled into surgery. Shortly after the stabbings, Ida and her husband, Otto, moved to a smaller apartment at 409 East 84th Street, with steel bars on all the windows and multiple locks on the front door. A year and a half later Otto died.

Kip was found guilty by reason of insanity and put away in a psychiatric hospital in New Jersey. While hospitalized, Kip wrote to Tante Ida in 1954 and said he was sorry, he didn't mean to kill Doris—just Ida—and if he got out he would kill her, too. How

---

28. This indeed was a life-changing experience for Carl. Up to that point, according to him, he was heading down the wrong road. After the tragedy he straightened out, completed high school, and found a full-time job. From that day forward he never took life too seriously. Carl said he "turned to God, not knowing His ways as to why things happen, but to trust in Him."

on earth can psychiatric hospital officials allow such letters to be mailed to the victims, continuing to victimize and terrorize them?

After receiving these threatening letters from Kip, Tante Ida went to her lawyers and asked for protection, to have him kept permanently institutionalized. Tante Ida feared that the released murderer, after being judged sane, would someday come after her. Her lawyers would not help her, though they said they could have sued the City of New York for $1 million in 1953, after the murder, which he was able to commit because he had escaped from the state mental hospital. (Kip had just walked out of the hospital and Carl had met him in the neighborhood, two days before the murder, drinking on First Avenue. Carl told his mother and they reported this to the local police precinct. Carl says the police did nothing. Carl talked to the detective and the detective said he was sorry.) Our aunt, being very religious (Mom used to say she lived in the church), wanted nothing of the so-called "blood money" and therefore would not sign any papers to sue the city after the stabbings. One million dollars was an extraordinary amount of money in the early 1950s. It seemed the lawyers now wanted to keep their distance from her, since there was no longer any monetary incentive in it for them. It was too late to sue.

Kip was eventually released on parole in 1961 and sent back to the South, where he was from, with the stipulation he never return to New York City. After living alone for decades, Tanta Ida had an opportunity to move to Green Valley, Arizona, closer to her son. She lived there for a few years before passing away.

On a much lighter note, some years ago, while Ida was living in Arizona, I once called her to say hello and ask what she was doing. She told me that her television was not working. I asked if she had the remote control in her hand. She said, "Yes." I told her to "take the part that's touching your belly, turn it around, point it the opposite direction towards the television, and then click it." Tante Ida did so and then blurted out, "You fixed my television!" I smiled. I am always willing to help wherever and whenever I can, even from great distances.

Tante Ida and son Carl in Green Valley, Arizona, 1998

Friends

We were taught from a young age to address all adults by calling them "Mr." or "Mrs.," never using their first names. It was a sign of respect.

Mrs. Paloosa and Joey

Mrs. Paloosa was a family friend from Germany who lived in Jackson Heights, Queens. She was eccentric. She usually wore hats with large plumed feathers, flowers, and sometimes even fake fruit fastened to it (I even think she once had a full three-pound fruit cake in her hat). In 1955, she and a lady friend drove from New York City to California. This was quite a feat for two ladies to do themselves at that time, before the interstate system had been built. Mrs. "P" sent the Gindeles a post card and in all seriousness wrote, "We drove to San Francisco and ran over a Chinaman." The way she wrote the card made it sound like this was their objective, but it was just a car accident and thankfully nobody got seriously injured or killed. She probably meant to say "struck" rather than "ran over." Some people sure have an interesting way of expressing themselves.

Mrs. Paloosa had a son named Joseph, about our age. I guess he didn't much care to study, since his grades weren't that good. She used to tell him over and over again that one day he would be shining Sasha's (our) shoes for a living, since we were more serious about studying.

Mr. and Mrs. Novacek

Mr. and Mrs. Novacek were also dear friends of the family. They were elderly immigrants who also came from Czechoslovakia and were like grandparents to us. Mr. Novacek, who we called *Strycek* (Uncle), was generally found smoking his *fajfka* or cigars. He had worked in the cigar manufacturing industry in the city, which employed many Czechs who hand-rolled cigars. John and I attended elementary school at 82nd Street between First and Second Avenues. Since Mom worked away from home and Dad slept during the day, John and I walked to the Novaceks' apartment at lunchtime. They lived two blocks from school, on York Avenue between 81st and 82nd Streets.

John and I usually had a cheese sandwich, milk, and a bowl of Campbell's tomato soup for lunch. The soup had a huge dollop of butter floating on top—to die for. We remember the soup spoons were as large as miniature "shovels." When we ate hot dogs, also a favorite food for us kids, Mrs. Novacek delighted in asking us if we wanted "baby shit," meaning mustard, on top of them. That's the phrase she used. Mrs. Novacek thought it was so funny and laughed hysterically in her high-pitched nervous voice. She, as well as Mom and Mrs. Chaloupka, also convinced us that eating burnt toast— instead of discarding it—would make us good looking when we got older. They were terribly mistaken. This was their way of not having us waste good, or at least edible, food. We are certain they colluded.

Another favorite saying of Mrs. Novacek was, "When you have your health, you have everything." We heard her saying this many times. She was a realist and pragmatist and didn't take anything for granted.

The Novaceks lived in a tiny apartment in a building built between 1879 and 1901. An apartment perhaps 12-feet wide and 40-feet long *with* a small air shaft, it had a front room, kitchen with bathtub, and small bedroom. (See Figure 1.) They had their own minuscule toilet attached to the bedroom. However, it had no sink. You had to use the kitchen sink to wash your hands. Except for the air shaft, there were no glass windows between the kitchen and front room, only a large windowless opening that received light from the window in the front room that faced York Avenue. The kitchen and bedroom had two small windows opening to the air shaft. Each apartment had a meter in the kitchen that regulated and dispensed a measured amount of gas for the stove. The meter was operated by a coin. Once money was inserted, gas was available for

Teta Chaloupka, Mrs. Novacek, Anna Novacek
(daughter), and Mom in Carl Schurz Park, 1945

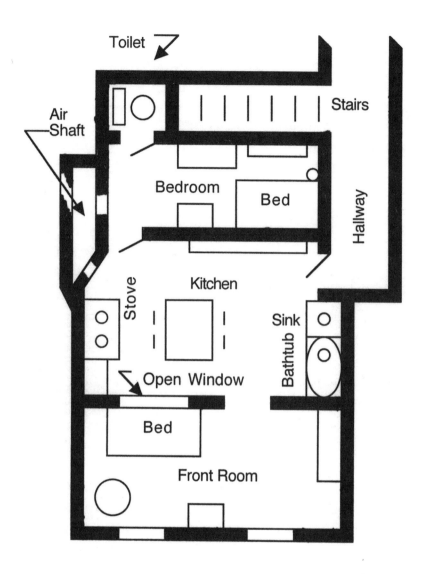

Figure 1. Mr. and Mrs. Novacek's
Three-Room Tenement Apartment

cooking. To save money and game the system, some tenants made coins out of ice, inserted the ice coins, obtaining gas. Of course the ice then melted, destroying the evidence. Free gas. Sometimes free is good. Sometimes free is necessary.

Mrs. Novacek occasionally helped Mom get needed rest and peace by taking us by subway to the Bronx Zoo and up to Pelham Bay Park, where we would picnic. We always enjoyed riding the subway, hearing the wheels of the cars screech as they turned around bends, smelling the "electricity," hearing and seeing huge sparks as contact was made between the subway cars and the third rail, and feeling hot, stale air blowing across our faces. We brought raw potatoes along with soda, chips, salad, sandwiches, marshmallows, and some charcoal. We made a fire in one of the public grills, placed the hot dogs on the grill and potatoes directly on the hot coals, and baked the hell out of them. The longer the potatoes baked—and many times they were overcooked—the thicker and blacker the outer skin would become. Many times it was difficult to discern the burnt potatoes from the charcoal. We burned our tongues eating the hot potatoes. For desert we had fun toasting and eating the roasted marshmallows. Mrs. Novacek also accompanied our family to the park or at celebrations.

One day after a Czech festival at National Hall, after the elders had danced their last dance ("*Tales from the Vienna Woods* Waltz," the "Blue Skirt Waltz" or "Blue Danube Waltz," "Beer Barrel Polka" or "Pennsylvania Polka," Hungarian *czardas*, "Edelweiss" or "Moonlight and Roses")[29] and were full from drinking beer all evening and we were full of soda, the adults and children began to walk the nine blocks home to our various apartments. Mrs. Novacek, then in her late 70s, couldn't hold it anymore. She straddled herself between two parked cars on 71st Street, lifted her dress, and pissed a river through her bloomers.

---

29. See Appendix C, Item 1e, Memories, Dances and Songs: Dances.

She once told us when she was a little girl in the old country she was arrested for stealing an apple off a neighbor's tree. She spent the night in jail. We were aghast and shocked. We kids couldn't even imagine such a thing happening to her or anyone else. She was the first "jail bird" we ever met—*and she was caring for us.*

Mrs. Novacek was 98 years old when she passed away. God bless her. She was a living treasure. She was the closest thing to a grandparent that we had ever had, and we all loved her.

Alex

Alex went to school with Otto and lived across the street over Frank's Bar and Grill. His apartment building was 70 feet away from ours. Since neither of our families had telephones, when they found it necessary to communicate with each other during the day one of them would flash a mirror, reflecting sunlight into the other's front room window. The whole room seemed to light up with flashes of dancing light. If someone was home, this signaled the person to come to the window so that information could be shouted across the street. Of course, this communication system had limitations. It didn't work on cloudy days or at night or when the sun was not right, and one had to be near the window by the street.

Alex's family had a farm upstate, in Cobleskill, west of Schenectady, New York. It was used mainly during hunting season. One Thanksgiving weekend, five people—I, Dad, brother Otto, Jr., Alex, and Alex's father—drove up there. Otto was behind the wheel; Alex sat in the passenger seat. We left Manhattan at 4 a.m. It was pitch black outside and the darkness remained for a few more hours. Since it was a blustery cold November day, Dad retrieved a paper bag containing a bottle of Four Roses whiskey. Keeping it in the bag, he twisted the cork off and took a chug. With me sitting between them in the back seat, Dad passed the bag to me to give to Alex's father so he too might imbibe. The bottle was passed back and fourth numerous times. I decided to intervene and take a few swigs myself. After all, I was 15. Soon the three of us were all warmed up. I had no intention of being left out of any party.

Freddy

An acquaintance, Freddy, was a year or two younger than us. He lived on hot dogs and soda. That's probably why he looked malnourished. For dessert, he generally picked his nose and ate the boogers. The longer the boogers, the tastier they seemed and the more satiated he appeared. I saw him do this numerous times.[30]

Another gross experience we had was when an older brother of one of the kids on the block twisted and took out his eyeball, showed it to us, then popped the glass eye back in. We damn near passed out.

Fat Mary

Fat Mary—that's the name we all referred to her by at home—and her husband owned a hotel and bar and lived in New Jersey. We remember visiting them and being at the bar on a Saturday night. Fat Mary's apartment, as well as rooms they rented out, was above the bar, and it was difficult for us to sleep because of the music and noise below. It was also difficult trying to sleep with the aroma of cigar and cigarette smoke and stale beer in the air. When we woke up on Sunday morning, Fat Mary opened the bar especially for us kids and gave us each a free bottle of soda. John and I thought we had died and gone to heaven. The soda was sweet, but more importantly it was *free*, and we *each* got our *own* little bottle—our treasure—that we didn't have to share with anyone else. Halleluiah. Life was good and promising. It was indeed very special.

---

30. John asked me why he did it. I said he must like the saltiness of his snot. John then inquired how I knew boogers had a salty taste. I pled the Fifth Amendment.

Mr. and Mrs. Solar

As kids, we spent three to five weeks each summer on a farm in Connecticut. We loved it there. Mr. and Mrs. Solar, both from Czechoslovakia, were retired farmers and rented rooms to our family in their large nine-room farmhouse. Three generations of our family had been going there since 1937. (See Chapter 8 for detailed information about our country adventures.)

CHAPTER 3

Growing Up in New York City

Free Toaster, Anyone?

Lay of the Land

JOHN: New York City[31] is composed of five boroughs: Brooklyn
and Queens to the east (which is the beginning of the western
edge of Long Island, becoming Long Island along with Nassau and
Suffolk Counties), the Bronx to the north, Staten Island (formerly
known as Richmond) to the southwest, and Manhattan Island in
the middle, bordering New Jersey on the Hudson River. (See Figure
2.) The East River separates Manhattan from Queens and Brooklyn,
and the Harlem River separates Manhattan from the Bronx. Both
rivers are not actually rivers, but estuaries. Roosevelt Island (formerly Welfare Island) is situated in the East River, between Manhattan and Queens. Manhattan Island is about 13.5 miles long and 2.3
miles wide.

Manhattan is the smallest in square miles of the five boroughs (24), the Bronx (42), Staten Island (60), Brooklyn (82), and
Queens (112).[32] Most of Manhattan is laid out like a grid, with

31. See Appendix C, Item 1e, Memories, Dances and Songs: Songs.
32. *World Book Encyclopedia,* 2010 ed., s.v.v., "The City," 323.

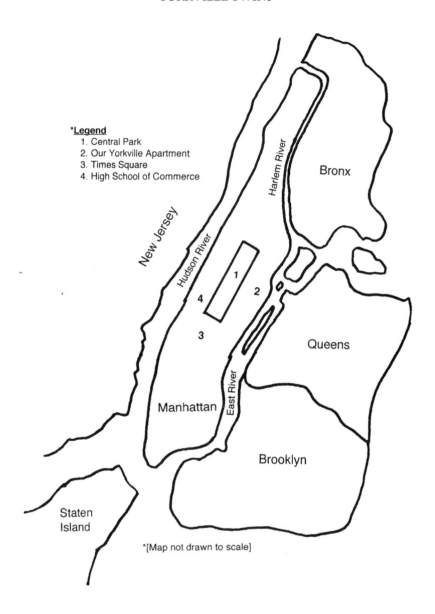

Figure 2: New York City (and Five Boroughs)

consecutive-numbered streets running parallel from north to south and avenues running parallel from east to west. Fifth Avenue divides the eastside from the west side. It is relatively easy to navigate the city.

Getting Around

As we grew up, all the boroughs except Manhattan were considered "foreign countries" to us. We hardly ever left Manhattan; we didn't have to since we had everything we needed right there. One of the great things about New York City is that it has delicious sweet water, piped in from northern reservoirs. Most people don't know this, but it is true.

The 77th Street IRT subway station on Lexington Avenue was a block closer to our apartment than the one at 86th Street. However, it was a local, slower train, stopping at each station. Whenever we needed to get downtown faster, we walked the extra block to the 86th Street station and took the express.

Public transportation in New York is great.[33] The subways are fast, but the busses offer more local stops and less walking. In our days, though, public transportation was perceived as being dangerous.[34] It also cost money we didn't always have.

In 1956, the cost of a one-way ride on the bus or subway was 15¢, which was considerable money to two young boys.[35] We sometimes

33. The Second and Third Avenue Els—elevated railroads or subways *above* ground—were built in the late 1870s and phased out in the 1950s along with trolley cars. (A new Second Avenue subway system is presently under construction and is expected to take 10 years to complete.) See Appendix C, Item 1a, New York City: Trains/Transportation.

34. As kids, we almost never went into Harlem for fear of being robbed, beaten, or stabbed. It was an area that had a lot of crime. Yet we had to travel through it to get to the Bronx on our way to Pelham Bay Park. Today, however, this area is being cleaned up—transformed socially and economically. Its main thoroughfare is 125th Street.

35. Today it is $2.25. One time Dad found out that the city was going to raise the subway fares. He thought they might be using the same metal tokens, so he collected and hoarded over one thousand of those subway tokens in an old whiskey bottle (we made sure it was first emptied, of course). His anticipation never materialized; the city did change the configuration/size of that token. Oh, well, he did try to save the family money.

77th Street Subway signage
(Roberto C. Tobar, photographer, 11/7/2008 [# 92965] adapted)

86th Street Subway signage
(Roberto C. Tobar, photographer, 3/6/2009 [# 92322] adapted)

walked downtown, then took public transportation home when we were tired and could walk no more. At other times we walked the entire round trip. Walking from street to street[36] is quick in Manhattan because the distances are short. However, walking from avenue to avenue is about two to three times further. Besides saving the fare, walking was good for us and gave us the opportunity to observe many different people (some of them crazy), stores, parks, traffic, and activities. Sometimes with the money we saved, we bought a hot dog from a pushcart vendor.

Eileen and son Dennis at hot dog stand, NYC

On rare occasions we took taxis, i.e., when Mom had to rush me to the emergency room of Lenox Hill Hospital because my face and body had swollen up. (We found out I had a severe allergic reaction to dust and feathers.) Another occasion was when she took us to Grand Central Station to catch a steam locomotive train to Fort Plain, N.Y.—but that was in 1948. We remember the

36. See Appendix C, Item 1e, Memories, Dances and Songs: Songs.

Checker taxicabs in the city. These taxis were very roomy inside, and if one needed extra seating, "jumper seats" unfolded from the floor for a few extra riders. Those were especially exciting for children to sit on, because we could ride facing backwards and see where we had been. It was fun and novel.

If one owned a car in New York City, as our parents did in the early 1950s, one either paid to park it in a garage—only the "rich" people did this—or parked it free on the street that did not have meters. Years later the avenues eventually got parking meters. Dad always parked on the street. However, if one did not take the car to work each morning, one had to move it to the other side of the street every third day, because street sweepers would come through and the owner of the car would receive a hefty fine and the car could be towed for hindering cleanup. Sometimes when we wanted to move our car closer to the apartment, where there was a parking space available, one of us got a garbage can and placed it in the middle of the space, or we just stood there, while Dad got into his car a block or so away and drove it to the new, closer space. This usually worked, but sometimes another driver muscled in and captured the space before Dad had a chance to claim it.[37] On other days water-tank trucks from the sanitation department drove through spraying the streets—they should have sprayed the sidewalks as well—to wash dog crap and other debris off of them. This could be done without moving the parked vehicles.

The challenge of getting around New York on little or no money prompted one of our longest lasting lessons about saving. When we were about 12 and saw a penny lying on the sidewalk, Mom would tell us to pick it up. We didn't want to. After all, it was not cool to do so and it was only a penny. Then she explained to us the significance

---

37. When I later taught on Long Island, I would drive into the city on Friday nights to spend the weekend with my folks. It took me anywhere from 30 minutes, if I was lucky, to one hour and 20 minutes, constantly driving around blocks to find an open parking space. Then I had to remember where I parked so I could retrieve it on my way out. Sometimes this was challenging.

of that penny. If you had only 14¢ in your pocket, you could not ride the bus or subway. That penny picked off the ground meant you could. This made sense. Ever since we have always picked up any change we saw lying on the ground. And who knows, another Depression might be coming; we have to be prepared.

Mom taught us about saving in other ways, too. When we were 11, she helped us establish bank accounts at Irving Savings Bank, a beautiful building with a street-level post office in its corner. It was adjacent to our apartment building at 81st Street and First Avenue. We regularly deposited money we got for birthdays and other events. She said we needed to save for a rainy day, and that was the only time we should take our money out. Joe was concerned and asked her, "What if we need it and it's not raining?" Luckily, her reply satisfied him.

Mom also helped us establish Christmas Club accounts at the bank. Each month we deposited a certain number of dollars into our accounts. It had to be before 3 p.m., because that is when New York City banks closed for the day. At the end of the year, a month

Irving Savings Bank with lower-level Post Office:
81st Street and First Avenue

before Christmas, we could take the money out (even if it was not raining) and have enough to purchase gifts for our family.

We also saved S&H Green Stamps. Beginning in 1951, they were given by merchants to customers as an enticement for them to spend more. Later Blue Chip and Gold Bond Stamps appeared. We, like millions of other people, pasted them into booklets. When enough had been saved, we redeemed them for toasters, coffee makers, and various other products. Merchants liked them because they encouraged sales. Customers liked them because they thought they were getting something of value for free. Who could resist a new toaster?

CHAPTER 4

Yorkville

The Constipation of Mr. Kovo

Ethnic Neighborhoods

JOE: The Upper East Side[38] of Manhattan stretches from 59th Street north to 96th Street, the beginning of Spanish Harlem, and from Central Park (Fifth Avenue) to the East River. This area encompasses the neighborhoods of Lenox Hill to the south, Yorkville,[39] and Carnegie Hill to the north.

Famous celebrities, affluent, and influential people have resided or still reside on the Upper East Side: the Rockefellers, Roosevelts, Kennedys, and Nixons, as well as other politicians and many actors and actresses. It was thought that anyone who made it big lived in this area. Today it is also home to notable museums and private schools. The Upper East Side is also known as the "Silk Stocking District" and Yorkville as the "Gracie Mansion District."

There has been some debate regarding Yorkville's southern boundary. Some say it started at 59th Street, others 72nd Street. Still others (especially today) identify 79th Street as the beginning of Yorkville. Still others believed Yorkville extended from 63rd Street north to 91st Street or 96th Street and between Third Avenue and the East River. (See Figure 3.)

---

38. See Appendix C, Item 1c, Upper East Side.
39. See Appendix C, Item 1d, Yorkville.

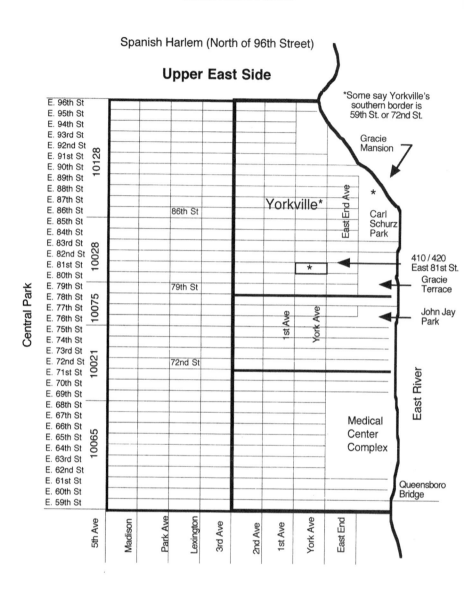

Figure 3: Yorkville on the Upper East Side

Yorkville[40] was primarily a German/Bohemian neighborhood, but Hungarian, Irish, Italian, and Jewish people also lived there. Many of these people, immigrants like our parents, were sometimes negatively referred to as "greenhorns," because they were recent arrivals from another country. Street vendors were common and could be seen pushing pushcarts selling frankfurters, pretzels, roasted nuts, vegetables, Snow-Cone treats, and Italian ices (shaved ice with flavored, colored, sugar syrup on top). Many of the carts were horse-drawn, and you had to be careful not to step in the horse manure when you crossed the street, lest you track it into your apartment. Organ grinders with their monkeys and people playing musical instruments performed for money and were common in the streets.

Today, Yorkville is home to, and a blend of, "high society's" rich and famous.[41] It is also considered a middle- to upper-level working class neighborhood. Years ago it was a poor working class neighborhood. Prior to the Civil War, farms were abundant in the area. After the First World War, mass transit—streetcars and elevated subway lines—brought in developers who built tenements for the influx of newly arriving immigrants.

Three main streets crossed Yorkville from east to west. The Bohemians lived primarily between 65th and 73rd Streets, with the wider East 72nd Street serving as its center of activity.[42] Bohemian National Hall (*Narodni Budova*) and Sokol Hall[43] were the ethnic gathering places for many of these immigrants. The halls provided food, gymnastic tournaments, live theatre, music, and dancing. Immigrants felt comfortable here, receiving support from people of their own language, nationality, and working class background.

40. See Appendix C, Item 1d, Yorkville: Ethnic Matters.

41. The reader may wish to do an Internet search for a list of notable or famous residents of Yorkville, then and now. See Appendix C, Item 1d, Yorkville: People.

42. Bodnar, Theodore A. (July 3, 1983). Letters; Yorkville recalled. New York: *The New York Times*, R7.

43. Bohemian Hall has since moved to 29-19 24th Avenue in Astoria, Queens. Some consider Sokol Hall to be a Czech version of the German *Turnverein*.

Czech butcher shops with poultry and meats hanging in the window and small independent grocery stores and shops selling imported ethnic goods and spices were found throughout this area. Praha was a Czech restaurant at 73rd Street on First Avenue. The Vasata was at 349 East 75th Street and Second Avenue. The Ruc was at 312 East 72nd Street.

National Hall: Friends of family, circa 1939

We remember when brother Tom had his wedding reception in the blue room of National Hall (321–325 East 73rd Street). Mom often brought her children there to see plays spoken in Czech. We didn't understand the Czech language, but we sure loved eating the twisted, salted bread sticks loaded with caraway seeds and playing hide and seek. Sometimes we even snuck a sip of *pivo*. Mom *never* knew. (Or did she?)

At Sokol Hall (420 East 71st Street) there was a dance party with prizes given away. John won a free *hoska*, a loaf of European twist bread, while I won a bottle of Three Feathers whiskey. We were 12 years old and ecstatic. Those in charge of the prizes didn't want to give me the bottle, but our family "protested" that this was won fairly. After all, this is America! I got the gift that was accepted by Dad, and the Gindele family walked home with heads held high to celebrate.

The Hungarians lived between 75th and 83rd Streets with the main area of activity along the wider 79th Street.[44] Ethnic food and Hungarian dancing were popular pastimes. Hungarian butcher stores and those selling imported goods and spices were also in abundance. We remember a Hungarian pork store, Tibor, at 1508 Second Avenue (78th Street), and Jos. Mertzl, on Second Avenue, offering smoked ham, *jaternice*, salami, etc., with meats also hanging on hooks in the window, with the aroma of meats wafting in the air, enticing passersby to come in and shop. Hungarian restaurants or bakeries like the Red Tulip (439 East 75th Street), Csarda (Second Avenue, between 83rd and 84th Streets), Hungarian Garden, Budapest Pastry (218 East 84th Street), Viennese Lantern, Debrechen, Tokay and Mocca (1588 Second Avenue, near 83rd Street) and Rigo Hungarian Viennese Pastry (318 East 78th Street) have since closed their doors.

We remember Hungarian spice importer, Paprikas Weiss, originally at First Avenue and 82nd Street, then Second Ave. and 81st Street. The store reminded us of a general store out west, similar to ones seen in Western movies. Walking into the store, one was greeted with a variety of sights and strong aromas coming from huge open burlap bags overflowing with fresh colorful spices from around the world. Standing on old worn creaking wood-plank floors, the proprietors spoke to customers in Hungarian or broken English. Mom also frequented Lekvar by the Barrel on First Avenue and 82nd Street. They sold not only spices and herbs but also baking accessories.

Orwasher's, a Hungarian bakery founded in 1916, is still in operation at 308 East 78th Street. They bake Eastern European/Jewish artisan bread of pumpernickel, rye, challah, small rolls, etc. We loved their salt-stick rolls and potato bread, especially with

---

44. Bodnar, Theodore A. (July 3, 1983). Letters; Yorkville recalled. New York: *The New York Times*, R7.

butter. Carl says, "Your brother Tom and I would go to Orwasher's each Saturday morning for your mother during the war years, 1941–1945, and buy sourdough bread. We also had a morning walk to your Uncle Tom's and delivered food that your mother prepared for him and Feeny."

Orwasher's Bakery, 2009

Later when we were teaching in Minnesota, our folks would mail us loaves of Orwasher's heavily seeded rye bread. We are not the only ones who enjoyed their breads from afar. Later in life we took a road trip through Alpine, Texas. We stopped at the Amtrak railroad station because they housed a Chamber of Commerce kiosk, and we needed travel information. We met an elderly lady who volunteered at the Chamber. She spoke with a heavy dialect and we inquired about her nationality—it was Czech. We got excited and learned she grew up in Yorkville and had been a frequent customer of this bakery. Now, living in Texas, she would fly to NYC once a year to visit friends, bringing two suitcases. One was empty, which she filled with Orwasher's bread. Back home she froze the bread and enjoyed eating it throughout the year. Another time we met an elderly couple on a cruise. He was Czech and told us he, too, once lived in Yorkville on 76th Street and enjoyed shopping at this bakery.

The Germans lived between 84th and 90th Streets with the wider 86th Street[45] serving as its center (sometimes called "Sauerkraut or German Boulevard"). Bars, restaurants, breweries, and ballroom dancing helped people relax after a hard day at work. During the 1930s this area was the national headquarters of the German-American Bund—a dangerous pro-Nazi group in America—led by Fritz Kuhn. This sometimes resulted in violent clashes between German Americans and pro- and anti-Nazi Germans.[46] Carl remembers,

> My father, in his drunken stupor, would take me along to some of these rallies. They would take place on 88th Street off Lexington Avenue in a downstairs gym. I, along with other German boys, would march around and work out. We spoke only German, which proved difficult with the Irish kids in school because of the accent.

In the late 1940s there was a shoe repair shop in our neighborhood that we frequented. It was possibly built during the middle to late 1800s. The shop was a huge open-air multi-story warehouse with 4- to12-inch-wide overhead leather belts, some 50–100-feet long, turning on pulleys and in many directions, operating different machines at various speeds for the repair of shoes. One central motor operated all the straps. The roar of the machines, the slapping of the belts, and the banging of hammers onto nails was music to our ears.

Other neighborhood bakeries were Fleischmann's Vienna Bakery (534 East 81st Street) and Finks on 76th Street. Finks, a commercial bakery, was up the block from the East Side House and John Jay Park. We remember Kurtz's German Konditorei bakery on York Avenue near 81st Street. We loved eating their sugar-coated, jelly-filled donuts (with red filling oozing out and sticking to our fingers, hands, and

---

45. Ibid.
46. See Appendix C, Item 1d, Yorkville.

faces) as well as their crumb buns. We could have eaten and enjoyed a bag of the butter and browned sugar-baked crumbs alone. They were all delicious. When one asked for coffee, the server, Frau Brunhilda, followed up with "Mit crème und zugar?" New Yorkers like lots of cream and sugar in their coffee. The more cream and sugar, the better. Other bakeries were Glaser's Bakery, 1670 First Avenue (87th Street), Kramer's Pastries, 1643 Second Avenue (86th Street), and Cream Puff, 1388 Second Avenue (between 71st and 72nd Streets). Roslyn's was on First Avenue between 79th and 80th Streets.

The evening bar/restaurant scene, especially along 86th Street, was lively and captivated one's senses with music, dancing, and the aromas of beer and food. This was a popular area to have fun and forget one's troubles.

The Irish were dispersed all over Yorkville along with numerous Irish bars. For many years we kids walked to Fifth Avenue to watch the St. Patrick's Day parade, which used to end up in Yorkville at Third Avenue and 86th Street. Today it ends at 86th Street and Fifth Avenue. This is still a popular area for Manhattanites to go and eat, although many of the old German and Irish bars are now closed as the ethnicity of these early neighborhoods has changed, blurring previously distinct boundaries. One German restaurant is left, the Heidelberg, 1648 Second Avenue (between 85th and 86th Streets). Dresner's Bar stood at 1479 York Avenue (between 78th and 79th Streets). A butcher and grocery store, Schaller and Weber, is still in business at 1654 Second Avenue (86th Street).

German restaurants that have since closed are the Hofbrau Haus, Jaeger Haus, Bremen House (220 East 86th Street), Café Mozart, Die Lorelei (Second Avenue at 86th Street), Gloria Palast, Café Hindenburg (86th Street), Café Geiger (206 East 86th Street), Kleine Konditorei (234 East 86th Street), and Ideal (238 East 86th Street, moving to 322 after a fire). The German Elk Candy store, once on 86th Street near Second Avenue, has also closed.

Luigi, an Italian immigrant and barber, had a shop down the

block. At Christmastime, when customers came for a haircut, Luigi had a bottle of whiskey and a shot glass on the table. A "shot" was offered to customers, even to us 17-year-olds, when we were getting our haircuts. But we didn't tell. Nothing like some spirits to lift one's spirit on a damp, cold, New York winter's day.

Of course, with lots of people living in New York, many pets resided there also. During the 1950s through early 1980s, people let their dogs do their business in the streets between cars. Some self-centered New Yorkers let their pets relieve themselves right in the middle of the sidewalks and did not clean it up. It is for this reason that most New Yorkers learned to walk with their heads down, so they could locate and not step in the dog shit. However, things have improved over the last few decades with New Yorkers cleaning up their act. Laws dictate that pet owners must clean up after the event, utilizing plastic bags or pooper-scoopers, or be fined.

Crime

Our family grew up on crime-ridden streets in Yorkville. Police and fire sirens were a constant presence, although you soon learned to "tune it out." In the early years—the 1940s and 1950s—Irish cops used to walk the beat. Now they patrol in cars and don't really get to know storeowners and citizens, as they once did.

At one time while living in our ground floor apartment, we heard sirens and saw the flashing lights of police cars driving down the street against traffic. We ran out and followed the noise. It seems this time the police cars were part of a movie-making set. The crowd, including us, was instructed to point across the street to a third floor window where a "murder" was staged. Later we found out the movie was going to be about the slums of New York. John and I fit right in, although we never did find out when the movie debuted or saw it.

When we were about eight years old, we were walking in Central Park with Otto when we got mugged—held up for 50¢ by an older Puerto Rican kid with a knife. We told the mugger to keep the money, but please leave us our cap gun. We told him we would have to walk "forever" to get home, since he took our bus fare. He wasn't fazed. We thought he was a nice mugger, though, since he did let us keep our cap gun (some protection).

We had gangs in our neighborhood. When we were teenagers, we would walk down the block to the store and if a group of older kids were congregating/loitering on a stoop or spilling onto the sidewalk in our path, we purposely crossed the street in order to avoid them and continued walking rapidly. They were looking for trouble. We also learned not to make eye contact with any of them and stared down hard on the pavement as we walked. Our block was famous for its bad reputation. We lived in fear. Kids who grew up a few blocks away on 79th Street near East End Avenue also feared the 81st Street boys. John Tauranac, one of those kids, said he led ". . . a generally idyllic life except for the fear we had of the 81st Street boys. When we heard they were coming, we ran home with our tails between our legs."[47] Kevin Boland, also a resident at this time, considered Yorkville to be "one of the toughest neighborhoods in the city referred to by many as a bucket of blood."[48] Sometimes our fear also carried over to subway rides, when one occasionally encountered a crazy or deranged person.

Tragedies #2 and #3: In the 1950s Mom had a family friend who was walking his dog on York Avenue between 78th and 79th Streets, when he was stabbed to death. He was an innocent victim of a random attack by a drunken, depraved man who just came out of a bar. In another instance, the family recalls a dentist being murdered at his office on 81st Street and First Avenue. (John and I had gone to his office for dental fillings—at $2 a tooth—and extractions, all

---

47. Harvey Frommer and Myrna Katz Frommer, *It Happened in Manhattan: An Oral History of Life in the City During the Mid-Twentieth Century* (New York: Berkley Publishing Group, 2001), 22.

48. Kevin N. Boland, *One Day as I Stood Lonely: Yorkville* (Bloomington, IN: Xlibris, 2010), 9–10.

without a local anesthetic such as Novocain. Ouch! We maintain our innocence.)

There are lots of mentally ill people living in New York, as in any major megalopolis. One day our sister was walking up 81st Street, near our apartment, when a stranger accosted her. She had her young daughter with her. Mary Ann was "frozen" in fear. Some garbage collectors were working the block and saw the incident. They yelled to Mary Ann, asking if the guy was her boyfriend or husband. She couldn't speak, but just slowly shook her head, "No." The sanitation men chased the guy away. Our sister thanked the men again the next time she saw them.

Years later, Mary Ann and her husband Joe went down to the street to get their parked car so they could drive to Long Island. They couldn't find it. It had been stolen. The cops said the car was probably on its way to South America where automobile parts bring in more money than a whole car. In the past they had had the hatchback window of their car stolen. After it had been stolen twice, the third time they replaced the hatchback window they *chained* it down.

While growing up, John was always nosy. Friends and relatives suggested he consider becoming a reporter. On one particular occasion, while sitting in our apartment, he once again heard sirens. The sirens seemed to be getting louder and closer. He was about 17 at the time and followed the sound, running down five flights of stairs and then running from 81st Street to 78th Street, where he saw police cars. While he was walking toward the police cars, a cop called him over. They took him into an apartment where two women lived and where someone had tried to break in. The first thing the cops asked him was, "What does your father do?" Perhaps they wanted to size him up, profile him. He thought, "What difference should it make *what* my father does?" He told them he was a baker. They tried to pin the attempted break-in on him when they noticed he was breathing rapidly and heavily, was sweating, and had scratches on his hands. He told them he ran downstairs from his fifth-floor apartment, then three to four blocks to see what was happening. He said the scratches were old, not fresh, and they were the result of refinishing a cabinet on the roof one week earlier. This was absolutely true. The cops scared the hell out of him and told him to get his ass home. He quickly followed their sage advice and almost got killed by a car while running across 79th Street on First Avenue.

When John was in high school, he worked part-time as a dry cleaning delivery boy in the neighborhood. Just across the street from the store was an Italian pizzeria where his boss usually ate. One time, shortly after his boss returned to his store after eating, some men went inside with guns blazing and murdered the pizza men. It was another gangland rubout. So what's new? We believe the intruder(s) saw his boss in the pizzeria and waited for him to leave before opening fire. It is one thing for gangsters to kill other gangsters, which doesn't usually get citizens overly excited, but it is another thing for gangsters to kill innocent bystanders, especially paying customers, which brings much negative attention and public outcry.

Two scams affected our family. A family, the Raubes, who lived across the street on 81st Street, was collecting money from residents to be used to throw a block party, a very local social event. This is where the police block off the street to traffic and people bring food, soda, and beer (Piels, Rheingold, Schaefer, and Knickerbocker beer were popular then).[49] Music, games, and dancing were to take place in the street. Our parents and others contributed money. The block party never materialized. The Gindeles later learned that the Raubes had suddenly become the proud owners of a new washing machine.

Another scam struck in the 1960s when Mom was caught up in

---

49. I remember having to go to the tavern for a neighbor, to bring back a two-quart cap-less porcelain jug full of sloshing beer. The bartender didn't question my age and I wasn't yet a teenager then. See also Appendix C, Item 1e, Memories, Dances and Songs: Songs.

a money swindle known as a "pigeon drop."[50] A woman stopped Mom on the street and asked her to take $3,000 out of the family bank account and let the woman hold it in good faith. Mom was told it was a sting operation and she was helping the police catch a crook who worked in the bank. Mom was told she would get the money back plus a reward for her cooperation, but she had to wait a half hour. Mom would help anybody and consented to help. During that time, the woman absconded with the money. Mom lost $3,000, the equivalent of picking up, washing, ironing, buttoning, folding, and delivering 20,000 shirts at 15¢ each. That's the price she worked for years earlier. Mom was so devastated, embarrassed, and angry because someone violated her trust and stole the family money. It nearly killed her, especially to tell Dad what happened. She kept saying, "Vhat vas I dhink-ink?" She did not tell her children about this, perhaps because she feared they would think she was stupid or weak. We learned about this years later.

At one time, one of our apartments was robbed of jewelry and some cash. It was an inside job. Our parents were on vacation for a few weeks and they gave the key for our apartment to the caretaker in the building. The caretaker was paid $10 to water the plants each week. (Mom and Dad loved flowers and we had lots of potted plants in the apartment.) We believe that a daughter of the caretaker and her boyfriend got the key and went into the apartment looking for valuables. A few gold earrings, pearls, and money were discovered to be missing upon their return from vacation.

One June day John and I were about to show some Minnesota relatives around Manhattan, when at noon, we heard on the radio, "This has been a most peaceful day in New York City. Only 11 murders have occurred so far." Oy vey!

---

50. Mom trusted people. She also believed anything printed in the newspaper had to be true, especially in her local newspaper and the national pulp newspapers she admired, otherwise it wouldn't be printed. She trusted the papers. "Dha newspapers dhon't phrint lies," she used to say.

Housing

One day a friend informed Dad that he might want to consider buying some real estate across the Hudson River in Fort Lee, New Jersey. A bridge was expected to be built crossing the river there. Dad couldn't afford it at the time. He didn't believe in borrowing money. The George Washington Bridge was eventually built in 1931. Our family could have been rich. Instead, the Gindeles settled for rental property in a steam-heated, hot-water (as opposed to cold-water) tenement-flat in Yorkville, with a gas stove, a porcelain bathtub, and an inside-your-apartment toilet. The inside toilet made up for missing out on the George Washington Bridge real estate property.

New York State passed Tenement Laws to protect tenement residents.[51] This was done for health and safety reasons. The "Tenement House Act of 1867" required new apartment buildings to have fire escapes and one water-closet, usually an outside privy, for every 20 tenants.[52] Because of the "Tenement Laws of 1879," when new apartment buildings were erected, air shafts were built in the middle of the apartment (in our case, with three windows—one facing each inside bedroom) so each room would have added light and ventilation.[53] The "Tenement House Act of 1901" required apartments to have even better ventilation, cold water sinks, heat and bathrooms on each floor to service the apartments.[54]

410 East 81st Street

The first apartment John and I lived in was on the ground floor of a five-story walkup, a railroad flat (these flats were common in brownstone buildings, many of which were built in the 1880s in New York City and San Francisco). Our family lived two blocks from the East

51. See Appendix C, item 1a, New York City: Tenement Living Conditions.
52. Richard Plunz, *A History of Housing in New York City* (New York: Columbia University Press, 1990), 22.
53. Jacob A. Riis, *How the Other Half Lives: Studies Among the Tenements of New York* (New York: Dover Publishers, 1971), 13.
54. Gale Encyclopedia of U.S. History: Tenements, http://www.fordham.edu/images/academics/programs/baahp/eastside.pdf [viewed February 14, 2012].

Air shaft between three interior rooms above the first floor

River and FDR Drive, 15 blocks south of Spanish Harlem, and eight
blocks from Gracie Mansion, the mayor's official residence, built in
1799. Alexander Hamilton slept there. Next to our apartment was
Irving Savings Bank. This bank was to change its name twice, first to
American Irving Savings Bank, then to American Savings Bank. I use
to fall asleep dreaming about drilling a tunnel from our apartment
building into the bank next door. I heard they harbored untold riches.
It was in this apartment where, at a very young age, we learned about
the benevolence of Santa Claus and the generosity of the tooth fairy,
who was usually good for 25¢ a tooth.

Our old building, typical of many buildings of that era, housed 10
apartments and was built in the late 19th century. There were two
apartments on each floor. The rooms were laid out like a railroad
track, with each "railroad car" representing a room. (See Figure 4.)
One entered the buildings' hallways through two doors. The vestibule
separated the outside of the building from the inside. This is where

the mailboxes were. It is here that one could ring the bell for individual apartments for entry. When the tenant returned the ring, the electric lock on the inner door was released, permitting entry.

John with homemade bike and nephew Tommy (at 410 East 81st Street), 1959

Access to our apartment was through a hallway door into the kitchen, which faced the back yard towards 80th Street. The door had two locks on it, painted over the years with at least 30 coats of paint. This was our security system at the time. There was also another door to the apartment, one we didn't use. A moveable bed or armoire usually blocked this to help secure the apartment. Its purpose, though, was

Gracie Mansion, Carl Schurz Park

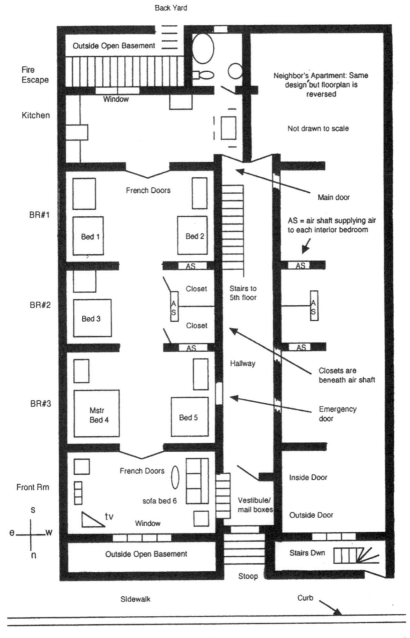

Figure 4: 410 East 81st Street
Five-Room First-Floor Tenement Apartment

81st Street looking west from East River, beginning of John Finley boardwalk (over FDR Drive) to Carl Schurz Park

FDR Drive, looking south from 81st Street overpass

79th Street looking west from East River, 1976

to enable us to escape the dwelling in case of fire, should the main apartment door not be accessible.

We had five rooms, consisting of a kitchen, three bedrooms, a front room facing 81st Street, and of course a small bathroom for seven family members. The middle room was the smallest, probably 7 feet wide, because of the air shaft. Three adjacent bedrooms had no doors for privacy, just curtains. We had to be real quiet when we came home from school so as not to wake Dad, who slept during the day since he worked at night. Whenever we had friends over after school, we walked through the bedrooms to get to the front room, where we played. Our friends couldn't help seeing a man sleeping two feet away as they passed by.

The walls in the apartment were made of thick-plastered laths; no sheetrock existed in the late 1800s. The kitchen had a patterned tin metal ceiling. The kitchen table had a steel porcelain top that could be extended and was covered with oilcloth. Mom first had an icebox for a "refrigerator." Block ice was routinely delivered twice a week. Carl remembers,

> Block ice usually measured 12" x 12" x 12" and cost 25¢. The ice was wrapped with newspapers to retard evaporation and melting to last longer. In the winter, people used window boxes made of sheet metal to store food. Daily shopping was the rule for butter, milk, eggs, etc., at local stores on the block, like Mellian's grocery store in the middle of the block on 81st Street.

The icebox had no light or electricity. When the ice melted, the floor pan had to be emptied frequently. When new ice was needed, one walked to the iceman's shop on 78th Street beforehand and wrote an order on a pad outside the store. Afterwards, Mom got a gas-operated Seville refrigerator, which periodically had to be manually defrosted.

The family also felt "rich" having their own toilet and bathtub in their very own apartment, since the building across the street, in which brother Otto's girlfriend had a three-room apartment, had only two toilets per floor (in the hallway), which were shared and cleaned by those occupying the four apartments on her floor. Our toilet had a pull chain with the wooden water box raised high, near the ceiling, which gave a great strong flush.

After Otto got married, he and his wife, Betty, lived in an apartment on 73rd Street near York Avenue. Their old apartment was "modernized" when the hall toilet was closed; new toilets were built into each of the four apartments on each floor. When Betty got a new toilet, it was built into the corner of her living room with a wall and door around it. The bottom of the door did not completely reach the floor. This "room" was not soundproof. It was so exciting. Ahh . . . those were some days. Assuredly, our family was moving up in the world. Since Betty's apartment was older than ours, a building as old as the Novaceks', built between 1879 and 1901, her bathtub was still in the kitchen.

Our apartment had steam heat and gas to cook with, and each room had a three-inch diameter pipe running six stories from the cellar to each of the other apartments above and through the fifth floor to the roof. Steam heat had to rise to the fifth floor from the cellar, and when it became warm enough on the top floor, we were "roasting" on the ground floor. Usually the top floor apartment never got enough steam to properly heat the rooms, as we later

Mary Ann in 410 East 81st Street kitchen with gas stove, circa 1949

experienced after we moved. The kitchen and front room had steam radiators below and in front of the windows. When we subsequently moved to a top floor apartment in another building, Mom, on a number of occasions, turned on the gas stove and opened the oven to get additional heat into our cold rooms. This, however, was not a safe thing to do.

The building, and most of the city, was first heated by coal. This was soft, bituminous, high-sulfur-content coal that was cheap at $10 to $13 a ton. On Park Avenue, the rich people had hard anthracite coal to heat their buildings. This coal burned cleaner, but it cost more. Trucks delivered coal on a routine basis. The soot the dirty coal deposited in the city was equivalent to every person breathing in the equivalent of two packs of cigarette smoke per day. When there was a wind, chimney soot blew into open window apartments. We remember our eyes burned from the coal dust in the air. Carl recounts,

> One major problem in those days was women washed clothes with their hands. They hung the wash outside on the wash line to dry. When the building's boiler was in use, soot blew out, which would ruin the nice clean wash and the women would have to redo it. We kids would feel sorry when we saw this, because we knew that washing clothes by hand was hard work.

You couldn't keep a washed car clean because a film of oily soot covered it in one day. Freshly fallen white snow blackened overnight. The boiler for heating the building was in the cellar. After the coal was burned and cooled, barrels of ashes had to be routinely brought up and disposed of. Later, oil was used for heat, which was a much cleaner fuel and ashless. If the air was too dry, open pans of water were placed on tops of heated radiators to add humidity to the room. It was our job to keep them filled. During the summer, when windows were open, the apartment was humid enough due to the surrounding coastal air.

In the early years we observed storekeepers early in the morning washing the sidewalk in front of their store with soap and water and a mop, then rinsing it. Building caretakers, as part of their job in living rent free, were also seen washing their stoops and sidewalk, and periodically they washed and waxed the hallways and stairs on each floor. They also collected rent from tenants for the landlord.

In 1955, we paid $38 rent per month for the apartment. Then the landlord had the audacity to raise the rent to $43—a 13% increase. Our parents never heard of such a thing. Forty-three dollars was a lot of money in those days, especially to a large family that had to be fed and clothed.

During the summers, neighbors leaned out of their windows, resting their elbows on pillows or bedding as they aired them out and carried on conversations with those on the stoop or street or even next door. We had no air conditioning, so fans were used to circulate air in the apartment. Blowing hot air was better than breathing stifling stationary air.

When we lived on the ground floor, there was sometimes a noticeable stench coming from the communal backyard, where dead cats, rats, and mice, along with their droppings, cooked in the heat. We had our share of rats, but mostly mice and cockroaches, especially when living above the cellar near the street, in spite of the fact that Mom kept the apartment spotless. In a manner of speaking, these were our *first* pets. We learned to coexist. We remember Dad "schmearing" J-o Paste on slices of raw potatoes and placing them in strategic locations along the baseboard of our ground floor apartment to kill cockroaches and large water bugs. It also killed mice and rats. It had an unpleasant odor. At times, we even hand-pumped a chemical called Flit to tackle mosquitoes. Both were effective.

Once we had a pinhole-size gas leak coming from a pipe connected to our gas stove. Mom called us and gave us each a piece of chewing gum and ordered us to "choo qhvickly." When the gum was pliable, even before the taste was gone, we had to give it up to wrap that gum around the pinhole to seal the leak. It worked. A few occasional coats of paint over an old large lump of dried gum on the pipe, and no one ever knew the difference. Light up that stove!

Later, we got parakeets, turtles, fish, and hamsters as pets. Once a week we let the parakeet out of its cage and allowed it to fly around the kitchen for exercise. At times, to thank us, it left its trademark by dropping a load in mid air. It must have been excited to be free. On one occasion we didn't realize the top of the window was down four or five inches, and the parakeet flew away.

The freedom-loving hamsters were placed in a cardboard box, which they soon chewed their way out of. Then they ran all over the apartment and under the beds, sometimes nesting in our shoes. When I was 9 years old, I tried to catch one with my foot as the hamster ran alongside the wall baseboard. I accidentally stepped on it, killing it. John caught the other one and put it in the bath-tub, knowing it won't chew its way out. However, it tried climbing up along the slanted back. Because it kept trying to climb out, our 5-year-old sister attempted to keep it from escaping by hitting it with an empty oatmeal box. Dead hamster number two.

Our family had old-fashioned iron beds with steel webbings for springs that sat high off the floor. These were the kind one found in hospital or mental wards in the 1920s. My mattress was made of stuffed horsehair. Every time I moved, the mattress talked back to me, making rubbing/crushing and creaking noises. In fact I am sure I was counting "Hee-Haws" as I drifted off to sleep. Shortly after turning off the lights, we could hear the "pitter-patter" of mice running across our linoleum floors.

Before John went to sleep, if he put his ear to the wall, he could hear the next-door neighbors yelling and quarrelling. Usually they were screaming and fighting with each other late into the night. Mr. and Mrs. Slowinski and their three 30- to 40-year-old bachelor sons lived there. We don't believe any of them graduated from high school. One might say they were "not too *swift* north of the collar-bone." During day and night we could hear Mrs. Slowinski cursing out her adult children. When they first got a television, before we got ours, we were invited to watch it with them. John and I went to their apartment, sat on kitchen chairs in their bedroom, and watched a small black and white television sitting on top of their refrigerator in the kitchen. When one of the older boys was able to drive, he needed the whole family to instruct him on how to parallel park the car in the street. At one time a neighbor from across the street, a son of Mrs. Raube, asked the Slowinskis, who usually sat outside on their stoop during the summers, to watch and hold a package for him. They held and watched it all day and later said to the Raube boy as he passed by on the other side of the street, "Don't forget the package we are holding for you." The response was, "Oh, you can throw it out. It's only garbage." This started another block war with yelling and cursing arguments between both parties across both sides of the street. The entire block was tuned in. Such was the entertainment for the time. It was free, spontaneous, and usually dramatic—never a rerun and never a commercial.

Mrs. O'Hara lived next door in an apartment directly over the Slowinskis. We remember waving to her, saying, "Good-bye, Mrs. O'Hara, good-bye Mrs. O'Hara," when men in white garb from the psychiatric ward of Bellevue Hospital came to pick her up. She was on a stretcher bound up in white cloth like a mummy and placed in an ambulance. Earlier in the day we had witnessed her throwing knives and forks out of her second-story window onto the sidewalk.

When John was between 5 and 7 years old and couldn't fall to sleep, he would talk to me in my bed, which was in the next, middle room. To get us to sleep, Mom who was in the next room tapped loudly on the wall to the hallway, saying that there was a policeman in the hall. Mom said there would be trouble with the policeman and he would come in and arrest us all if the talking didn't stop. We were terrified. This always worked and soon everyone was fast asleep. Mom was so smart. She must have completed a class in Psychology 101, specializing in terroristic threats towards twins.

At another time John slept in the bedroom next to the front room, facing the outside street window. Mom and Dad slept in the next bed three feet away. With the front room shade pulled down as far as it could go, there was still about a two-to-three inch gap of window glass and light showing. The height of John's pillow was such that he went to sleep every night watching the neon sign of Frank's Bar and Grill flash on and off across the street, next to a garage. Who needed to count sheep?

We heard drunks yelling and fighting on the street when the bar closed at one o'clock in the morning. Sometimes one or two stumbled into our apartment building, made their way behind the stairs to our apartment door, and fell asleep in front of it. That part of the hall is dark. Dad would come home from work at 4 a.m. and stumble over them.

I found out that Dad didn't always sleep during the day. Once when I was in high school, classes let out earlier than usual. I came home unexpectedly and walked through the apartment to the front room to get something. Soon I came across Mom and Dad, lying

John in bedroom #1 (410 East 81st Street), 1956

Mary Ann at 410 East 81st Street
(note: shade did not come down fully, radiator, water pan), circa 1949

motionless and pretending to be asleep. They must have heard me open the apartment door. They were hiding in plain sight. I apparently interrupted something. All three of us made eye contact for almost one nanosecond. Nary a word was said, yet volumes of "communication" were quickly exchanged. I think I noticed a twinkle in Dad's eye. After promptly analyzing the situation, I hastily got my butt out of there, quickly exiting the apartment. I don't know who was more shocked, my parents or me. Yet when I think about it, in fairness to them, they often didn't have much time or privacy to be a couple. Who could with five kids around and many rooms having no doors for privacy?

There was an automotive garage with an empty lot across the street adjacent to the 405 building and to the left of Frank's Bar and Grill. Gross Brothers had a body shop with many mechanics servicing cars all day long, six days a week. Loud and constant grinding and hammering on steel was heard. When the garage doors were open, one saw a shower of sparks when the hand grinder was used by one of the mechanics. There was a perpetual movement of cars into and out of the garage and lot. Besides parking cars in the small lot, many cars were double-parked on both sides of the street, up

Frank's Bar & Grill; to the left is Gross Bros. Garage
(damaged 1959 Volvo is ours), 1969

and down the block, before or after being repaired and serviced. When the cars were driven into the shop, they disappeared almost immediately from view, since they were being driven down an incline toward various work bays. At one time, the garage had been a movie theater—thus the slope of the floor.

When it was time to sleep and there was loud music or noise coming from the apartment above, where the neighbors did not have telephones, Mom or one of us twins banged on the pipes with a hammer or other hard device to alert them to quiet down. However, this method caused all five apartments above to receive the same "clarion call." At other times we banged the tips of broom handles on our ceilings to "communicate" with tenants above.

Each family had a small locked storage area in the basement to store items; we stored a bicycle, sleds, clothing, and some books there. Apparently mice and rats loved to read too, because they chewed on the glue of the bookbindings, which was a source of food to them. At least we had *educated* critters running around.

Mom sent care packages to relatives in Czechoslovakia, since they were living under Communism and were very poor. John and I helped stuff 10 to 15 pillowcases with clothing, sneaking in bags of coffee and other non-perishable food items. Much of the clothing was purchased from neighborhood thrift stores for very little money. I, being heavier than John, was designated to sit on each stuffed bag, compressing it, while Mom sewed it shut. She used a special lavender non-smearing permanent-ink pencil to write names and addresses on the cloth. She got the tip of the pencil to "print" by frequently touching it to her moist tongue. Sometimes we took

Mom in Czechoslovakia
with her newly arrived European bundles/care packages, 1972

turns with her. Then the purple-tongued brigade of three hauled the packages off to the post office for shipping. During World War II, regular postal mail sent between the U.S. and Europe—especially Germany, Czechoslovakia, and other countries—was delivered to the post office unsealed, ready to be read and censored by government officials. This was particularly necessary for homeland security.

Once John and I helped one of Mom's Hungarian friends, Mrs.

Kovac, with a similar task. As a tip, she gave Mom a small piece of furniture, which we had to carry four blocks from 77th Street to our apartment on 81st Street. Cockroaches started coming out of the furniture and running all over York Avenue. I guess they weren't thrilled about moving into a new neighborhood. Perhaps they, too, were terrified coming to 81st Street, after hearing of its infamous reputation.

Some people on our block also moved, but they did so involuntarily. In the 1940s and early 1950s we witnessed numerous evictions of tenants on our street and in the neighborhood because they couldn't afford to pay their rent. They were destitute. All their worldly belongings were brought down to the street. We remember elderly widows sitting on their sofas or wooden kitchen chairs at the curb, surrounded by what little furniture and clothes they had, staring with bewilderment and despair into space. It was so sad to see this. Mom felt very bad for those evicted. Whatever happened to them, God only knows.

We also remember seeing a grown adult sitting on a board with wheels, moving himself up and down the sidewalk using his hands on the sidewalk to propel himself. He had no legs. They were blown off in the war. I use to think, how did he go to the bathroom? How did he navigate crossing the street—the corner sidewalks had no disability ramps sloping to the street? How did he get up to his apartment? How did he live and support himself? How did he wash and clothe himself and prepare food? What was his life like? Whatever became of him?

To make playful use of our long apartment, John and I entered into some competitive marathon sports. It seems we were always competitive. One time, standing in our stocking feet, we ran as fast as we could from the kitchen through three other rooms, into the front room, sliding on our T-shirted bellies on the waxed floors from the last bedroom towards the window, in the direction of the cast iron radiator positioned just below it. (Smart, huh?) There was one slight problem, however—we couldn't stop. John slid head first at approximately 10 miles per hour into the radiator, splitting the back of his head open. Dad wrapped his head in a towel and hauled him off to the local pharmacist on York Avenue and 81st Street for medical treatment. Forget the doctor—he wasn't dead yet.[55] John learned that Mercurochrome antiseptic didn't sting as bad as iodine disinfectant. Ouch! When he recuperated, Dad gave him a beating, "to knock some sense" into his *dummkopf* son.

After many decades, the three-story corner bank and post office were torn down and replaced with a skyscraper, a new high-rise apartment building adjacent to our tenement building. The old sidewalk's slate slabs on First Avenue were going to be discarded, so our sister and her husband decided to take them and use them for landscaping at the new Massachusetts home they were building. A passerby remarked to her friend, "Would you believe it? Would you believe it? Look at that! They're even stealing the ____-damn sidewalk." As the bank was destined for demolition, our parents also received notice that our apartment building would also be gutted and renovated, so in 1960 the family relocated.

420 East 81st Street

Brother Tom and his family lived only five apartment buildings away, at 420 East 81st Street, in a similar five-room, no-elevator walk-up. However, he lived on the fifth floor. (See Figure 5.) Since he was in the process of moving to his first house on Long Island, our parents wanted to move into his apartment. Because decent rental apartments were difficult to come by, especially in our neighborhood, Dad made the landlord an offer he couldn't refuse. He was victorious, and we moved right in.

---

55. Talk about doctors. This was an age when medical doctors still made house calls (and to our apartment, only when extremely necessary). On more than one occasion, doctors came to our residence to treat a family member—usually an adult who was ill who found it very difficult to get to the doctor's office.

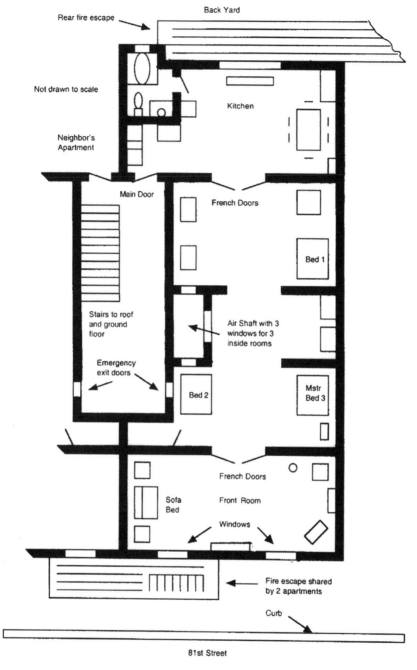

Figure 5: 420 East 81st Street
Five-Room Fifth-Floor Tenement Apartment

Walking up and down five flights of stairs daily was certainly different than living on the ground floor. The cardiovascular exercise kept our folks living into their 80s.

Mom went to the grocery store and brought food home in a folding shopping cart on wheels. She rang the bell signaling one of us to run down and carry up the groceries. Then once again, we had to carry the garbage down. Some people facing the back yard didn't carry their garbage to the trashcans, thinking it was easier just to throw it out the back window. What were they thinking, that the garbage would "walk itself" into a trash can? Those living on the ground floor had to smell the rotting garbage during those hot, muggy summer days. The authorities, however, got after the perpetrators, who were fined and re-educated.

The "420" apartment also used to have one toilet on each floor, shared by those living in the two apartments per floor. By the time our brother Tom moved in, renovation had occurred and every apartment had its own private bathroom with tub and sink. There was *one* occasion where this was *not* a welcome improvement. The bathrooms in our two adjoining apartments were tiny with toilets closely adjacent to each other—probably less than two feet apart—separated only by a plaster lath wall. Which made it freaky when Mom discovered that while she had been using it, her Hungarian neighbor Mr. Kovo, a recent widower, had been sitting on the other side for two days. (Talk about constipation!) He had died and rigor mortis had set in. No wonder Mom hadn't seen him lately. Mr. Kovo's son, Sandor, went to his dad's apartment and found him after not hearing from him for a couple of days. Rest in peace, Mr. Kovo. Your wife made the best Hungarian goulash, which she shared with our family. (She *really* did. That sweet paprika can spice up any meal.)

Our "new" apartment, unlike the previous one, had beautiful wooden parquet flooring in the front room, which we meticulously hand paste-waxed and buffed. Our parents purchased a Castro convertible sofa bed for this room, which was put to use daily. We

Old 420 East 81st Street building, 2nd building from left
(we lived on top floor, right two windows).

thought we were rich, with this sofa sitting on the parquet floor, especially since its brand was heavily publicized on television. It *had* to be good, after all, it was advertised on TV.

The problem with living on the top floor, the "penthouse," was that water sometimes leaked from the roof though the ceiling after heavy snow and rain, and the intense heat of the summer sun baking onto the black tarpaper lining the roof above heated and "cooked" the apartment even more. For most summers, living in

Our 420 East 81st Street apartment #5

Joe on stairs coming down
to bring up groceries

Kitchen

Middle smaller room (with full air shaft) look
ing towards bedroom and front room

Middle room with air shaft looking
toward first bedroom and kitchen

The only built-in closet
for family of seven

Front room looking through
all rooms toward kitchen

Bathroom

John, front room (420 East 81st Street)

this apartment was like living in an oven—living in hell. Many times it was just unbearable. Dad couldn't even install a window unit air conditioner if he wanted to, because the building's wiring was so old it couldn't handle it.

The old single-paned windows rattled easily in the wind. Our parents stuffed towels and rags around the windows to help stop the draft and cold in the wintertime. We were always amazed that the rickety windows with rotting wood frames didn't just fall out in a strong wind.

We remember Mom washing the outside of these windows. She would open the front room window, sit on the window ledge positioning her body outside the window, hold the inside of the window with her left hand and clean those windows using her right hand. While she did this, we each held onto one of her legs. We were very nervous she would lose her balance and fall out, tumble down five stories, and get killed. Only one of these two windows had a fire escape to catch her if she fell. The other had no such protection. When we got older, John and I also did this job. It was dangerous and scary.

Living just under the roof had its advantages, though. Dad got his suntan on our tar "beach," lying on the roof on a blanket just one floor up. We also played on the roof occasionally, although we had to be careful. When we walked on the roof in the summer, the tarpaper flexed and it felt spongy and bouncy under our feet. We were nervous about falling off the roof or down the air shaft, since the ledges, especially to the air shaft, were only about 8-10 inches high off the roof. A false move or trip could have led to our demise five stories down. We also used the roof to get from one apartment building to another to visit friends. This was sometimes a shortcut from going all the way downstairs and up again through another building. A number of people throughout Yorkville also used their roofs to dry laundry and raise homing pigeons.

Three events affected our family on the 15th of March in 1962—the Ides of March (the anniversary of the day Julius Caesar met his Waterloo). On this same day one of our brothers had an accident with his Volvo (previously pictured, damaged, and parked outside Frank's Bar and Grill), the parents of his fiancé announced their impending divorce, and Mom's clothesline full of wet clothes broke off the pole and fell five stories down in the back yard.[56]

Sometimes the clothesline just slipped off the pulley on the pole, 35 feet away. This, too, had to be fixed. Mom had to hire a lineman to climb the five-story 60-foot pole to reconnect the clothesline so she could hang her laundry. In those days linemen would walk through the neighborhoods with 80–100 feet of clothesline slung over their shoulder, shouting, "Lineman here, get your clothes-line fixed." Not many linemen wanted to climb five stories up a pole, since it was very dangerous work. However, a generous offer would soon remedy the situation. There was no other way out. The

---

56. See Appendix C, Item 1a, New York City: Tenement Living Conditions.

clothesline was attached from the pole into the brick wall outside our fire escape, which we called our "terrace." At this time Mom had a portable washing machine with wringer in the kitchen. She could not afford a dryer, and even if she could, she had no room for it. So a clothesline was essential. Eventually, when her wringer machine finally gave up, Tommy encouraged her to buy a new automatic washer. It was paid for on time payments, the first time she ever owed money and ever heard of an "installment" plan. (Our parents knew nothing about credit cards, and if they did, Mom and Dad would *never* have used one.) Carl relates, "We would often hear women got their fingers caught in the wringer. In those days, we had a standard saying when women would yell at us kids, 'Hey, don't get your tit caught in a wringer.'"

Moving into this apartment was also our family's first real introduction to the use of the telephone. A working vintage rotary-dial 1930s telephone came with the apartment, left by the second previous renter. Dad thought you had to *yell* into the telephone for it to work properly. So he did. It took some time to convince him that he only needed to speak in a normal voice. He really didn't want a telephone, saying, "If sumvhon vhants me, dey know vhehr to fine me." We still remember some of the older telephone numbers, such as BUtterfield 8-80xx, REgent 7-60xx, IVanhoe 5-26xx, and TRemont 7-91xx.

During those hot summers, we took turns sitting on the stoop or our fire escape. Hey, a hot breeze is better than none! At one time our sister was sitting on the stoop when a pigeon sat on the fire escape above and did its bodily functions on her head, blessing her. Ugh! One resident of our building lived a few floors up and didn't like kids (to put it mildly), especially kids who sat on his stoop. On many occasions he poured a full bucket of water on our heads through the fire escape from his window. He was such a nice man—kind, compassionate, friendly, and patient. He was always successful in scattering us.

Stoop (420 East 81st Street)

One of the best ways of cooling off from the heat, Dad suggested, was to drink something hot. It sounded strange to us, but we tried it and it seemed to work.

Because the building was so old, it had settled unevenly, making the floors slant. Maybe this contributed to John's scoliosis. Pieces of wood had to be wedged under appliances, beds, armoires, book-cases, and cabinets to level them off.

Mom, Dad, and Mary Ann went to Europe in June 1962. When

they returned, John and I had a surprise for them. While visiting their families overseas, they were not able to attend our high school graduation and watch us accept our coveted diplomas, so other relatives took their place. After graduating and successfully completing all of our Regents exams, we went to Martin's Hardware store to buy paint with our own money and painted the entire apartment, ceilings and all. We think the paint cost $35 total. At the time, our parents were paying $87 per month for rent, while a neighbor living directly below them was paying $250 per month. We were under the city's "rent control" program, but the neighbor wasn't.

At another time when Mom went to Europe, her suitcase got lost. She had a friend in Czechoslovakia who was an advocate, a lawyer. He made telephone calls for her and Interpol (International Criminal Police Organization) got involved. They found the suitcase on the Swiss border, full of holes. John and I don't recall if they were bullet holes or why the suitcase wound up there. We think it was because the suitcase came from America destined for a Communist country.

Eventually, our second apartment building also was going to be renovated. Our family could have purchased the building, with all 10 apartments, for $90,000, which was a *lot* of money in those days. Over the years, most of the 10 families had moved out, except for (1) our parents, (2) our sister and her husband, and (3) two other families. John and I were living in Minnesota at the time. Hookers and bums started to occupy some of the abandoned flats. Some of the mentally ill ones got into the ground floor apartments and burned wood in the gas oven. Some of them slept on the stair landings. Mom was very nervous, smelling smoke in the middle of the night, thinking the building would burn down with everyone in it. And she was afraid of the new "tenants." Dad told the landlord, "You vhant us out? Vhee [all four families] vhant $100,000 each." The landlord settled for $27,000 each, and in the early 1980s our folks moved to Long Island to live with brother Otto and his family. Mary Ann and Joe left their second floor apartment and purchased

Newly renovated 420 East 81st Street, now seven stories high

a fifth-floor walkup co-op apartment at 320 East 83rd Street. They were very lucky to get that small-boxed three-room apartment in the neighborhood. The other residents moved elsewhere. God only knows where. Thanks, Dad.

About 1981 the old "420" building was gutted and soon a new seven-story building with seven large apartments was built in its place. But instead of having two apartments per floor, the new building had one large apartment per floor, with an elevator, fire-place, terrace and hot tub. We heard that each new apartment commanded $2,600 per month ($31,200 per year) in rent, where our parents were paying $87 per month—$1,044 per year—for half the floor space. So, at the end of each year, renters had $31,200 in rent receipts with no equity. Many times apartments like this had groups of mobile single people living there, such as airline pilots, stewardesses, etc., sharing the rent and utility bills.

CHAPTER 5

Amusements and Entertainment

"Going Down"

Inside Our Apartment

JOHN: Although television is now ubiquitous in American homes, we fondly remember listening to radio before we ever had television. *Listening* to radio programs made us use our imagination, because we had to create and supply the action scenes in our mind. We think this made the listener more closely engage with the contents and characters of the programs and form closer relationships with those characters. One had to focus and pay undivided attention to what was transpiring. We listened with delight to *Abbott and Costello, Amos 'n' Andy, The George Burns and Gracie Allen Show, The Goldbergs, Gunsmoke, The Lone Ranger,* and *Sherlock Holmes.* Later, these radio programs evolved into television programs.

Our new 19-inch Emerson television arrived in the early 1950s, when we were 8 or 9 years old, bringing many hours of enjoyment to our family. The shows were all in black and white—colored TV did not become affordable until the late 60s. Rabbit ear antennas sat on top of the television and were adjusted to length and rotated and angled to obtain the best picture quality. There were no remote controls. One had to get up each time and turn a knob to change channels or regulate the volume. The television could show some pseudo colors if owners purchased a piece of colored translucent plastic and placed it over the screen. It had a gradation of colors (i.e., blue, red, and green) that helped the viewer infer that there was some semblance of a colored picture. It worked best when the scene on the TV was outdoors. You had blue for the sky, red for the middle, and green for the bottom grass. This was our first *color* TV. In addition, there was a thin plastic Fresnel-like lens one could purchase which, when placed over the TV screen, made the picture appear larger. Our TV stations went off the air at midnight, just after the national anthem was played. The stations came back on around 6 a.m. We wonder why the anthem isn't played anymore, even in between late-night programs.

During these early years it was fun watching TV. There was no *real* violence (the closest, perhaps, was in Westerns or some slapstick comedy) and no sex or cussing—an enormous contrast to current television programs. Even the word "pregnant" was not used, lest it offend someone. We had only five or six channels to choose from. We enjoyed viewing many shows including Westerns. Every time Gene Autry stopped singing in the saddle, shooting would break out in "them thar hills." We also watched *Hopalong Cassidy* and *The Roy Rogers Show*. Adventure shows included *Ramar of the Jungle* and *Robin Hood*. Detective shows included *Boston Blackie* and *Dragnet*. *Flash Gordon* and *Sergeant Preston of the Yukon* provided additional action. Popular movies included the Marx Brothers and Mae West. Good clean comedies included *I Love Lucy, Laurel and Hardy,* and *The Three Stooges*. There were game shows such as *I've Got a Secret* and *The $64,000 Question*. Other family programs included *Father Knows Best* and *The Ed Sullivan Show*. Joe and I once sat in Ed's audience viewing an elephant act when the elephant urinated on stage. When Ed said, "Well, that's show biz," the audience roared. Kids enjoyed *Howdy Doody*. I once met Clara-bell the clown when I worked one summer doing air-conditioning work at Flower Fifth Avenue Hospital. We also watched the *Mickey Mouse Club*. Joe always wore his official Mouseketeer ears; the show seemed more exciting to watch that way. A few years later Disney produced *Spin and Marty*, for the older kids. Sunday mornings were especially entertaining when viewing *Ted Mack's Original Amateur Hour* and Jon Gnagy, the artist.

Our family also liked musical programs. We ran home after school to watch and hear Kate Smith sing "God Bless America,"[57] followed by the talents of Liberace playing the piano with his brother George on the violin. We also enjoyed watching Molly Goldberg with her famous "Yoo-hoo" call. Mom especially liked *The Lawrence Welk Show, Guiding Light,* and *General Hospital.* Years later her most favorite program was "dha Vheel." She loved the *Wheel of Fortune* and its host, Pat Sajak, who she believed was Czech.

We kids liked watching horror movies on Friday and Saturday nights. *Frankenstein* was one of our favorites. When we watched and learned that Count "Alucard" was "Dracula" spelled backwards, we almost filled our pants. Watching *Dracula,* especially at night, and especially during thunder and lightening, was the scariest black-and-white thriller. The nightmares continued.[58]

We enjoyed playing High-Fidelity 45 rpm records on our record player. They were later replaced by the larger 12" 33-1/3 rpm Hi-Fi LP (long playing) vinyl platters. Mom was somewhat in awe of this technology. Later in life when she heard Nat King Cole's records playing, she would say, "Vhood you believe it, vhood you believe it? Ova thwunty yhears he's dhead, un he's still singkingk."

For other forms of entertainment, we spent many hours work-ing on our coin and stamp collections. Joe collected coins and

---

57. See Appendix C, Item 1e, Memories, Dances and Songs: Songs.
58. See Appendix B for a comprehensive list of popular radio and television shows, movies, and the actors and actresses that entertained us.

worldwide stamps, while I only collected United States stamps. On many occasions we went downtown to Macy's Department Store or up to 86th Street to purchase stamps to update our collection. Through these hobbies we learned much about the names of other countries and states, their history, and geographic locations. We firmly believe our stamp collections are, in reality, miniature art collections. Some stamps are extraordinarily beautiful. I collected stamps at age 11, but I don't anymore, since they were in a suitcase that was stolen.

We enjoyed creating things such as building structures with the A.C. Gilbert Erector Set and building houses with American Plastic Bricks, two of the most creative toys ever invented. We built a little village and Joe declared himself "mayor." He said he was older than me and he should be the boss! TinkerToys, Lincoln Logs, yo-yos, Slinkies, marbles, jacks, Mexican jumping beans, and the hula hoop were toys that we played with. We even had an ant farm. We oil painted canvases by the numbers, painted pages of special coloring books with brushes dipped in clear water, with different colors magically appearing on those white pages, and molded with clay. We mixed and poured plaster of Paris into rubber molds, making animals and statues that we painted. We made periscopes out of milk cartons, cardboard tubes, and mirrors. The most creative, wondrous, and least expensive "toy," however, was a large empty appliance box that we used as our fort.

Having inquisitive minds, we also enjoyed taking things apart to see how they worked. I once took a lamp apart while sitting on the floor in the front room, but I neglected to pull the plug out of the wall socket first. I certainly got a charge out of that project. I never forgot it.

In another instance, I explored the back of our 1930s floor-model radio and found some blue wires that had been cut. During WWII, wires were cut for homeland security reasons so the populace could not receive short-wave radio signals. Well, I thought what the heck;

let's see what happens, so I connected the wires. I thought I could pick up Berlin. Sparks flew and half the lights in our fifth-floor apartment blew out. I almost wound up in Berlin. The entire apartment only had two screw-in glass fuses. They were located near the ceiling in the hallway, and I needed a flashlight and stepladder to replace them. Mom was mad as hell and yelled at me. (My efforts were not a complete failure: Like Edison, I discovered another way that did not work.) Off to the hardware store I ran. It's a good thing this happened during regular business hours.

Joe and I also liked building electronic kits such as a police radio, to keep up with the latest happenings around town and in the neighborhood. I built a HeathKit transistor radio, but it didn't work, probably because of having too many cold solder joints. I had thought, "If a little solder is good, more should make it work better." I had to mail the radio to Benton Harbor, Michigan, to be repaired.

I also burned out many transistors as I tried to solder them into the kits with a soldering gun. I didn't have a soldering pencil or know about using heat sinks to draw the heat of the soldering gunpoint away from the transistor. These transistors cost about $13 each—a lot of money in those days, especially for a teenager. I killed two or three of them. Ouch! But it was a learning experience. I took the IRT subway to Canal Street in Chinatown, where I purchased additional transistors, radio tubes, and other electronic parts and equipment from army surplus shops.

Joe and I also built a HeathKit speaker enclosure, an Allied AM/FM radio, and an amplifier with vacuum tubes for our Hi-Fi system—this was before the introduction of stereo. (With vacuum-tube portable and car radios and TVs, one had to wait 20 to 30 seconds for the tubes to warm up before they worked.) We were also in awe when we learned we could generate heat and fire using a magnifying glass. No one was safe around us.

We played board games such as Checkers, Monopoly, chess, Scrabble, dominoes and Ouija. While playing on the Ouija board on our kitchen table at 11 o'clock one night, we even contacted a Viking in the 1500s. It scared the hell out of us. We played cards, built "card-houses," played with Chinese handcuffs, and worked jigsaw puzzles, which were kept on a wooden board and stored under our beds between uses. We collected bottle caps, dug the cork out of them to see if we won any prizes, played pick-up sticks, and made yurts and tents out of chairs, blankets, pillows and cushions, and yes, large cardboard boxes on the couch. We made airplanes out of balsa wood, driven by a rubber-band "engine," and later assembled destroyers and air-craft carriers and planes from plastic model kits, which we painted and applied decals to.

We collected, read, and traded comic books along with baseball and cowboy cards. The cards came in a packet with a slab of dried pink bubble gum. "Delicious!" If we accidentally dropped gum or candy on the sidewalk or street or if one fell out of our mouth, we quickly picked it up, blessed it by making the sign of the cross with it, and popped it into our mouths. ("Quickly" was the operative word. The faster we picked it up, the fewer germs it collected—or so we thought.) We were immune to practically every disease known to man as a result of these precautionary and meticulous hygienic practices.

We also collected real estate. In the early 1950s we enjoyed eating cereal for breakfast—especially the cereal that gave away deeds to free land in Alaska. So what if the deed was for a one-square inch of land—it was real—we kept telling Mom to buy more. We felt like land barons or the Rockefellers. We had deeds to at least 11 square inches of property—not necessarily adjacent to each other. Who knows, there could be gold deposits under our land. We were on a real estate *roll!* For safekeeping, we hid these deeds. We did it so well that to this day we don't know where they are; they are lost forever. We think we hid them inside the backs of framed pictures that hung on our wall. These probably wound up in thrift stores when we moved.

Lionel electric trains were fun to play with. We connected a line of straight tracks together with one end on top of the front-room radiator and the other end extending to the floor of the next room—about 15 feet long without any middle support—letting the metal cars speed down the ramp to see what would happen. The cars always seemed to crash. It was fun, though. But we didn't think Otto was amused since the trains belonged to him. He beat the hell out of us. Oh, those black-and-blue marks on our bodies. We still remember those knuckle punches. It's amazing we ever survived those early years.

We also loved listening to music, especially Czech and German music (even though we couldn't understand most of the words) and later folk songs, bluegrass, and Irish revolutionary songs.

Outside Our Apartment

Summer

When we were about 10 years old, with encouragement from friends and relatives, Mom took us to an audition of *The Ted Mack Amateur Hour* television program, to get us on television. Joe and I sang, "You are My Sunshine" and "On Top of Old Smoky," two of our favorite songs.[59] We were unsuccessful. Apparently the talent agency didn't recognize and appreciate really good talent. At least we thought we were good. After all, we *were* twins and we *were* cute—truly a winning combination. The organization tried to get Mom to sign a contract for singing lessons, to help us boys along. Mom said, "Nhuttin dhoingk." The money was better spent elsewhere, like on food and underwear.

There were lots of other things for us to do in the summer. When we were very young, we sometimes had a little picnic in the park or played on a blanket spread out on the concrete sidewalk in front of our apartment building or further up in front of the bank, closer to

---

59. See Appendix C, Item 1e, Memories, Dances, and Songs: Songs.

the money. We chalk-marked a game board of squares on the sidewalk and played hopscotch ("Potsy"). We played jump rope, "Ring Around the Rosy," and "Red light, green light, one, two three."

Dad took us to the zoo in Central Park (64th Street and Fifth Avenue). We went roller skating, had picnics, and launched our toy boats on Sailboat Lake. We rode the carousel and caught the steel ring each time the carousel rotated. If we were lucky, we got a gold-colored brass ring that we could turn in for a free ride. As we walked through the tunnels in the park, we screamed until our vocal cords almost burst and heard our voices echo competitively against each other.

When it got really hot, the kids on the block opened up the fire hydrant in front of Frank's Bar or even further down the block, using a stick of wood and a wire as a makeshift wrench. It usually took two or three kids to turn it. Then they put a board in front of the flow of water, fanning the water spray out across the street, washing whatever cars were parked nearby or drove by. Those walking by sometimes got their clothes washed for free. Some of them needed it. Sometimes the neighborhood kids took an old metal garbage can, kicked out the bottom, and dropped it over the hydrant, causing a two-story geyser. If you lived across the street from the hydrant and your front room window was left open, you got your floor and walls washed for free. The water spray actually hit some of these open ground floor windows. It happened to Teta Chaloupka, with the water coming into her first-floor front room. Remember it was hot. Sometimes drivers brought their convertible cars up the one-way street with their tops down and could not back up due to traffic behind them. The whites of their eyes would show. If they were nice to us, we let them through without washing the *inside* of their cars. What *power* we had. A few times, one or more of the neighborhood kids got struck by vehicles coming through, when the force of the water pushed them into oncoming traffic. One kid got killed this way when a truck ran over him.

While all of this went on, a kid served as a sentry, perched atop a second-story fire escape, looking east for the cops turning west into our street from York Avenue. If the cops were spotted, the kid yelled out, "Chickee, the cops," and the munchkins scattered into their apartment hideouts. The cops were angry, and it would take one or two of them, using a heavy wrench, to *tightly* turn off the hydrant and secure the cap. These "shut-offs," however, usually didn't last very long, because when the cops left, and/or as the days got more hot and humid, the kids turned on the same fire hydrants again and again. Once this happened seven times in one day. The cops were really pissed. Survival kicked in. (Let it be stated that Joe and I *never* took part in these activities. It was the *other* kids down the block who took the initiative. We just secretly cheered them on.)

Some of our friends were involved in throwing water balloons off the roof, sometimes splattering innocent pedestrians. We later had some high school friends who stuffed a pair of pants and an attached shirt with newspaper, to resemble a mannequin. Our friends threw the mannequin off the six-story-high roof and screamed a blood-curdling shriek. Little old ladies looked up and came close to cardiac arrest when they saw a "body" jumping or being thrown off the roof, crashing to the ground. (We twins, again, participated *only* as observers in these creative extracurricular activities. Such activities, we thought, kept us out of trouble.)

We built a communication device by attaching a string to match-sticks, which were inserted inside of two empty soup cans, each with a hole in its bottom for the cord to go through. By pulling the cord taut, one could talk into Can "A" while the other person could hear the first person through Can "B." This is the way it was supposed to work. However, Joe thought we heard each other talk because we yelled into the can—of course I was on the other end, 25 feet away and couldn't help but hear the loud words yelled out on the other end. Anyway, we felt like Alexander Graham Bell, and we didn't have to go through an operator or party line.

We played handball against the bank wall, using Spalding (also called spaldeen) balls, high-bouncing pink rubber tennis balls with no outer fuzz, and stickball in the streets with friends, dodging dog crap and using a broomstick as a bat. (If we did accidentally step in dog shit, which happened enough times, we had to get a twig or small used ice-cream stick and dig it out of the deep bottom grooves of our sneakers. Otherwise it was tracked into the apartment. We usually got most of it out.) If one of the broomsticks broke, the neighborhood kids pooled their money and one went to the hardware store to buy a new broom, then proceed to saw off the handle. One of the mothers shouted not to saw the handle off the new broom, but to exchange it for her older worn broom, which could then be sawed off. This mother appreciated the value of a brand new broom, and the kids were just as happy with an old broomstick. After all, it could still hit a ball—and it even seemed to work better. It was aged, had character and experience, and "knew" precisely what to do. We played in the street or park until the streetlights came on at dusk. This was our signal to come home.

We wanted a bicycle but could not afford a new one. Over the period of a year, brother Tom picked up pieces of discarded bicycle parts from throughout the city with his air conditioning truck, when he was going to or from work. We used these parts, purchased new tires and inner tubes, and assembled and painted the bike in our front room. It weighed a ton. We sanded the bike, painted it with a Rust-Oleum primer and then with glossy red paint, and attached trading cards to the wheel spokes with clothespins, which made fluttering sounds as you drove it. This alerted folks that there was a motorized vehicle approaching them from behind on the sidewalk and it was not to be taken lightly. Now we were in business and could explore the outer reaches of the neighborhood, expanding our "world view." Many older kids and some young adults explored the city with free transportation, although this was a precarious thing to do. They hitched rides dangerously hanging onto the back of city busses or trucks that drove down the avenues or streets. A few of them were killed doing this.

We roller skated with metal skates that clamped to the sides of our sneakers and were tightened with a special square key. We skated in our apartment, in the street, on the sidewalk, and in the park. Our entire bodies vibrated violently as we roller skated on cobblestones on Second Avenue—the rougher the more stimulating. After we left cobblestone pavement for a smoother sidewalk, the vibrations seemed to continue for a while. While riding on the sidewalk, especially with our scooter or Radio Flyer wagon, Joe and I went around tight corners of buildings so fast we sometimes lost control and crashed into unsuspecting people's legs. That certainly didn't gain us any friends. We played handball and Kick the Can; we stomped on empty soda cans to make elevated metal shoes out of them and walked around like Frankenstein, making noise on the concrete sidewalk.

When we got older, we went by ourselves to the Museum of Natural History and Planetarium, the Museum of Art, and the Guggenheim Museum. When we didn't walk, we took the 79th Street crosstown bus.

The kids on 81st Street "fought" the kids on 80th Street—our mortal and eternal enemies—using broomsticks and garbage can covers as shields, like the Vikings used. Joe even had snowball fights with kids from 80th Street, but he packed snow around ashes from burnt coal to make harder snowballs. Boy, when you got hit with one of those, you were smarting. Since Joe and I had long legs and were fast runners, we remember running into our ground floor apartment while being chased by a dozen or so 80th Street "thugs," slamming the door hard, and locking the door quickly behind us, which resulted in long wood screws actually popping out of the rickety old doorframe. While the door rattled on its old, weak hinges, Mom once again screamed at us in Czech, "Jezis Maria!"

When it got really hot and humid, which was the usual case

each summer, we took the subway downtown to Macy's, Gimbels, or Bloomingdale's department stores, rode their wooden escalator steps up and down to cool off in their air-conditioned building, and watched "rich" people buy things. Rich people were anybody who had discretionary money to spend or at least more perceived money than we had. Sometimes we went all the way down to 14th Street to visit Klein's Department Store.

We also rode the subways down to the Battery and South Ferry (where trains reversed direction) and up to Pelham Bay Park and Orchard Beach in the Bronx, sometimes doing this on local trains two or three round trips a day. For 15¢, we could ride the subway from one end of the city to another, getting a hot breeze across our bodies. As long as we didn't exit the station, we didn't have to pay another 15¢ for the return trip. We had it all figured out. (Once or twice we took the subway to the South Ferry station, exited, and took the ferry to Staten Island for a visit. It seemed like a whole new world there, like being in the country while still being in the city.) Riding the rails was more comfortable than sitting and sweating in a stifling *hot* apartment with little air movement. Carl recalls,

> Tommy and I did the same thing years before. The subway ride cost 5¢. Many times we timed the trains' door and ran under the turnstile [illegally] and rode for free. Trolley car rides were the same and we would go in walking backwards as people were exiting the rear door. With the 5¢ saved, we bought an ice-cream cone or Mello Roll.

During New York City's sweltering summers, we could stand in our fifth floor apartment at night, with lights off, and scan over rows and columns of other apartments across the street to see what we could see. This didn't work when living on the ground floor. The higher the temperature, the more windows, drapes, and shades were open, since air conditioning was not in vogue, affordable, or doable in our old neighborhood in those days. Scanning towards the east and west and north to south was quite an education, observing the things people do in their apartments as well as folks "cooling off" in the "fresh air" while sitting out on their fire escapes. We grew up fast. It was better than watching television, without any commercials. If looking north through the front room window was boring, we could change geographic locations 180 degrees and look south across the back yard through the kitchen window.

When the summer heat became too oppressive, some neighborhood children spent the night sleeping on the fire escape outside the window of their fourth or fifth floor apartment. This afforded them some relief, but it was also a dangerous activity, in case they would fall off the fire escape.

During the Fourth of July, kids put firecrackers in dog shit, lit it, and ran. It flew everywhere with an explosive force. You were lucky to have your mouth and eyes closed when this happened. We had a small piece of old rope, and we burned one end with a match. This end of the rope flamed out, but the fire within stayed lit and smoked for a long time. It became our flexible match. Sometimes we used smoking punks. We thus had a constant source of heat to light sparklers and hundreds of firecrackers. We lit firecrackers, ash cans, cherry bombs, etc., threw them, and then ran like hell. At times our hands got burned if we grabbed a recently burned-out sparkler that was still hot. Invariably, we heard some kid got a severe hand injury when these fireworks inadvertently exploded in his/her hand; fingers were even lost. We learned that sparklers generated heat to 1500 degrees Fahrenheit. Friends shot off roman rockets. If your front room window was open, your front room could receive such a projectile; as the rocket hit the building across the street it swiftly serpentined up the side of the building like a snake looking for an easy opening. Each year the drunks came out of Frank's Bar to celebrate, causing explosions with cobblestone bricks and their secret ingredients. The explosions sent pieces of brick and shrapnel far and wide in every direction. We were surprised no one got hurt. The more inebriated the men were, the more chemical they used. This may be one reason a lot of parking space was available during the Fourth. People either parked in garages or "got out of Dodge" to save their cars from dents, window and paint chips, and other damage.

Sometimes we stuffed white flour into Mom's long, used sheer hosiery and chased after each other to hit the other person with it, leaving large white "gotcha" marks. This invention was probably the precursor of the paint gun. We also burned cork, which then turned black, and smeared the carbon it produced onto our faces, making us look like Indians or Negroes, depending how the carbon was applied. During Halloween we dressed up in Mom's old dresses, filled with bouncing balloon bosoms, and high heels, and went trick-or-treating. With the high density of apartments on the block, we didn't have to go out of our neighborhood to accumulate a largess.

We made homemade scooters (go carts) from wooden vegetable or soda crates stood on end, with metal roller skates that were pulled apart anchoring one set of wheels under each end of a wooden 2 x 4 using nails or screws.[60] Two flat sticks served as handles, and beer caps, as well as various soda bottle caps, were hammered into place to serve as decorative and identifying ornaments.

Homemade rubber-band guns and sling shots were another of our specialties, as well as peashooters. In using these weapons we were lucky that no one was hit in the eye by the projectiles.

When I was about 6 or 7, my nosiness got my head caught between vertical wrought iron bars at the wading pool in Carl Schurz Park. The fire department had to be called to extricate me. (Hey, this once happened to Joe, too—what a dummy. Who knows, it could have been between the same two iron bars.) We also played in the sand box, on the seesaw, and swings. At one time, I was standing too close to the moving metal swings and got my head cut open after being struck by one of them.

Joe and I sometimes swam in the pool at John Jay Park (situated across from the East Side House). They had a building where we

---

60. See Appendix C, Item 1a, New York City: Tenement Living Conditions.

Carl Schurz Park wading pool and sprinklers for small children

changed into swimsuits. We placed our clothes, shoes, and valuables (coins, cap guns, gum, etc.) into a wire basket and gave it to the attendant, who then issued each of us a numbered metal tag with an elastic strap attached to it. We then placed that strap around our arms or ankles and proceeded to the pool. When done swimming, we exchanged the tag for our basket of clothes. This way, our clothes, shoes, and valuables were secured and protected.

At one time I dove into the pool headfirst with my arms and hands to my side—a big mistake! "Vhat vas I dhink-ink?" I hit my head on the bottom of the pool, which resulted in a large welt on my head. Mom was horrified. Someone was looking out for me. You'd think by this time that all these experiences would have knocked some sense into me.

While walking home from the pool, some of the neighborhood kids had the good sense to stop at Fink's Bakery nearby, to purchase freshly made rolls. They only cost 5¢ each. Those were just some of the treats we enjoyed. During the summer Good Humor or Mr.

Softee trucks would drive slowly down our street ringing bells and playing a tune on their loudspeakers. Kids ran out of their apartments from every direction to buy ice cream. One double orange Popsicle frozen ice, with two inserted wooden sticks, could be split and shared between us. Chocolate Fudgesicle ice cream bars were also a favorite. At the park, the Good Humor man peddled his tricycle down the walking paths with a box of frozen delights. We also enjoyed their ice cream sandwiches and vanilla ice cream bars coated with a thin layer of frozen chocolate, which cracked and bit into our tongues and the roof of our mouth when we chowed down on those ice-cold treats.

We loved eating orange Creamsicle ice cream bars at John Jay Park, and eating Clark, Mars, 5th Avenue, and Sugar Daddy candy bars and rock candy. We ate Wax Lips and Bazooka bubble gum candy, candy from a Pez dispenser, and bubble gum cigars and chocolate cigarettes and drank colored sugar water from tiny soda bottles made of wax. We bought strips of paper with small half-mooned candy buttons attached. They were colorful and always sweet tasting. At home we poured orange juice into ice cube trays, froze it, and sucked on very cold freezing orange-juice ice cubes until our throats burned and our teeth and head ached.

Drinking egg cream sodas at the corner soda shop at 81st and First Avenue or Sal's Ice Cream Parlor at 80th Street was always a treat. It was a phosphate-type drink that didn't contain any eggs or cream. Go figure. If you ordered "Two cents plain," you got a glass of plain seltzer water for 2¢. Carl reveals,

> Tom and I did the same thing. They cost 8¢ and we could listen to the jukebox. In wintertime we had hot chocolate for 10¢ while listening to 78-rpm records played on the Seeburg [jukebox] at the cost of 5¢ a song and the older kids kept feeding it money. We loved it, and if there were pretty girls in the booths, we fell in love just looking at them.

When we were between 4 and 5 years old, Mom took us to the park and brought chocolate milk, a mixture of Hershey's syrup mixed with milk, but stored in empty brown-colored Old Brau beer bottles. Passersbys were astonished and scolded Mom for allowing her young kids to drink "beer." Anyway, the "beer" worked. It kept us quiet, happy, and sedated. At home, we enjoyed drinking chocolate milk through clear Zip 'n See straws, watching milk go round and round in the hard-plastic pretzel-like twisted straw. Our favorite drinks were Bosco or Hershey's syrup in milk as well as commercially bought Yoo-hoo chocolate drink in 12 oz. bottles. When we drank Ovaltine chocolate drink, we made sure we drank it in our official plastic, insulated Ovaltine mug. It seemed to taste better that way. Nehi orange soda was also a favorite thirst quencher.

At a very young age, whenever we would hurt ourselves playing, by scraping a knee or arm, we'd cry. Mom always kissed the "wound" to make it better. It seemed to work. We think there was some type of psychosomatic hocus-pocus going on here; however, we were and are true believers to this type of medical practice without a license.

Winter

During the 1940s and 50s, New York City used to have lots of big snowstorms.[61] Maybe we thought they were big because we were so small. Sanitation workers opened up manhole covers and snow was shoveled into them. Dump trucks picked up snow and dumped it into the East and Hudson Rivers. We loved all the snow, because we could pull each other in sleds up and down the middle of the streets, since there was little or no traffic. We even went to Central Park to sled down the hills. Some of us used inverted garbage can covers as sleds. Sledding seemed best, though, when school was called off. We remember how gleeful we felt when Mom came to our beds early in the morning to tell us we didn't have to get up to go to school that day.

We also made ice and snow igloos in the streets that we could

---

61. See Appendix C, Item 1d, Yorkville.

Snow, 410 East 81st Street, 1951

crawl into. There seemed to be hardly any cars in those early days of our youth. Perhaps most folks couldn't afford or didn't need one, since public transportation was easily available.

When our steam-heated radiators operated during the winter, we children took crayon stubs and melted them in used metal peanut butter or jelly caps on top of the radiator. As the colored wax melted, we placed our thumbs in the hot wax, took our thumbs out, and peeled the wax away from our skin, leaving a clearly visible thumbprint. We mixed the colored crayons in the cap producing a *nasty* looking black-olive hue. For some reason, this repulsive outcome always surprised us. We had obtained similar results when mixing leftover Easter egg dyes.

The Gindele family always had a Christmas tree, sometimes two. We purchased the tree by Thanksgiving. We hung chocolate ornaments on some of its branches. Sometimes during the night, especially when we lived on the ground floor, mice found the low-hanging ones and chewed on Santa's feet. Much evidence was found the next morning.

We were blessed as kids. We usually got a toy or two and some

Otto (with Lionel train), Mary Ann, Mom, John and Joe, 1952

clothes. It was a lot more than Mom and Dad got, judging from how they described their childhood Christmases to Julie, their 8-year-old granddaughter, in 1977 for a school assignment.

MOM:
Dear Julie,

When I was a little girl in Pole, Czechoslovakia, I lived in a little house in a small farming village. In fact, my house number was 4. We were the 4th house built in the village. There were eight other houses in our village.

We got our Christmas present a week or two before Christmas on St. Nicholas Day. We usually got stockings to wear or an orange to eat and cookies. If we were bad, we got coal in our stockings.

My father would chop down an evergreen tree in the woods. He would cut a hole in a log and stick the bottom of the tree into it. We decorated the tree with all kinds of cookies and candies and real candles on the outer edges. We put an angel on top. On the heavier, lower branches on the tree, we hung little apples and walnuts.

My father made figures of shepherds and lambs out of noodle dough. My mother baked the dough and we put the figures under the tree.

On Christmas Eve, at 6 pm, we would sit down to dinner and eat carp (fish) and cooked barley and mushrooms, kolache, apple strudel with rum, and coffee or tea. (The carp was freshly caught and we kept it in our wash tub for a few days before we killed and ate it.) At midnight we went to Mass in the larger neighboring town of Kadov, three kilometers [1.8 miles] away. Of course, we had no electricity at that time, so we burned candles and used a kerosene lamp for light.

The village shepherd, who took care of all the sheep, would walk from house to house and blow a horn. The people gave him cakes and sometimes money.

On Christmas morning, we went to church again. The next day, we got an apple or orange as a present.

So you see, Christmas was different from today, with so many presents exchanged. And we didn't have such tree ornaments as you have. But it was lovely, just as it is for you.

Love,

Oma

DAD:

Dear Julie,

I was a little boy in a little town of 210 houses in Ersingen, Germany. We chopped down our own tree in the woods and decorated it with cookies, pears, apples, nuts, and glass balls. We put matchsticks in the nuts and put wire on the sticks to attach it to the trees. By the time Christmas came, all the cookies were gone, and a few days later, the trees were all empty, except for the glass balls. We had no electricity, so we put real candles on the outer branches of the tree. We used kerosene lamps to light the insides of the houses.

On Christmas Eve, we went to Church at 6 pm. When we came home, Santa Claus came. It was a lady dressed in all

white, like an angel. She was called Christkindle. And a man
came, too. He was called Plznickel and he was dressed all in
black and carried a sack with two legs sticking out (they were
fake) and a chain. Christkindle would give out the gifts to the
children and Plznickel would take you downstairs if you were
bad. You would yell and scream and be so scared and tell him
you would be good from now on. Then he would let you go
and you would run up the stairs so fast until you were back
with Christkindle and then she would give you your present.

We only got one present a year. It might be stockings to
wear, or an orange, a ball or a harmonica. Sometimes we got
slippers made of straw. When we were older, we got ice skates
and passed them on to our younger brothers or sisters. We
might get a bar of chocolate or maybe the whole family would
get a sled.

Then we would have hot chocolate and a special white
bread made just for Christmas. It was wonderful and we always
had a lovely time.

Love,

Opa

We usually didn't get rid of the tree until February in order to get
maximum usage out of it. Because it was so dry, the needles would
fall off if it was dragged down the five flights of stairs of our 420
apartment building. Who would want to sweep all of that up? So,
Joe was the designated sentry who went down to the street, direct-
ing away pedestrian traffic. When the all-clear signal was given, I
shoved the tree out of our fifth-story front room window, watching and hearing it crash to the ground. (I was lucky that the rickety
window itself did not grab onto the tree and join it in its descent.)
When it landed, most of the needles fell off the branches.

Usually a week or two after Christmas, the neighborhood
kids gathered up all the dried discarded trees and dragged them
near the fire hydrant, a space which was open since cars are not
allowed to park there. The trees were set ablaze, and a roaring rapid

thunderbolt was heard as flames violently and quickly shot up over 20 feet high. (Occasionally people got concerned that the lead car, the one with its gasoline tank closer to the hydrant, would explode. Never happened. We didn't need to attract any more cops into the neighborhood, that's for sure.)

All Year

Our parents' friends often came over on Friday nights to visit and play cards, eat, drink beer, and smoke their pipes and cigars in the kitchen. During one of these gatherings, one of Mom's friends brought us two small bottles of "grape soda" that they had gotten from a liquor store while buying a bottle of wine for our parents. The guests actually thought it was soda, but it was indeed wine. Mom was probably distracted and also thought it was soda, since the bottles were so small, and she gave it to us, telling us we could have a little each night.

We were between 8 and 9 years old. We drank it all and crawled under our beds. After a while, Mom thought that there was something wrong. "It's too qhviet, vhehr ahre dose guys?" she inquired. She was soon to have another "Jesus Christ, Mary, and Joseph" moment. When we got pulled out from under the bed, we were drunk, spread-eagled, trying to keep the floor from moving (which it *was* doing). It was like lying on the deck of a small ship that was moving up and down and sideways, simultaneously, in rough, very rough, high seas. I am surprised we didn't die. Thank God for the bathtub—which was in the bathroom, not in the kitchen under the barrel of beer, headcheese, *jaternice*, and seeded rye bread. It was more easily accessible and made a great trough as we half ran and crawled to it, upchucking.[62]

---

62. As a kid living in the 410 apartment, I also sometimes had nightmares when I slept, thinking that I was being pulled like a magnet into the clothes closet, where the boogieman lived. The more I tried to yell to Mom and Dad for help, the fainter my voice became, the more strongly I was "pulled" into the closet, and the closer the boogieman was to me. As a pre-teenager, I figured out how to end dreams that terrified me: I would mentally "jump off the 59th Street (Queensboro) Bridge" into the East River. Each time I "hit the water" I awoke from the dream only to realize that I had wet the bed. "Hey, Joe, how come you had the same sweet dreams about the boogieman that I had?"

Dad had a few rules for us. He told us when traveling around NYC we were not to get ourselves into a crowd and never run from the police. As young kids, Joe and I usually spent New Year's Eve watching Guy Lombardo and his Royal Canadians on TV. As we celebrated, we gorged ourselves with potato chips, pretzels, nuts, and soda. At midnight we opened the windows to the cold, damp blustery air and took pots and pans and banged them together as hard as we could, as well as hitting the hot hissing steam pipes and radiators with hammers to usher in the New Year. We are convinced that it was only through our planned, concerted, diligent, and untiring efforts that the New Year always arrived. (One of our nephews and his friend went to Times Square one New Year's Eve and someone standing next to them was shot. They got away from the crowd and ran to Penn Station to take the train home to Long Island. They never did see the ball drop at midnight.)

In regards to marijuana, Dad said in his caring, sensitive way, "If I eva khetch yous takin mhareewhana or dope, I'll fix your vhagon." (We knew what that meant—a fate worse than death itself!) Our response to him was, "We don't know what marijuana or dope is or where to even get any." I guess drugs were starting to appear on the streets in the early 1950s. They might have started previously and possibly from the G.I.s returning from the Korean War. Carl comments,

> Marijuana was known to us kids in the 40s being used in Harlem by band players, but not evident in Yorkville. Beer was the big thing along with "sneaky pete," $1.25, a pint of whiskey that bums would buy. The drink of choice at the Bowery.

In the 1950s we went to 86th Street to watch movies. The RKO movie theater was on Lexington Avenue and Loew's on Third Avenue. Twenty-five cents got you in where you first watched the news of the Korean War, then the movie, all in black and white. There was no color at that time. (How did we *ever* survive?) We enjoyed going to the movies. We remember one in which we had to wear special cardboard glasses with colored film lenses to view the show in 3-D.

Carl reminisces,

In the 40s Tom and I would go to the Monroe movie house at First Avenue between 75th and 76th Streets on Saturday mornings and watch 21 cartoons. Cost was 11¢. We were always counting them to make sure there were 21. Sometimes there were only 19 and the kids would yell out *boos* and the matron would come down the aisle and tell us to shut up, shining her flashlight in our face. She would try to grab us and try to throw us out. This most always started a rumble and maybe 100 kids would throw things at her till she ran away into the lobby. If it got too out of hand, the projectionist would stop the film and turn on the lights until order was restored. As kids, we just loved it. Good clean fun we thought!

The Annex movie house in the block on 74th Street was known to us kids as the roach or bedbug house. They showed only B movies, low budget commercial films, and weekly chapters. We always had rumbles there rolling down the aisles and yelling. For some reason we never went to the Colony at 79th Street and Second Avenue. The 86th Street movie houses (RKO, Loews, Grande*)* were more upscale theaters. We would get in free by collecting the torn-in-half stubs and sticking them together with gum. We had a field day when they had an old-timer ticket collector. One day we got caught when I think Herbie H. had just used new chewing gum and the guy took the ticket and the gum stretched with each half. We would now resort to going off the street into the back alley and barging in through the back stage door. This got to be stressful at times when the maintenance man was around and we would run up the aisles and dive into any empty seat. When things got quiet we would try and locate one another and sit in the balcony and smoke a cigarette. We all thought we were cool. After all, the movies we were watching on screen showed everyone smoking. I don't remember Tommy ever smoking. You could buy cigarettes at that time for 2¢ each or three for a nickel; they were called "loosees." We had a strange vocabulary in those days, but the kids all knew what we were talking about. Example: If you were walking along and picked up something the kids would yell out "haggies." This meant they got half. Whenever you were playing a game and wanted to go last you would yell out "larry." Hide and Seek was "hangleseek" and everyone would yell out "Not it" and sometimes kids would say it so close to each other it was deemed a tie you had to choose with throwing out your fingers and say odd or even as you tried to match your opponent. Street rules. There were many other events that took place during that time but should not be published. Tommy and your entire family had good parents and you all learned and listened well.

During special holidays or events, Dad took us to Madison Square Garden to see the rodeo with Roy Rogers and his horse, Trigger, or to Fifth Avenue to see the St. Patrick's Day or Thanksgiving/Christmas parades. We were excited to see Trigger before he died and was stuffed. When the circus came to town, we went up to First Avenue and watched a line of elephants walk down the avenue the wrong way, against traffic, with movement of cars blocked by police. Usually this occurred late at night or in the wee early morning hours when automobile traffic was minimal. This Manhattan safari was a great sight to watch as each elephant walked holding the tail of the elephant in front with its trunk. When Memorial Day came, we did our patriotic duty and went to First Avenue and saluted marching soldiers as we waved American flags. As the end of the parade came up, we would join the marchers and parade with them for a few blocks. There was true American pride and patriotism everywhere in those days. What has happened to American patriotism today?

Going to the beach at Coney Island, we had a chance to ride a regular roller coaster or the monster of them all, the Cyclone. Since the Cyclone was bigger and higher, we thought we would get more for our money and it would be more fun. So we rode it. There was a sign that said riders with eyeglasses should take them off and give them to the attendant for safekeeping. I did not trust this idea and put the glasses in my pocket. The ride was very scary. Sheer-terror-like would be a better description. When it was over, I took the eyeglasses out of my pocket and found the lenses broken. I should have listened. Another whack to the head.

We went to Jones Beach for picnics and swimming in the Atlantic Ocean. At one time Joe almost drowned when he went into the water and rip currents started pulling him out to sea. He had learned earlier if this ever happened to try to move parallel to the shore instead of perpendicular towards it. This worked and saved his life.

I brought brother Tom's old portable Philco radio with me to the beach. It had a very large battery, which was expensive to replace. The battery's size (10" x 4" x 2") made it heavy and bulky to carry around. The radio, with vacuum tubes, was replaced a few years later with lighter transistor radios, one of which I assembled from a kit.

When Joe and I came home from elementary school, we walked to the East Side Settlement House. It was founded in 1891 and a new building was built in 1901.[63] It was located on 76th Street by the East River. (It closed in the early 1960s when attendance dropped.) We spent many years in after-school endeavors there and one summer at their Stepney camp in Connecticut. Recreational and creative activities allowed us to play in the gym, work with arts and crafts, use the game room, or work in the wood shop for an hour or so. On Friday nights they showed movies to keep the kids off the street and out of trouble.

We enjoyed the wood shop and cutting up wood. We liked the smell of freshly cut wood, the sawdust it produced, the vibrations, and hearing the whirl of the woodworking machines. Joe broke so many blades on the jigsaw that he was banned from its use. He tried to cut pieces of ¼" thick plywood making quick, sharp 90-degree or more turns. The stress on the cutting blades became evident. (Little did Joe realize that one day he would become an industrial education

<hr>

63. Survey—East Side House (11-12-07), page 2, http://www.fordham.edu/images/academics/programs/baahp/eastside.pdf [viewed February 14, 2012].

teacher,[64] teaching woodworking classes, including the proper use of the jig saw and responsible care of its blades.) We were proud of the napkin holders, clay ashtrays, and other useful high-end avant-garde art we could craft and bring home. So were Mom and Dad. Some of our paper art went right up on the already crowded refrigerator door. The East Side House kept us busy and out of trouble while Mom either worked or got some deserved peace and quiet.

---

64. In his teaching career, Joe would eventually teach many other subjects besides industrial education.

PART II

The Learning Years

P.S. 190, 2009

CHAPTER 6

K–12 Public Schools

No Reservations

Elementary School

JOE: Our early schooling (K–6, ages 5–11) was from 1949 to 1956, when we attended P.S. 190, the Paul Revere Public School, at 311 East 82nd Street. This school later became P.S. 290, now called the Manhattan New School, a special K–5 school well known for its writing program. The five-story structure, situated between First and Second Avenues, was built around 1900 and located two blocks from our apartment. The classrooms had very high ceilings. At the request of the teacher we opened and closed windows from their tops using a long wooden pole with a brass hook on the end, being careful not to break the window. One of the least desirable things about *older* school buildings was the water there tasted putrid, perhaps due to contaminants found in the pipes, and water pressure from drinking fountains was minimal. Next to the school stood Sam's Candy Store, which we frequented often.

Our formal early education began shortly after World War II and continued through the Korean War. As a result, during the 1940s and early 1950s, like all students, we were required to wear metal "dog tags" throughout the building. When the air raid sirens sounded, we had lots of opportunities to take shelter in the basement, cafeteria, bathrooms, and under our desks covering our necks with our hands.[65] Dog tags were to be used for identification purposes in case you were injured or killed during aerial bombings. Wearing them left green rings around our necks from reactions to the metal chains. We remember many blackout drills at home as well, when air-raid sirens blasted, street lights were turned off, automobiles stopped and shut off their headlights, and we pulled down window shades and shut off our apartment lights. This was a test in case New York City came under enemy aerial attack.

In 1954 we remember teachers asking students, "What newspapers and magazines do you get at home?" "Vhy vhood dey ask dhis qhvestion," Mom asked? Were the teachers spying on immigrant families? Who wanted to know? Was this pervasive throughout the city or just in our ethnic German neighborhood? Was our government spying on us?

Every day in homeroom at the beginning of school, our class stood up, faced the flag, placed our hands over our hearts, and recited the Pledge of Allegiance.[66] This occurred throughout our building and in public schools throughout the city. Were you, the reader, and students in your town required to say the pledge? Do your students still recite it in school?

We hated having the teacher call on us in class to answer questions, especially if we weren't fully prepared with our work (this was infrequent, but did occur). After all, our peers were focusing in on us. Likewise, we didn't like having to stand up and recite anything, because we felt very self-conscious. We are sure our peers felt the same way.

In fifth grade we were very excited to take a class field trip to Cushman's Bakery in Queens. It was fun being "out of school" and traveling by bus across the Queensboro Bridge to a "foreign land," observing people driving and walking freely on the streets. We

---

65. I used to internally question this practice, thinking that being in the building under our desks wasn't going to help us if the building was bombed or collapsed on top of us.

66. See Appendix C, Item 1g, Miscellaneous.

thought they were so lucky because they didn't have to be stuck in school, like us. We were especially excited to each receive our very own small loaf of white bread upon completion of the tour, freshly baked just for us. We didn't have to share the bread with anyone. We felt important and respected. What a special, grand feeling. And it was a *full* loaf, at that.

During recess, the teachers closed off the street to through traffic and older kids played in the street. The younger ones played in the school's back yard. We were both members of the School Safety Patrol, wearing white plastic across-the-chest belts and badges, safely assisting children in crossing the street. We did this daily before and after school. We felt proud. We felt like the "high sheriff."

At lunchtime students could eat all the soup and peanut butter and jelly sandwiches they wanted, for free, but at least one of the slices of bread had to be *whole wheat*. That's the only way they were made. Oh, well, we *would* do anything to eat peanut butter and jelly. What tricks these adults play on us defenseless and unsuspecting kids. There ought to be a law, I thought. White bread rules!

John's friend Thomas flunked kindergarten. (John sure knew how to pick friends.) John and Tom ran away from school one day, when their group was about to be bussed to the Guggenheim Dental Clinic on 72nd Street near York Avenue, where dental students practiced their torture by giving free care to children. To this day, on blogs, adults who reflect upon their visits here during early school days actually refer to the clinic, time and time again, as a "Torture Chamber." They didn't like all the drilling and pain. All dental work was done without painkiller or anesthesia, and children were strapped down into dental chairs. As patients, we remember seeing and smelling "smoke" coming out of our mouths when dentists drilled. When visiting the clinic on previous occasions, John and Thomas had been terrified to find out they were assigned to the dreaded third floor area, where the specialty was tooth extractions. They trembled at the thought of having it done again and were not going to chance it. When the mothers found out about the disappearance, they brought them back to the principal's office. Mom dragged John two city blocks by his ear lobe to "straighten him out."

In another incident, when John's friend Barry and he were in the sixth grade, they went to St. Monica's Church after school to get their throats blessed. As the priest started to bless their throats with candles, they began giggling. When they could not stop, the priest asked them to leave. They left without the blessing and three days later John developed a sore throat that lasted for two weeks. Could this have been an omen?

Up through eighth grade we were dismissed early from school on Thursdays and were bussed to St. Monica's Catholic school on 80th Street for religious instruction. The school was in back of and connected to the church on 79th Street. More studying. The nuns used metallic "clickers" to catch our attention. It sounded like croaking frogs. At times when we were not prepared with our homework or had not learned our prayers properly, we had to hold out our hand, palms down, and the nun whacked us over our knuckles with a wooden ruler. Boy, did that smart! At age 14 we left the program.

I was generally a better student than John. This seemed to be the trend throughout our lives. John says I was more studious than him. Maybe that's why I didn't get into as much trouble as John. I would come up with ideas and projects, and John would generally follow my lead and start to get involved with me and my activities. I would generally take more challenging classes that John knew would be more difficult for him (i.e., third year of German, solid geometry, and physics in high school), in which case, John did not follow in my footsteps. In fifth grade John received a few unsatisfactory grades in arithmetic, social studies, literature, and music—just a *few* "unimportant" curriculum areas, he thought. In the closing weeks the teacher said he was very disorderly. However, that behavior didn't last long. "Whack." Thanks again, Mom and Dad.

Whenever we performed in school plays, Mom would almost

always attend. Occasionally, Dad would too. When Mom was not able to make it, Teta Chaloupka, Tante Ida, or Mrs. Novacek would fill in for Mom. On other occasions, they all were there with Mom. We were covered from all angles.

In fifth grade, my class was going to put on a play about Abraham Lincoln and they needed someone to play Lincoln. I got my friends to vote for me, and I won. However, once I won I decided not to continue. I guess I just like entering into competitions. My teacher, Mrs. Greentree, was furious. Mom was called to come to the school. I was let out of the play, and my classmate Tony Bendazo got to play Abe. Hey, he could have been our first Italian president. Mrs. Greentree found out that Mom was a domestic. She asked if Mom wanted another job, cleaning Mrs. Greentree's apartment. Mom graciously declined, since she had enough work, and with the two of us, Mary Ann, and two teenage sons, her plate was already overflowing.

In 1955 I went downtown and saw President Eisenhower being driven in his motorcade. I got a few snapshots of Ike, as he was only five feet away. A few years later I saw former President Harry Truman taking his daily constitutional walk down Park Avenue with reporters in tow.

On yet another occasion, Fidel Castro was in town. Our government was on good terms with him then. He held a rally in Central Park and we went to see him. It was a hot, still, humid June night, and you could have cut the air with a knife, the cigar smoke was so thick and heavy. In short time, someone shoved a large banner in front of me and I grabbed one of the supporting poles. Later that night I saw myself on the Walter Cronkite-anchored news holding the banner, which said "Viva La Revolucion." Otto said I would never get a government job. Castro stayed in a hotel in Harlem and it was alleged that he brought chickens with him that ran up and down the halls of the hotel.

In those early days of the 1950s when we were in elementary and junior high school, immigrant adults held teachers in the highest regard. Immigrants knew that education was the key to success for their children, to get them out of poverty and into a better life than they had. They knew that teachers were instrumental in providing this opportunity. When Mom and us kids walked down the street and passed by one of our teachers, that teacher greeted Mom. Mom was a bit nervous and embarrassed because of the huge difference in their educational levels, but she was still very proud and honored as a new American to have a teacher greet and speak to her. Teachers were her heroes. Without exception the conversation was cordial and affirming. We also remember that whenever we may have caused trouble in school and were disciplined by the teacher or principal (which was very rare) or didn't always do our best work, when word about it got home we were in double trouble and got additional punishment. Embarrassing or disgracing the family for not behaving well or not working up to our full potential was not tolerated.

One of my elementary teachers asked me to stop at the drug store to pick up Bromo-Seltzer antacid for her on my way back from lunch at the Novacek apartment. This was a weekly occurrence every Monday, and she always gave me the money beforehand for it. Mom thought the teacher's headaches might have been from too much drinking the night before. If so, what might have caused her to drink? Surely I had nothing to do with it. Maybe her headaches were from excessive use of the spirit duplicator ("Ditto" machine) or a combination thereof.

In the 50s teachers used mimeograph machines to reproduce worksheets and tests for students. The spirit duplicator replaced this messy process, but it required the use of an alcohol-based solution. Of course, when the teacher handed out freshly made copies, the fumes from the still damp paper almost knocked you over. OSHA would have had a field day. Actually, I didn't mind the fumes so much. I liked the smell. Instead of getting black mimeographed

Fire at P.S. 96 (built in 1890s), York Ave and 81st Street, circa late 1950s

copies, we were now getting light-blue copy that faded out with each successive copy being made. Some of these copies were barely readable. What a difference quality high-speed laser copiers can produce today, although emissions causing indoor air pollution remain an issue.

There were times in elementary school when I feigned illness at home (must have been those fumes), so I wouldn't have to go to school that day. I was scheduled to have a test and a few times I wasn't prepared. I am surprised that I was able to fool Mom the two times I pulled this.

Generally after school, we rushed home to watch our favorite television programs. At other times, our part-time jobs began after school.

P.S. 96 was an old junior high at the end of our block on York Avenue. The building caught fire and soon thereafter closed down.

Junior High School

In most of our grades, the teachers separated John and me from being in the same class. How could they be so cruel and insensitive and do such a thing, we thought? We didn't like it one bit, but somehow we survived.

From 1956 to 1959 (grades 7–9, ages 12–14) we attended P.S. 167 (Senator Robert F. Wagner Junior High School), the new $4.5-million, coed school at 220 East 76th Street, between Second and Third Avenues. Had this school not opened when it did, we would have gone to the old P.S. 30 on 88th Street, an eight-block walk each way. Our walk to Wagner was seven blocks one way. We never knew that there was such a concept as a "school bus" to take students to and from school.

Students were assigned classrooms according to their intelligence or ability. For instance, we had 16 sections of seventh grade classrooms. Sections 7-1 to 7-14 and 7SP1 and 7SP2. I was in section 7-2 and John was in section 7-3. The smartest "regular" kids were in 7-1, with the less capable, or should I say, more educationally challenged, in section 7-14. The kids in 7SP1 and 7SP2 were the brightest of the bunch. They went immediately from seventh grade into ninth grade the following year, totally skipping eighth grade. Our sister and her daughter were in such a group, although at a later time.

Seventh graders were required to take typewriting class. Students had to memorize the keys since lessons were learned on tall, heavy, manual Underwood typewriters with unmarked keys. If our memorization was faulty, when we wanted to know what character was associated with a particular key, we stuck our finger in the typewriter, typed on it, then looked at our finger to determine what character we typed. Of course, the image appeared in reverse. When the typing teacher was absent and there was a substitute, students pulled out the ribbons and hung them out the three-story window, where they waved in the breeze—like streamers in a military parade—greeting the citizenry and taxpayers passing by.

P.S. 167, Wagner Junior High School

In seventh grade English class we were required to read *Pride and Prejudice*, a book by Jane Austen. Ugh! I hated that book. First of all it was very thick and heavy, and it hurt my hand and arm to carry it. Second, it was about a bunch of young women in England and their romantic adventures. Who cares? I didn't. They couldn't even talk right. Maybe it would have helped if they talked my language. I could not identify with the characters or the era and had absolutely no interest in their story. Yet we had to carry the book back and forth from school to home—14 blocks each day—and read it in its entirety. We also had other books to carry. No wonder one of my arms is longer than the other.

In the eighth grade there was a big focus in school for everyone to be involved in a geography fair. The school sponsored a "Ge-O-Rama," with *all* classes—no matter what subject—actively participating, demonstrating connections between their subject and geography. It was a big successful affair, generating lots of publicity, and got our school celebrated in city newspapers. Many outside visitors attended this widely acclaimed festival.

In German class, teacher Herr Lobel played his mandolin and we all learned to sing *"Muss I Denn* (Wooden Heart)" and *"Röslein auf der Heiden* (Little Rose of the Field)."* He, being the wonderful man that he was, introduced us to the voice of Marlene Dietrich, a German singer and actress.[67]

We were required to take physical education a couple of times a week. We hated Phy Ed. My friends and I had to form a volleyball team and give ourselves a name. Because we equally disliked English, to be spiteful, we decided to call our team "The Adjectives." We got to play our rivals, "The Adverbs." (They hated English, too.) I don't know which team played better. I honestly didn't care. We also abhorred changing in and out of our clothes and going through the showers like a herd of cattle. But we were not alone; others felt equally self-conscious.

In our last-hour eighth-grade science class, one of our friends, who had band the previous period, brought his trumpet in its case to class with him. He allowed John and me and a few other friends to hide our squirt guns in the case in a secret compartment under the trumpet. These guns were forbidden to be seen or used in school. As a result, we had our squirt guns readily available for use after school as soon as the bell rang.

In 9th grade science, John was told to guard the lab bench since a delicate apparatus was set up. He was fooling around and picked up

---

67. Decades later we were thrilled to see her in a live one-woman concert in St. Paul, Minnesota. The 79-year-old arrived in a chauffeured 1929 Duesenberg. She sang most of the songs in English, which disappointed us. We had expected the majority of them to be sung in German. Of course, "Lili Marleen," our favorite, was sung in German. *Es macht uns sehr glücklich.* The reader may wish to do an Internet search for these songs, listening to them sung in German, English, Czech, or other languages. (See Appendix C, Item 1e, Memories, Dances, and Songs: Songs.) Years later, just before we were going to tour Scandinavia, we made a special effort to stop and visit her grave in the Friedenau Cemetery in Berlin. I laid on her mother's grave adjacent to hers and John photographed me next to Marlene. The small cemetery was difficult to find, since it was in a residential area. This side trip cost us $500 extra, but it was well worth it! Marlene had left a lasting impression on us. *"Danke schön,"* Marlene and Herr Lobel.

an open cardboard tube to playfully hit another student, and a long, expensive mercury thermometer—one of the items he was supposed to be protecting—flew out, hitting the floor and broke. His teacher was pissed.

For the most part, New York City teachers were either Italian or Jewish. We got in good with the music teacher, Mrs. Antobeli, because we always polished her piano or cleaned the piano keys. We also liked the way she smelled. We figured that collecting "brownie points" never hurt anybody. After all, we might need them someday. Most of our teachers, however, were Jewish. We were also grateful for that, because Jewish people have a long tradition placing a high value on education. We appreciated learning from the best.

During lunchtime, students had a choice of eating in the lunchroom or were allowed to leave and go home for lunch. Usually we went to a restaurant around the corner on Third Avenue to have a tuna fish sandwich on toast, along with a pickle and a Coke for 65¢. Yummy. At other times, we walked briskly with a group of friends ten blocks along Third Avenue to the Horn & Hardart Automat restaurant on 86th Street. This restaurant chain was unique; we loved eating there. Upon entering the store, you gave the cashier, also known as a "nickel thrower," a dollar bill, and she quickly and literally threw out the exact change in 20 nickels, since nickels were the only coins that could be used in the machines. Food was in dishes located in little "mail boxes" with windows. If you placed three nickels into a slot, you could get a hot macaroni and cheese casserole to die for. Yes—for 15¢. Five cents bought a crusty Parkay dinner roll with real butter. In 1950, 10¢ bought coffee; it went up to 15¢ in 1966. Fifteen or twenty cents got you a sandwich. Lunch was under a dollar. Hot dog! This chain of restaurants opened in 1902[68] in Philadelphia and New York City[69] and, unfortunately, closed in 1991 because of fierce competition

68. Lorraine B. Diehl and Marianne Hardart, *The Automat: The History, Recipes, and Allure of Horn and Hardart's Masterpiece* (New York: Clarkson/Potter Publishers, 2002), 28.
69. Ibid., 30.

from growing fast food restaurants.[70] Customers' eating habits were changing. The chain sponsored the *Horn & Hardart Children's Hour,*[71] a weekly television program on Sundays, hosted by Ed Herlihy. As kids, we thought this was one of the most entertaining programs on television—a performance of our peers—and we always watched it. Hoffman beverages sponsored the program;[72] we especially loved drinking its' cream soda.

On other occasions, we walked to 73rd Street to an apartment where Mom worked as a domestic and had lunch with her. She cleaned two apartments for three spinster English ladies, a male preacher, and one widow. The preacher and three women shared a six-room boxed-room apartment with a man-operated elevator and a doorman. The three aforementioned ladies lived into their 90s. We are convinced that their longevity—quite a feat in those days—was due to their nutrition. They lived off of white Arnold Bread toast (delicious), Earl Grey English tea with Carnation Evaporated Milk, and Gordon's Gin (not necessarily in this order). The widow, Mrs. Williams, was a writer for the *Perry Como* and *Ed Sullivan Shows,*[73] and rented a separate apartment.

One day, while working in Mrs. Williams's apartment, Mom made us a light lunch (soup, tea, and toast—hold the gin, as we had to get back to our junior high after lunch). John helped her clean by polishing brass items, while she told me to take the Hoover vacuum and clean the living room. I vacuumed around the fireplace when I accidentally knocked over a piece of metal. The brass cylinder, which popped its lid off as it hit the floor, ejected dirt onto my newly cleaned carpet. When I told Mom, she quickly figured things out and got upset. It seems that the "dirt" was the ashes of Mrs. Williams's cremated husband. I collected and put back what I could and

---

70. Ibid., 123.

71. Ibid., 86.

72. Ibid., 88.

73. John and I got free tickets to sit in the audience of these shows. We even watched Bud Abbott (of Abbott and Costello fame) perform on the Sullivan show.

vacuumed up the rest. How does one explain to Mrs. Williams that half her husband wound up in the bowels of the Hoover, but the worse part was we didn't know which half? We said nothing. Mum's the word. What a terrific, powerful, unforgiving, non-discriminating cleaning machine, I thought.

There was a time when Mr. Beem, a science teacher and also a lunchroom supervisor, and I didn't get along. We got into a power struggle over not allowing me to leave the building during lunchtime to have lunch with Mom. I told John I mumbled a few things about Mr. Beem under my breath. Unfortunately, days later Mr. Beem jumped out of a 17-story window.

During the summer of 1959, at the age of 15, just before John started high school, he wanted to exert his independence and travel to Minnesota and spend some time on the farm with Uncle Hugo and Aunt Lilly. He had been there eight years earlier with our family and had fond memories of it. Also our cousin David and his wife were just married that year and drove to NYC for their honeymoon to visit us at our 410 apartment. This was the year our families exchanged visits.

The 1,000-mile airplane ride from New York to Minnesota took six hours with loud propeller-driven engines that sent vibrations throughout the aircraft. John had an idea what Wilbur and Orville Wright must have felt like. Commercial jet planes had not yet arrived on the scene. Three days after arriving on the farm, John became homesick and put up such a fuss that Uncle Hugo took him to the airport for a return flight home. He got home around 7 a.m. and quietly knocked on the door. Mom opened the door and was shocked to see him. He went round trip in three days and arrived home *before* our parents received his post card saying he had arrived safely and was having a good time in Minnesota. He attributes his change in behavior to (1) immaturity, (2) cultural shock, and (3) fear. He was out of his element. I guess he wasn't so independent at that age after all.

Joe, Cousin Dave, Mary Ann, Dad, Mom, John, and Otto in 410
(notice clothesline), 1959 (Rose Ann Gindele, photographer)

We were the first graduating class ever to complete grades 7–9 in our brand-new junior high. In a few months we would be ready for high school—which would turn out to be a vastly different experience.

Senior High School

High school was a time for wearing penny loafers, a time to be cool. From 1959 to 1962 (grades 10–12, ages 15–18), we attended the High School of Commerce located near "Hell's Kitchen" at 155 West 65th Street. Andrew Carnegie actually laid its cornerstone on December 14, 1901. Commerce opened in 1902 and was an all-boys school until about WWII, when girls were permitted to attend.[74] It was demolished in 1965 to make way for The Julliard School at Lincoln Center for the Performing Arts.

We could have attended a number of high schools in various boroughs. Joe took the test for Stuyvesant High School in lower Manhattan, but didn't pass it. Like Otto, we chose Commerce

---

74. See Appendix C, Item 1b, Manhattan.

because the school was located in Manhattan and although it was on the West Side, it was close by. We did not want to attend Franklin High School (35 blocks north) because it was located in Harlem on 116th Street, overlooking the FDR Drive. Thinking about its reputation of gangs and violence put "knots in our stomachs" and made us nervous. We actually feared for our lives. We soon found out that things weren't much different at Commerce, but we knew that Otto survived it and so we followed in his footsteps. (We don't know why Tommy chose to go to Seward Park High School, which was located further downtown on the East Side, instead of Commerce.)

Although this was a nothing-special, very average, typical public high school, attending this school was a completely different experience for us. We had to take two city busses each way and do a fair amount of walking, too.

We were required to put book covers on all of our textbooks. The school offered durable coated paper ones for 25¢ each. Coated covers lasted much longer. Joe and I didn't want to spend that much, so we cut out uncoated brown paper grocery bags for this, while other students showed up with durable green vinyl covers—which were slashed out of the soft seat covers from the rear of public busses. (This was before steel and fiberglass seats became the norm.) Obviously, the vinyl covers lasted much longer than the paper bags, which didn't last as long as the coated ones.

When we attended Commerce in 1959, the six-story building contained a *new* annex, which was 45 years old at that time. Composer/musician George Gershwin attended Commerce but dropped out in 1914 at age 15,[75] while baseball player Lou Gehrig (who lived in Yorkville at 309 East 94th Street) graduated from Commerce in 1921.[76]

75. Alan Kendall, *George Gershwin: A Biography* (New York: Universe Books, 1987), 17.
76. Ray Robinson, *Iron Horse: Lou Gehrig in His Time* (New York: HarperPerennial, an imprint of HarperCollins Publishers, 1990), 44.

In 1962, the school's clientele consisted of 30% Negro, 30% Puerto Rican, and 40% White. These terms were part of the vernacular of the time. Today the terms would be African American, Latino, and Caucasian, respectively. There were holes in the blackboard of the third-floor German classroom. (I think they were bullet holes. I can understand why—more about this later.) Commerce had gangs and cops were constantly in the building. We lived in fear of being harassed and bullied. We were. On a daily basis. And we hated it! (Not much seems to have changed, as bullying is still very much alive in schools today over 50 years later. Perhaps it has gotten worse.) Our safety was always on our minds, and we looked out for each other and over our shoulders every day we attended. We wore garrison belts at home. These were wide, thick leather belts with a heavy metal buckle as seen in *West Side Story*. Some people identified them with gangs. Because they could be used as weapons, we were not allowed to wear them at school. (Decades later, when John taught at a junior high in Minnesota, students would ask him if he saw *West Side Story*. John's answer was, "saw *West Side Story*? I LIVED it!")

During our free period, we did volunteer work as part of the Audio-Visual squad, delivering, setting up, and returning large, bulky 16-mm movie projectors and other equipment to class-rooms throughout the building. We felt special, because we could travel freely in the building while other classes were in session, as long as we had our wooden AV pass, and could use the elevator, which was hand-operated by a woman. (Little did we realize that one day, we too, would be employed as AV Coordinators in public schools in the Midwest.)

The lunchroom was in the basement; the gym and track were on the fifth and sixth floors, respectively. Our gym teacher, who was overweight and could have benefited from exercise himself, had students do calisthenics for five minutes, then disappeared into in his office while most others played basketball and a few studied. Commerce had some good award-winning teams that played at Madison

Square Garden. The rest of the students, including John and me, sat on the track and did homework. We just had to turn our feet in and sideways to allow track students to run by. Students wore their street clothes—there were no gym uniforms—because the showers hadn't worked for 30 years. None of the students ever saw the inside of a locker room, probably for decades.

Public school food was prepared by prisoners on Riker's Island and then transported in heated trucks to the schools. I once received a partially green liver for lunch. Yes, they served liver in those days. Can you believe it? I wanted to throw it in a shoebox and mail it to the New York City Board of Health for inspection. I should have.

Commerce wasn't like the Bronx High School of Science. Commerce offered three different types of diplomas.

First, there was the non-academic track General diploma, also known as the attendance diploma—you get your butt to school, attend class, shut up, and you graduated. "Cooperate and graduate" was the theme.

The second was the Commercial diploma, offering business education courses—typing, filing, shorthand, etc.—to get you immediately employed when you graduated. There was a need for workers with these skills after WWII and the Korean War.

Finally, there was the academic-track Regents diploma, the one that prepared students for college. With the encouragement of family members, we enrolled in this track. Students were told they *had* to take this more *rigorous* track of courses to be able to: (1) get into college and (2) have a chance of surviving there.

In 1962 and before, one of the requirements for being accepted into college was that you had to have a *minimum* two years of foreign language. If you didn't successfully complete two years of a foreign language, you didn't get into college. Period. The foreign language requirement was a gatekeeper to academia. We took German in junior and senior high school. I completed three years of high school German when only two were required. The German teacher saw promise in me and he had the counselor sign me up for a third year of German. This was not my choice. I struggled and disliked it for the most part, so naturally I voluntarily signed up to take German in summer school, to advance myself so I wouldn't have to spend the *entire* next school year taking *two* semesters of German. *Wunderbar*. In my junior year I only had the sixth semester of German, since I completed the fifth semester in a six-week rigorous course during the previous hot summer, attending a non-air conditioned high school below 14th Street where I commuted daily by subway. Since I was spending 15¢ each way to take the subway downtown to take German, I wanted to get my money's worth and decided to also sign up for a solid geometry class too. It was free, was not offered at Commerce, and fit into my schedule. I had taken all the math classes Commerce had offered. In six weeks both classes were over and I still had time to work my various summer jobs. Unfortunately, my summer school German teacher decided to drop dead a couple of days *before* the Regents exams were given, taking with him all the brownie points I had accumulated. The French teacher, who also was fluent in German, read the oral parts of the three-hour long German Regents exam for me and others to translate.

Dad tried to help us, but he spoke country or "low" German, "Swabish Deutsch." In high school, we were taught formal or "high" German. I survived, but John did not. There were a half dozen ways to say the word "the" in German. John balked at this, thinking, "I'm not learning this; they (all the Germans) will have to change it to one word." When Herr Helmut Schmidt, one of the German teachers, asked John, "*Wie heissen Sie?* (What is your name?)," John replied, "*Heute ist Montag!* (Today is Monday!)" To make a long story short, John got kicked out of German and into Spanish. ("*Ya! Ya! Er war ein dummkopf.*")

When the bell rang for classes to change, Herr Schmidt beat the students out of the classroom door, making a beeline to the faculty lounge, a very large dark closet with tall narrow windows. He was a chain smoker. Rumor had it that he might have had a bottle of schnapps stored in his locker as well. (*Prost!* Maybe he hated German, too.)

John completed Spanish, which he loved and excelled in. *Mucho bueno!* He said, "Spanish has only one word for the word 'the.'" This made it much easier to learn.

About the time we graduated, state law changed to allow computer languages to be used in lieu of any foreign language when applying for college. Some folks thought this was dumbing down the curriculum.

Our chemistry class had five different teachers in one year. In the lab, kids slept with their coats on and their heads on the lab tables, just inches from the gas jets. Some kids lit the jets, turned them fully on, and an 18-inch jet flame emerged and blew by the side of one's head like a miniature flamethrower. That was one way to wake up the sleeping beauties. Students stored their notebooks and textbooks in the lab drawers. The drawers were watertight—as students learned when a quick hose connection from the water faucet into the drawer caused the books and materials there to bob up and down.

Our social studies teacher, Mrs. Benson, taught class by having her students copy word-for-word out of the textbook into their notebooks. This kept the students busy and quiet. The more you wrote, the higher your grade. I guess the teacher thought by transcribing the text, the contents had to pass through the student's brain, and therefore they would learn the material. We would imagine the principal enjoyed passing this room as he walked the hallway. He certainly would think the teacher had complete class control, since the room was quiet, and the students were actively engaged in serious learning. Good job, Mrs. Benson.

One of our English teachers, Mrs. Harding, had us diagramming sentences. She also gave us 20–25 new spelling words each day. Yeah, would you believe it? *Each day.* Did she think this was the *only* class we had? And we had jobs after school, too. We had to look up each word and define them in a sentence. One day I admonished her, "This is just too much. I'm sick of it. You're giving us too much work." Nothing changed. (Thank you, Mrs. Harding.)

Once a week our English teacher brought us into the library to receive library instruction and select books to read. I didn't have much of an interest in reading, and the librarian sensed it. The librarian brought me over to the bookshelves and told me to select a book. I looked and looked, searching for the thinnest book I could find. Since I couldn't find a matchbook, I settled for another close in size. As soon as I took it off the shelf, she loudly ordered me to reshelf it. (I thought libraries were quiet sanctuaries?) She stood there until I chose a thicker book, which I did just to get rid of her. I could care less what the subject matter of the book was. Little did I know that one day I would become a licensed and degreed librarian and media generalist in public secondary schools, offering library instruction and helping kids select books from the shelves. (Mom always said, "Vhat goes rhound comes rhound.")

One of my high school classes was challenging and rigorous. I hated my teacher. The teacher had a lousy personality, never smiled or joked, was rough and didn't have patience with students. However, I had the highest respect for him as a great teacher—one who knew his subject matter and taught students well. I learned that just because you don't like someone doesn't mean you cannot learn from them.

As extracurricular activities outside of school, we were involved on our own in citywide science fairs over three years. We built a lie detector, a battery rejuvenator, a wireless transmitter, and other electronic gadgets. We enjoyed making things and entering into contests. I received an honorable mention and even won a $25 Pepsi-Cola scholarship for my science exhibit. "M.I.T., here I come!" I was on a roll.

When each new semester started, teachers issued Delaney cards to students. These were small, 2" x 3" cards with a place for students'

Joe, Science Fair, NYC, 1961

names and a calendar of days printed on them. If a student was absent, the card's box was appropriately marked with an "X," or if tardy, a "T." It was an easy and quick way for teachers to take attendance. During the first day of class, blank cards were handed out and students printed their names on them and handed them in. One student had an extra card and printed the name, "Hurts, Dick." The language teacher, Mrs. Murano, kept asking in her broken English, "Who's Dick Hurts?" since that name did not appear on her *official* class roster. Three or four 15-year-old guys raised their hands partially and sheepishly under their desks or slightly into the air behind the backs of students sitting in front of them. Other students did all they could to contain themselves from breaking into laughter or falling off their chairs. Who said school was boring?

One of the least boring classes was art. John excelled in it because it was so subjective.

At one time John and I switched classes when John sat in on one of my law classes in lieu of me. The teacher never found out, but the other kids knew about the switch.

John with high school art teacher, Mr. DiGemma, 1960

At another time the shop teacher, Mr. Beller, came looking for recruits to bolster attendance in his industrial arts class. I was in a study hall doing my homework and was recruited. When the shop teacher asked the students what they wanted to build, the consensus was "gun racks" to store and display their weapons. (We had a working rifle range in the building under the bleachers—another after-school activity.) The shop class was located in the bowels of the building next to the boiler room. Of course. Where else to hide it? One of my tasks was to plane a few wooden boards by hand and assemble it into a gun rack. When I got through planing the boards, they were wavy and thin. I never did make my gun rack. But I got a decent grade in shop anyway, not because of my craftiness, but because, according to the shop teacher, I could take tests well. I knew how to read (at least my reading ability was better than some of my classmates in wood shop). Well, of course I could. I was in the Regents program and had won that $25 Pepsi-Cola scholarship. Remember? I was no dummy. I didn't know it at the time, but I would later become an industrial arts teacher myself and teach a few woodworking classes. Not only that, I would earn my doctorate in industrial technology. So would John. My overall high school grade was an 82 (B average). John's high school grades were okay except for chemistry and German, where he struggled to survive. Let's not go back there—please. Later in life we looked back at our academic performance and determined we were late bloomers. Our future academic endeavors and successes would demonstrate more promise.

Finally it came time to take state Regents examinations. All students throughout the State of New York were given the same exam at the same time, so you couldn't call your cousin in another school district or across the state and tell him/her what some of the questions were on the chemistry test, for example. The tests arrived at school in armored trucks and were then locked in the school safe until test time. Since it was always hot and humid in New York at the end of June—the school year is this long because of all the Jewish holidays during the year—the classroom windows were opened for "fresh" air. These three-hour Regents exams were required to be completed in *each* major subject area such as English, social studies, science (with separate three-hour exams for each science area like biology, physics, chemistry), including various math classes, etc. Busses, trucks, motorcycles, racing police cars, and other traffic drove by the school honking their horns and sirens blasting, emitting engine noises and noxious exhaust fumes, while construction workers were dynamiting across the street to build Lincoln Center for the Performing Arts. The date was late June 1962. So much for an educational environment conducive to learning and test taking.

Early on in high school, John and I were given the nickname "String Bean" because we were tall and lanky. One weekend when he was a sophomore, John took a bus with his friend Joe Paloosa and another friend to New Jersey at night. They all sat in the rear of the bus. They were "half-in-the-bag," having polished off a few six packs before boarding the bus. One of his friends had to pee, but there was no bathroom on board. It was dark out and the bus was traveling 55 mph, so John's friend slid open the side back window and started to relieve himself. In turning toward the window, he accidentally brushed an important working member of his body against the hair on the back of the head of the lady who sat in front of him. She didn't seem to notice or move, thank goodness. Maybe she was dead. The wind took the pee and sprayed it all over the outside of the side and rear windows.

They got off the bus at the wrong stop, several towns away from where they were supposed to get off, not knowing where they were. John asked his friend, Joe Paloosa, remember, the one whose mother said he would one day shine Sasha's shoes? "Where are we going to sleep?" He replied, "Here, at this house," which he pointed to. John went to sleep on a couch on a porch and the other guys disappeared. Around 4 a.m. the owner of the house came home, awakened John, and demanded to know who he was and what he was doing there. John told him his friends had made reservations. Then he figured out the entire story was a lie—they did not get the owner's permission for him to stay there. He profoundly apologized to the homeowner and thanked him for not calling the cops, which would have precipitated a call to Dad (remember, we *had* telephones now), who would have had to come to get him, which John perceived would have been worse then death itself. He never told our folks this story. His friends slept elsewhere, having had "reservations" at other houses. They later caught up with John in the morning, hung around town for a couple of hours waiting for a return bus back to Manhattan, taking with them a new sobering experience. Another exciting weekend.

While in high school, John remembers many times going to sleep in our fifth floor apartment with his self-built HeathKit transistor radio against his ear, listening to distant stations. He picked up a radio station over 1,000 miles away in Waterloo, Iowa. Little did he know then that he and I would be living in Waterloo decades later, pursuing post-graduate studies in nearby Cedar Falls.

CHAPTER 7

Part-Time Work

Got a Quarter, Mista?

Elementary School

JOHN: We were budding entrepreneurs early in life. During our elementary school years, we got an allowance of 10¢ per day. On major purchases, our folks believed that if you didn't have money to buy something, you didn't need it, because you couldn't afford it in the first place. This was a strong belief, since it was before the invention of the installment plan in the 1950s and certainly before credit card use became the norm.

Lemonade

When we were 8 or 9 years old, we set up a lemonade stand in front of our apartment building at 410 East 81st Street. The profits were great since we didn't have to pay for the water, ice, sugar, or lemonade. We had a built-in vendor who supplied the latter two items for free—Mom. There was no government agency to license, regulate, inspect, tax, or shut us down, and if there was, we would have moved and set up shop elsewhere under another name.

Shoe Shining

Next, we branched out and expanded our business adventures to include shoe shining. Each of us had our own shoe shine box and we stood on different street corners trying to "drum up business." At the end of the day, we compared notes on how much money we made. If there was very much of a difference, the one who made less was jealous of the one who made more. Then we saw who had the better "real estate" location. This spurred fierce competition between us. It seems we were always competitive. We had to be. Each of us had to survive.

Potholders

At 10 years of age, while vacationing in Connecticut, we, along with our sister, designed, manufactured, and sold 100 potholders using potholder-making kits. Joe "hired" other rural kids to work for our "Gindele Enterprises." So already he was moving into management and entrepreneurship. Then he drove Mary Ann on his bicycle from farmhouse to farmhouse, having *her* knock on doors to make the big sale. Who could resist buying potholders from a sweet 6-year-old girl? (Joe was applying psychology before he even knew how to spell psychology.) When the farm dogs started barking and running towards them, Joe sped off on his bike (Joe was applying survival skills), leaving our dear sister to fend for herself and make the sale or become "lunch" for one of the dogs.

Supermarket

Joe started working regularly when he was 11 years old. There was a New York City law that a kid needed working papers to get a job. Child labor protection laws, you know. This was good. Joe applied for the working papers, but they said he was too young to work, that he had to be 14. This was bad. Well, he was angry, stubborn and determined to work, so Joe, a sixth grader, started his own business as a carry-out boy standing in the front line of checkout counters at the local A&P supermarket on the corner of 79th Street and First Avenue. This supermarket did not have any such program to assist shoppers. They did not have baggers or carriers. No one came to grocery shop using his or her car. People walked from their apartment to the supermarket and walked back home up flights of stairs with armfuls of groceries. Aha! Joe found a niche. He stood at the end of the checkout line and asked people if he could carry their groceries with them to their apartments only for a tip, the amount of which they decided after the fact. Mostly it was a quarter per customer or ten or fifteen cents. The supermarket paid him nothing, nada, zilch! He hustled before it was legal for him to work and generally grossed about $18 to $25 a weekend, working only Friday nights and all day Saturday. By law, grocery stores were *not* open on Sundays in 1955. Too bad for Joe. On one occasion he had one lady's groceries all over the sidewalk on First Avenue, since the two fully loaded paper sacks, one in each arm, were heavily laden with cans of food. He did the best he could. He really cared about doing a good job servicing *his* clients and he put forth a great effort. Who knows, one day he might run for office and need their votes. It made him feel good that he was putting his best foot forward, helping others, earning his own way, and learning responsibility. Our parents were proud; we weren't idle; we kept out of trouble.

Come to think of it, he still got a tip for those spilled groceries, since the lady felt sorry for this puny kid from an immigrant family who had a speech impediment. Yeah, Joe was in a special speech class in elementary school and junior high. But he had good caring teachers who helped him improve his speech. He had other various interesting jobs after that, including work at a butcher shop, poultry market, and dry cleaners.

Junior High School

Butcher Shop
When we were very little we accompanied Mom to the butcher shop. Louie the butcher always cut a slice of bologna or hard salami

for us kids to eat. We liked it, and Mom purchased some to take home, along with kidneys, liver, heart, and other inexpensive cuts of meat. She frequently brought home stewing or roasting chicken and, on very special occasions, duck.

When Joe got older, he got a job working six days a week delivering meats from Louie's shop on York Avenue, between 79th and 80th Streets. Mom actually got him that job. She did a lot of shopping at this Czech-owned, sawdust-spread-on-the-floor meat market. One day she asked the butcher-owner, with a blood-splattered apron, "Vhy you ahlvays hirhing Eyerish kids to deliva meat for you, vhy not hirhe a good Czech boy, my shon. He's lookkink for vhoik. I spend plendy money here." That did it. The butcher was convinced of Joe's stellar capabilities. So he was working again, since delivering meat was a six-day-a-week job instead of working only the weekend. At the meat market he had a steady flow of income. He was moving up in the world—on his way to untold riches.

One rainy day Joe was hurrying to deliver pork chops. He tripped and the wet paper bag opened, spilling six pork chops all over the sidewalk on York Avenue. He thought the meat missed some of the dog poop, but he was not absolutely sure. He quickly wiped the pork chops clean on his dungarees (blue jeans) and threw them in the bag, lest another customer see him, and delivered the meat. The next week the maid informed the butcher that Madame said, "They were the best tasting pork chops ever." Joe didn't tell the maid, but he thought to himself, "Of course they were. They were specially seasoned. Thank *me!*"

Once he found a dollar bill lying on the floor of the backroom of the butcher shop, the room where he changed school clothes to working clothes. He didn't know what to do with it at first, but he did turn it in to the boss. The boss accepted it and thanked him. Did it fall on the floor by accident, or was his boss testing Joe's honesty and character?

Poultry Market—To Die For

While in high school, Joe got a better paying and more satisfying job—that of killing and cleaning chickens at the New Jersey Chicken Company located on 80th Street between York and East End Avenues. In the early 1900s this building used to be a livery stable for horse-drawn carriages. His boss told Joe a man was once murdered here. A lot of chickens certainly were. Yes, they were alive *before* Joe "processed" them. Every Saturday he took a spatula and scraped chicken shit off the bottom of the now empty cages, since the chickens had met their demise and were now in chicken heaven. He had to hose the cages down for return delivery to the company in New Jersey to pick up a new load of live poultry. He even hosed and scrubbed down the white tiled walls adjacent to the cages. Boy, did his clothes stink. Did he stink. His boss was Murray. What an Irishman. He ran the business during the day and studied nights at NYU for six years to become a math teacher, which we heard he eventually became. Good for him.

When Joe killed chickens, he held them in one hand, pinched their wings together, and held the head back with his thumb. With their throats exposed, he slit them with a knife and immediately threw the chickens head-down into a metal conical trough with a two-inch opening in the bottom for blood to drain. The birds remained momentarily still, then became agitated and, as their feet thrashed wildly, they defecated. Joe learned pretty quickly to keep his mouth and eyes shut, since chicken shit would fly up into his face. Wearing eyeglasses helped a little in this regard.

Once a bird was dead, he dipped it into boiling hot water, holding it by its feet. Then he laid it over a machine with a revolving steel drum with rubber fingers to remove the feathers. Then he gutted them. Sometimes the heart and attached liver continued to pulsate and "flop" up and down on the cutting board. This freaked Joe out. His boss explained that it was only muscular reaction and not to pay it much mind. Joe thought the gutted chicken was still alive.

During the fall hunting season, hunters drove up and Joe had to remove half-rotting birds from the trunks of their cars, which had been there for days. Joe had to clean them while trying very hard not to puke. He was not always successful in doing so.

Some of his Chinese customers liked to eat pigeons (squab), and he made regular deliveries to Park Avenue where a very elderly customer, Madame _____, owned a two-floor, 14-room apartment. At one time, he was told, her family dynasty owned one-third of China. They were really into the real estate business. He knew why they were so rich, because they never tipped—not even a dime, not even for Chinese New Year.

Joe worked in the chicken/pigeon business for a few years and then moved on to a bigger, better, "drier and cleaner" job. Delivering dry cleaning would now be his business.

Senior High School

Dry Cleaners: Joe

Joe worked as a delivery boy at a dry cleaning establishment in the neighborhood for 90¢ per hour. The dry cleaner was on the street level and part of a 35-story apartment building above it. It is now closed, consumed by an expanded grocery store.

By law, one had to have working papers and be 16 or older to work in a dry cleaning establishment, because of the machines and toxic chemicals used. One day the dry cleaning machine door was inadvertently left ajar. The machine re-cycled and many quarts of cleaning fluid shot out onto the linoleum squares on the floor. Immediately the squares turned to dry powder and fumes heavily saturated the air. A few workers as well as Joe got drunk just breathing the toxic fumes. His boss said prolonged breathing of that chemical would put holes in your liver. Joe's must look like Swiss cheese. They were more careful next time.

One of the more pleasant experiences with this machine was when its dry cleaning operation was over. Upon opening the door, many coins could usually be found just inside the door lip. People who brought in clothes were not always diligent in removing change from the pockets. Tip time.

Once Joe delivered dry cleaning to Mr. Grief, a customer who lived in a penthouse suite of a high-rise building. He also owned the building. Delivery people are *supposed* to use the delivery entrance and service elevator and not the main elevators reserved for residents. Well, one day Joe was in a hurry. The delivery elevator did not come, so he used the main elevator instead. When the door opened at the top floor, Mr. Grief was standing there. He read Joe the riot act, told him *never* to use this elevator again. Not a smart move. Joe thought, "He shouldn't have messed with String Bean." As he had with Mr. Beem, Joe mumbled a few things under his breath. Mr. Grief died two weeks later of a heart attack. His body was taken down, not in the main elevator, but in the *service* elevator. Now, he too, knew what the delivery entrance was like, probably experiencing it for the first time in his dead life.

Dry Cleaners: John

While Joe delivered clothes at his dry cleaners, I did the same at a competing dry cleaner one block from Joe's store. Our Jewish bosses were in competition with each other. So were their Gentile delivery boys.

However, the only famous person I delivered dry cleaned clothes to was Dr. Schwartz. He worked in a high profile forensic lab in New York City. Rumor had it he had body parts in glass jars displayed in his lab. One burnt specimen in particular (now residing in a jar of formaldehyde) had been taken from a man who was said to have urinated onto the electrified third rail in the subway. The man got electrocuted and partly fried. Ouch!

Many of our customers didn't know that we were twins or even brothers. For example, people stopped me on the street and gave me a tip, thinking I was Joe, and visa versa. I said, "Hey, anyone who gives me money is okay in my book. I won't complain." When customers switched dry cleaners and saw the "same" delivery boy working there, they thought the kid held two jobs and was really "hard-up" for money.

One day, when delivering clothes to a lady on East 79th Street near York Avenue, I could not immediately see her when she opened the door. She was on the floor, drunk as a skunk. As a teenager, I was not used to seeing such adult sights and it frightened me. I asked her if she was okay and gave her the newly cleaned clothes, which she took directly to the floor, soon, no doubt, to be dry cleaned again. My heart was racing and I ran out of the building, vowing for my peace of mind to have some semblance of protection the next time I had to return there. So what did this high school student do? I became a (cap) gun-toting hombre, packing heat that offered me, at least psychologically, protection and solace.

Not only did I deliver clothes, I also cleaned toilets, swept, washed and waxed floors, and shut off the boilers in the cellar before closing time. I was multi-talented and always left the place spotless. I took pride in my work. You could eat off my cleaned bathroom floor. Thanks again, Mom.

We went to school with another friend who worked for a different dry cleaning establishment outside the area. He told us that his establishment took in customers' fur coats to be kept in "cold storage" for safe keeping over the summer. That's what their customers thought. The coats allegedly were hung in protective thick-paper-sealed bags on bending water pipes in a filthy, hot, humid basement boiler room, guarded by mice, and were "refreshed" just before delivery to the customer prior to the onset of winter. Our friend told us that the customer was charged the appropriate "cold storage" rates.

Through various job experiences, Joe delivered meats, poultry, and dry cleaning to many famous movie stars and celebrities in

Bi-level FDR drive entering under the boardwalk
on East River (81st Street) looking north

our neighborhood (Paul Muni, William Holden, James MacAr-
thur, etc.), various diplomats from the Middle East embassies, and
customers who attended JFK's inaugural ball in Washington. Joe
spotted actor Don Ameche walking past the chicken market numerous times per week. He and variety show host Arthur Godfrey,
comedian Red Buttons, and news anchor Walter Cronkite all lived
in our neighborhood, within a few blocks of our apartment. (The
Marx brothers grew up at 179 East 93d Street,[77] and at one time it
was reported that President Barack Obama lived at 339 East 94th
Street[78] during his college years.) Comedian Red Buttons waved
to Joe from his balcony above the East River Drive, near where
the FDR drive goes under the Board Walk. Joe waved back with a
chicken leg—or was it a pork chop?—in his hand.

77. Harpo Marx and Rowland Barber, *Harpo Speaks!* (New York: Proscenium Publishers, Limelight Edition, 1962), 12.
78. David Remnick, *The Bridge: The Life and Rise of Barack Obama* (New York:
Alfred A. Knopf, 2010), 114.

The reader is encouraged to check the Internet for additional information regarding other famous residents. Who are these people who lived in Yorkville or on the Upper East Side, then and now?[79]

Early College Years

Air Conditioning

Joe and I also worked at an air conditioning/heating and refrigeration company during the summers of our early college years. Brother Tom started there as a mechanic, before he became manager and ultimately vice-president. In 1955 Tom was making $45 a week with an old air-conditioning job, then got a raise to $65 a week in his new a/c job. We thought our family was on the fast track to hog heaven. Life indeed looked exceedingly promising.

One of my jobs was to go to movie theaters to replace dirty air filters with clean ones. My partner and I literally walked inside the air conditioner. Commercial air conditioners are the size of very large rooms. Even though it was 95 degrees outside, we wore coats inside these rooms. Filters get dirty quickly, especially in New York City. Filters cost money to keep replacing or cleaning, so many movie theater managers simply didn't clean all of them. Some permanent filters that were designed to be steam-cleaned, were removed and not replaced. The result was that moviegoers "thought" they were breathing fresh, clean-filtered air, but they were not. My partner and I pulled out dirt, soot, rat carcasses, rat tails, dead mice, etc., from air ventilation ductwork—at least six paper grocery bags-full from one theater alone. (Watch out for "specks" on your popcorn. They may not be pepper or spices.)

As a teenage mechanic's helper, Joe was working with a partner on the roof of a six-story building in downtown Manhattan. The lead mechanic asked him to go down to the street and return with

---

79. See Appendix C, Item 1d, Yorkville: People.

a specific tool. Joe climbed down the ladder, then walked down six stories to their truck. He really was not familiar with most of the tools. Not to disappoint his co-worker, he returned with the entire toolbox. The mechanic wasn't too happy with Joe. This was Joe's first introduction to identifying tools—a prerequisite to becoming an industrial arts teacher, which he ultimately became, later teaching students tool identification.

When I was 19 years old, I had a harrowing experience while driving across the 59th Street (Queensboro) Bridge from Manhattan to Queens in my company's truck. I was smoking a cigar and placed it on the dash of the Jeep pick-up truck while I was on the way to the shop to pick up supplies. I forgot about the cigar as I was trying to stay in my lane while driving over potholes in heavy traffic. The cigar fell to the floor and under the driver's seat into oily rags that began smoldering. I panicked, envisioning flames burning my backside and engulfing the truck as I drove 50 miles an hour across the bridge. There was no way to pull over in the heavy traffic. As soon as I made it across, I quickly removed the smoldering rags, just prior to flashpoint.

We once worked a job at a manufacturing plant in Harlem. I was a first-year summer helper sent along with one of the mechanics. The plant was not getting cold air out of their system. We couldn't solve the problem, so another mechanic who was in the neighborhood came to help. He also couldn't solve it either until a third mechanic arrived. This mechanic was also an expert electrician. It seemed an "engineer" for the manufacturing company either had been fired or quit. He was angry and decided to "get even" with the company. He did something with the system. So now the fan that used to blow cold air from the air conditioner *out* through the ductwork into the room was blowing it *back* into the air-conditioning unit. The mechanic made a simple adjustment of wires; suddenly cold air came billowing out of the ducts. The management was so happy they gave each mechanic and their helpers a $2 tip. This was the early 1960s. Of course the company was not told what caused the problem or how it was solved. Much time and labor was spent on that job, and the company was billed accordingly.

One of the jobs we had was servicing a funeral parlor in Brooklyn. I accompanied one of the mechanics, and when we got into the elevator to get to the basement where the air conditioning unit was, one of the funeral parlor workers got out a tape measure to measure the mechanic, by height and width, implying he was going to get a correctly sized "coffin" ready for him. The mechanic, who was nervous as hell to be in a funeral parlor in the first place, freaked out. When we got to the basement to look for the air-conditioning unit, there were eight doors to select from. One had the a/c, the others had God knows what behind those doors, and we weren't eager to find out. We finally opened the correct door, serviced the unit, and "got the hell out of there" as quickly as we could. Before departing, the funeral director laughed and told us, "It's not the dead ones you should be worried about, they can't hurt you; it's the live ones you need to watch."

Our company had a contract to service the Playboy Club in Manhattan. Just before Labor Day, Tom got a call at home to come to the club and check to see that the air-conditioning system was operating at peak performance. It was. The club was expecting huge crowds of people that weekend, and management wanted to make sure nothing would break down. It was Sunday and he took Joe along. Joe had never been in the club. The Playboy Bunnies were very nice to them and some gave them a personal tour of the facilities, showing private back rooms, etc. Joe remembers being in a *small* elevator with a couple of these *large* gorgeous Bunnies, going from floor to floor. He thought, "I don't want this elevator to ever stop. Life is good, it's really good. How lucky could an 18-year-old guy be?"

Joe and I have always been conscientious and passionate about our work. When we were mechanics' helpers, we were told by some of the workers not to work so fast, "You'll get us fired." I was told this again later in life when I worked part-time in food service.

We knew of an air-conditioning mechanic who was in a lady's apartment trying to install her new window unit. It was a hot, muggy summer day. All she did was complain and complain that he wasn't working fast enough. Finally he had enough of her whining and the window unit accidentally "fell" out of its frame, crashing 15 feet below to a concrete patio. Of course the company had insurance to cover the mishap and a new window unit would be ordered immediately, however it would take at least a week to arrive. The moral of this story: Don't "tick-off" your service personnel, because it can come back to haunt you.

Here's an air-conditioning tip that can save you or someone you know money and make you more comfortable. We were told about a person who had a new house. It was a hot day and very humid outside, so this person turned on the air conditioning. It quickly got real cold in the house and then the air conditioner shut down, but the inside air remained uncomfortably muggy. I was puzzled. I asked my nephew Tommy, Jr., who owns his own commercial air-conditioning company[80] about it. His first response was, "These must be wealthy people or people of means." I said I think so, but how would you know? He replied:

> When people have money, they tend to purchase the biggest air-conditioning unit they can buy, because they think they are getting and can afford the very best, but in the air-conditioning business this is simply not true. You have to get an air-conditioner that matches the size of the interior of the house you want to cool, not any more or less. The first thing an air conditioner is supposed to do is take the humidity out of the air, *then* cool. What is happening in this case is that the air conditioner is so powerful it is cooling the air much too rapidly and then shutting down, thereby not letting the air conditioner take the humidity out first. I see this all the time.

---

80. Air Comfort in Amity Harbor (Long Island), New York, www.aircomny.com

Our Philosophy of Work

We never sloughed off on our jobs. When it was time to quit or prior to starting a new job or college, we worked even harder during the last week or so; when we finally left the job, we wanted our bosses to really miss us. The old saying, "You don't know what you have until you lose it" is really true.

We also felt that whoever hired us were the lucky ones. We were loyal and productive. We did our best to work hard, like our role models, Mom and Dad. It gave us a real sense of self-respect, self-esteem, and responsibility. You couldn't buy this feeling. We knew what we were worth and we were going to prove it.

Besides working in these junior high and high school part-time jobs after school from 3:30 p.m. to 6:30 p.m. every day, we studied three hours per night, from about 7 p.m. to 10 p.m., doing homework. We used whatever time we had on weekends, generally Sunday, to do major projects, term papers, library research, etc. When we were home studying, our parents would be quiet so as not to distract our learning. Joe and I placed wooden boards across the arms of our armchairs or on our laps and did homework on it. This was our portable "desk," and it worked perfectly.

All of these employment opportunities looked good on our résumés when we applied for college admission. We gained a sense of self-worth, responsibility, and independence and learned to appreciate the value of a dollar. We grew. We also learned how to relate to and deal with people, show up at work on time, and solve problems. Work was great, but we always tried to keep up with our studies, especially in secondary school.

One thing Joe had a passion for besides working was to *save* money. In the sixth and seventh grades, he washed his coins and dollar bills (money laundering), even ironing the currency. (He thought he could make the bills "crisper.") When we were in secondary school we each paid Mom $20 a week for food and to help with the rent, making only one major purchase a year—a portable Remington manual typewriter one year, a $100 reel-to-reel Wilcox-Gay tape recorder the next, and later a Hi-Fidelity music system that we built from a kit. The rest of the money went into taxes (Ugh! Whoever dreamt *that* up?), buying clothes, and having a little entertainment and spending money, as well as saving money. When Joe left for college in 1962 at the age of 18, he had earned $5,500 gross from work since he was 11 years old. (Joe kept tabs on everything.) That was a lot of money in those days. From this he managed to save $2,500 net for upcoming tuition, room, and board.

Sometimes when we wanted to eat steak at home, we gave Mom extra money and the family ate steak. This was the only way the Gindeles could really afford it. To help feed the family, Mom made meals from scratch. We ate liver and liver dumplings and kidney stew with rice (yummy—really). You just have to soak the kidneys in clean water for a few days, regularly changing the water to rinse the kidneys well. She soaked them and let them drain over the bathtub. She made homemade soup from boiling chicken feet in a large pot to make flavorful stock, and hamburgers were made with lots of bread and onion filling to extend the meat, thereby making more burgers than was possible with the meat alone. But we wouldn't trade that life or experience for anything.

It was not easy for our parents to support seven people, especially teenagers with bottomless stomachs and attending high school and going to college. But the family managed. The Gindeles wanted to succeed and achieve the American dream. We did. All of us children worked long and hard and contributed, but again our studies came first. Our parents put their five kids through college, always insisting that education was the *first* priority, and they sacrificed and made their children's home environment conducive to studying. They didn't just talk the talk, they walked the walk! Dad believed that in life, "*Wie man sich bettet so liegt man* (What you do to prepare yourself in life determines what you will get out of life)."

"Schtick your noss in a book," Dad shouted again, when he saw us sitting idly around the apartment. Sometimes it was sickening to hear. It didn't seem as much fun as doing other things, and of course, it wasn't. But it was more important for Joe and me at that time than being frivolous and wasteful with our time. During the formative years we siblings had adults (uncles, friends or acquaintances of our parents, employers and local store owners) tell us over and over "Get a good education or wind up shoveling shit in a coal mine." That's exactly what they said. We didn't challenge them. We took their sage advice. They were older, more experienced, and knew better. We were just too scared not to. Our parents knew what a hard life they had because they didn't have enough of an education themselves. They remembered their early immigrant years as well as living through the Great Depression. They were trying to help their children not make the same mistakes they made, but more, to recognize and accept opportunities that were freely available to us. Back in those days, the phrase "It takes a village to raise a child" was accepted practice and expected from people in the community, from those who had any contact or relationship with a kid as well as those who didn't, who were complete strangers. This social custom was supported and encouraged by parents. It is sad to say that this practice is almost non-existent today.

In 1962, when Joe attended the University of Minnesota as a freshman, he paid all of the $2,500 he saved up for tuition, room, and board. He and I then got a special educational student loan from our bank (Irving Savings Bank) at 6% interest. We only had to pay back 3% and the State of New York paid the other 3%. We didn't have to start paying the interest and loan principal until after we graduated, when we started our teaching jobs. It took years, but we finally did pay it all back. What a great feeling!

Years later when we purchased our house, Mom and Dad tried to give us a large interest-free loan for a down payment. We insisted, however, that they charge us 8% interest on that loan, the going rate at the time. We didn't want to take advantage of them. We didn't want to mooch off them. We paid it all back, principal and interest. We wouldn't have it any other way. Mom and Dad did more than enough in raising us. They were not people rich in tangible assets, but they were millionaires in many other respects. We didn't want to be coddled; we didn't want entitlements, for this would have weakened us and made us dependent on others. We wanted to be strong, independent, and responsible and stand on our own two feet. After all, we had our pride and self-respect. We knew what was right and what we had to do.

CHAPTER 8

Vacation Days/ Special Days—Playtime

Outhouse: Family Bonding Time

Family Visit to Minnesota

JOE: Our first big family vacation was when all seven of us drove from New York City to Albertville, Minnesota, in the summer of 1951 in our new black four-door Chevrolet Deluxe automobile. There were no seatbelts, air bags, padded dashboards, air conditioning, GPS systems, satellite radio, phones, or electric windows in the car. The windows were cranked manually by hand. There was no power steering, and the tires all had inflatable tubes in them. The windows were not made of safety glass. They had not yet been "invented." In its lifetime that car gave our family 125,000 miles of pleasure. The 1,200-mile journey to see Dad's brother, Hugo, and his farm family, took three days. Tom and Dad drove. Joe and I were about 7 years old. We remember running over a chicken and encountering a police roadblock—not because we ran over the chicken. Tom was the driver and felt awful.

Mary Ann was about 3 years old and slept on the huge rear windowsill of the car. At motels, she slept in a dresser drawer, then later in a closet, with the door open, although somehow someone

Our 1951 Chevy Deluxe, 1957

Uncle Hugo and Aunt Lillian on a Minnesota farm, 1927

kept shutting the door. We tried sleeping over the hump on the rear floor of the car. This didn't help the curvature of our spines. Perhaps it caused it. Mom loved drinking coffee at home. When the can was empty she recycled it. So the family wouldn't have to stop so often, Mom brought along an empty coffee can for us kids to pee in as we drove. The container proved to be a time-saver.

During the early 1950s, a television commercial for gasoline said to say "Amos 'n' Andy sent us" whenever we filled up our car at a Texaco gas station. We kept out of trouble along the way by trying to locate Amos 'n' Andy's house. The route was along two-lane state roads passing through towns and cities of varying sizes. The interstate highway system was four years away from being constructed.

Our family arrived at the farm around dusk. We remember the delicious malted milks Aunt Lilly made, sometimes with raw eggs; we fondly remember her playing the piano as we all sang along.

The farm had a party-line telephone, a system allowing many people to subscribe to and share one phone line. This was prevalent in the U.S. over 70 years ago, mostly in rural areas. All members of the party line heard all the rings of everyone else, but each party had its own unique ring to signal that the phone call was for them. Anyone could eavesdrop on another members' conversation just by picking up the receiver. Although this was against the rules, many people *did* listen in to what their neighbors were saying, thus fueling the gossip mill.

Having watched Westerns most of our lives, we thought Minnesota was the Wild West where shootouts occurred at high noon. Well, that's what we saw on television. (In Minnesota we dressed as cowboys, with boots, spurs, whistles, hats, and bandanas.) Later as John told his third grade teacher about our trip to Minnesota in search of cowboys and Indians, she used it as a teachable moment and asked the class to describe another name for "Indian." John quickly raised his hand and, jumping halfway out of his seat,

John, Mary Ann, and Joe, circa 1951

shouted, "I know, I know, Teacher, it's savages." "No," the teacher said, to which he replied, "That's what they're called on television."

The farm had everything a city slicker could want—chickens, geese, horses, cows, pigs, dogs, cats, tractors, animal manure, and a barn with pitchforks and hay. It was a great experience for some of the kids, except for the younger ones. We hated the geese, because they chased us all over the farmyard and bit us. They knew we didn't belong there—we were "*auslanders*."

John's curiosity got him into trouble. He was in the farmhouse snooping around the cellar one day and got his hand and fingers caught in a fox trap. He can attest that the trap functioned properly. He was lucky it didn't chop off any fingers.

Being on the farm gave us the experience of seeing chickens butchered—the heads were chopped off with an axe, but the dead chickens were still "running around." Were they undead? This terrified us, since we never experienced anything like it.

We also remember going into Monticello, a neighboring town, with Uncle Hugo to pick up a calf that was then transported home in the back of his car, with the seat removed. Well, the calf made a mess all over the floor en route to the farm. We were in the back, slipping and sliding, holding a rope around its neck. Mom and Aunt Lilly were angry because the car had to be cleaned in time for church the next day. What about us? "Hose 'em down, those varmints!"

Connecticut

Every summer for well over 30 years, Dad brought the family to spend part of the summer on an old farm in southwestern Connecticut. Over the years, other friends of the family were invited to visit. We kids generally spent three to five weeks at a time there. Toward the end of his employment Dad got four weeks off with pay. He took an additional week off without pay to be with us for an extra week. It was in the Derby/Shelton/Southbury and Oxford area, actually about six miles from Derby, off Route 34. Eighty miles away was considered New York City *and vicinity.* Since we grew up in the concrete jungle, going to the country and having grass under our feet was something really special.

Mr. and Mrs. Solar were retired farmers from Czechoslovakia, and they took in renters. They had 40 acres of rolling land, woods, pastures, and an "Eight-mile Brook" that crossed their property. The farm was situated on Coppermine Road (now called Bowers Hill Road), two and a half miles from Stevenson Dam, a popular beach area on the Housatonic River.[81] (Presently, the 1919 dam, which created Lake Zoar, is scheduled to be replaced with a newer one upstream.) We walked and drove our bicycles over the dam along Route 34 past Lake Zoar towards Stepney Camp. We remember walking along Laughlin Road (which intersected with Coppermine Road—that's where the farm was) when it was a single-lane gravel road used only by the mailman. We children followed a cow path through the woods to the brook. The brook was rocky and ice-cold when we floated on our inner tubes. The brook was also our bathtub. The Solars and our parents were not going to use good water

---

81. See Appendix C, Item 1g, Miscellaneous.

Mrs. and Mr. Solar in Connecticut

Stevenson Dam on the Housatonic River

Dad, Mom, Tommy and dog in Connecticut by the woodshed, 1938

Friends visiting in Connecticut, 1957

Eight-mile brook in Connecticut: Tommy with Tom, Jr.

Brook in Connecticut: Family and friends washing in brook

that required the cost of electricity to pump it into the house for us kids to bathe in. The brook was a good relief during those hot and humid August days. We went rock hopping and stone skipping and caught small fish for our fish tank in New York. But the fish died shortly after being placed in the tank. It seems freshwater fish are not accustomed to swimming in chlorinated city water.

The Arbuckles were the Solars' neighbors. We were told that Mr. Arbuckle lost his life savings in the 1929 stock market crash. Further down the road a farmer had hung himself in the barn. We were not sure why.

This section of the country, New England, has a rich history and related artifacts from the time of the American Revolution. On our adventures, we found real Indian arrowheads in the woods. Joseph and Josephine Solar slept on a bed that was manufactured in the 1700s. They had lots of antiques in their attic and the attic of their garage. They gave us an 1887 Seth Thomas mantel clock manufactured in Waterbury, Connecticut, along with some oil lamps, all in working order. We went for rides in Mr. Solars' old Model T Ford (converted to a dump truck to gather wood and rocks) that needed to be cranked up to operate and in Mrs. Solar's 1938 Chevrolet automobile. When she came home from work, Mrs. Solar delighted us on many occasions by driving us from her front lawn into her garage, a distance of perhaps 30 feet. It didn't take much to please us at that age.

The Solars had a root cellar where they kept canned jars of food they made from their garden. It had a dirt floor and was always damp and musty-smelling; cobwebs, spiders, and other lurking and crawling creatures seemed to be everywhere. It was dark and creepy to go into it, but the canned butter pickles and peaches tasted fresh and delicious, right out of the glass Mason jars.

Many times we saw Mr. Solar cut grass with his manual push lawn mower. He used a scythe on the longer grass that grew next to the chicken coop and behind the outhouse. Vegetation

The Solars' Model T Ford, 1958

Joe, Mary Ann, John, and dog Iggy in Connecticut, 1953

seemed to grow taller near the outhouse. He sharpened the cutting blades on an old grindstone wheel that he rigged and wetted with water held in a half-cut tire attached to its underside, operating the circular stone with a foot pedal. All his life he and his wife were self-sufficient. They had a wood-burning stove in the kitchen that was in constant use. Mr. Solar and Dad sawed and chopped wood that John and I stacked in the woodshed, using a wheelbarrow to move it. The pile of wood was heavy—we were only 12 or 13 years old—and it was hard work. Mrs. Solar rewarded

Mrs. Solar, John, Mary Ann and Joe, ready to ride into the garage, circa 1950

our work by driving us to an ice-cream parlor in Derby to get a banana split, malt, or tutti-frutti ice cream.

In our pre-teen years, we walked down to the brook from behind the barn, walking over rocks, passing "wild beasts" like cows and sometimes bulls, following the cow path adjacent to a barbed wire fence that separated it from an open field. We had been told to stay away from the bull that would be there on occasion. One day John went to the brook by himself, but instead of walking along the fence, he walked straight down the middle of the cow path and began sinking in mud that rose up to between his ankles and his knees. The mud was a mixture of sand and clay, cow manure, and urine. He was terrified, thinking he was sinking in quicksand and

The Solars' house from pasture, 1957

the ground was about to swallow him up. He started to cry, tried to make amends with God, and pleaded with God to help him, saying, "If you save me, I'll be forever good and do anything you want." Thanks, God!

We flew our balsa-wood airplanes and homemade kites in the hilly cow pastures. Our kites wouldn't stay up, so Mrs. Solar helped us by making a 6-foot-long tail tied with fabric remnants that was attached to the bottom of the kite. We made slingshots and shot stones at objects, including beehives, and were rewarded with a few stings. When walking through woods and fields, brushing against foliage, we sometimes got poison ivy. The rash on our skin itched and turned red. Mom and Dad kept Calamine lotion close by to treat the affected area.

We also picked pears, apples, and red and black plums off trees and ate them until our bellies bulged and ached. I was always amazed that the fruit we ate cost nothing; it was picked right off the tree for free, whenever we desired it. We also ate watermelon outside on those hot days and were allowed to spit out the seeds on the ground—something we couldn't do in the house or in our apartment. We had contests to see who could spit the farthest.

Japanese beetles were a threat to the fruit trees, so Mrs. Solar gave us an empty milk carton with some kerosene in the bottom, and we shook the beetles off the leaves into the carton. The beetles either died immediately or were roasted when we threw the partially filled carton into the fire pit. No matter how hard we worked, we didn't solve the beetle problem.

We searched for and picked four-leaf clovers, Concord grapes, wild blueberries along the road, blackberries, and raspberries on the hill and made jam out of the fruit; we picked wild mint leaves and sour grass and hunted for mushrooms. We sliced and dried mushrooms in the sun on newspapers placed on screens on two wheelbarrows. The dried mushrooms were robust in flavor, making absolutely delicious soup and scrambled eggs. Mrs. Solar knew edible mushrooms from the poison ones and evaluated each one carefully. Some of these fungi grew to enormous sizes, especially a day or two after a good, long, hard, steaming rain.

When it rained, we usually played Monopoly or other games in the family room by the porch. We also enjoyed being outside on the porch, sitting in rocking chairs and being protected by the overhang as a hard rain poured down in a thunderstorm. Only when lightning was severe did we run like hell at the last minute and seek shelter inside.

We helped collect eggs from the chicken coop, often getting pecked, and participated in killing chickens for soup and for dinner. Solars' dogs, a collie, Lassie, a German shepherd, Iggy, and later a black lab, Prince, waited in eager anticipation for the chicken heads. A retired Polish farmer, Mr. Poposki, delivered glass bottles of fresh milk to the farm. Sometimes I would ride my bicycle about a mile up Coppermine Road to his farm and pick up milk. The cream separated and floated to the top neck of the bottles, since the milk

The Solars' house with porch in Connecticut

Dad and Mr. Solar, 1958

Tommy (nephew) at the Solars' drinking well

was not homogenized. When it rained, family members sat with the dogs in the open woodshed listening to stories of yesteryear while Dad and Mr. Solar, who was then in his 80s, puffed on their *fajfkas*. Joe and I pulled ice-cold sweet-tasting water up in a wooden bucket from a real well in front of the house and explored the barn and other neighboring Laughlin, Freeman, O'Neill, Bowers Hill, and Quaker Farm roads by foot and bicycle. In fact, I buried some money—coins and memorabilia—in the ground behind the barn. It should still be there. I once came face to face with the head of an upright copperhead snake when walking behind the barn. I don't know who was more mesmerized, the snake or me. God must have been with me. The dogs enjoyed following family members walking along the road and through woods and fields, chasing woodchucks and other wild critters.

It was a peaceful life for us kids, wonderful, adventurous, and carefree, a life and time never to be repeated. We are grateful for the memories. (Thank you, Mom and Dad.) We are grateful that

Mary Ann, John, and Joe in Connecticut, 1951

generations of our family and friends shared these experiences. Thank God for the cherished fond memories we have of our youth and time spent in Connecticut with the people we loved.

For additional entertainment, we designed skits and put on talent shows with our sister and other children. We loved singing our favorite songs, "You are My Sunshine" and "On Top of Old Smoky."[82] When brother Tommy drove up with his girlfriend Eileen (whom he later married) from NYC for the weekend, he reluctantly took us with them to the drive-in outdoor movie in the Derby, Shelton, and Ansonia area. We saw Debbie Reynolds in *Tammy and the Bachelor* under the stars, all of us sitting in the car with a speaker attached to the car's inside front window. Hundreds of other cars

82. See Appendix C, Item 1e, Memories, Dances, and Songs: Songs.

Dennis (nephew) exploring woods/fields in Connecticut

surrounded us. There was a stand serving popcorn, beverages, and other treats. We were half-asleep in the back seat when Tommy drove home to the farm after the show, late at night, up and down hilly and winding roads through mist and fog. Why he was reluctant to take us along just to see a movie we will never understand. Tommy was all right, though. He did look out for our interest. He even taught us that we didn't have to sleep with our socks on at home, that we could take them off, that they would be there in the morning to wear again, that we needed to air out our feet (not to mention our socks). What a mentor! What a mensch!

Although there was indoor plumbing, our family members, especially us kids, were encouraged—instructed in no uncertain terms, in fact—to use the outhouse instead of the inside toilet. The outhouse had three different size openings and could accommodate three people at a time, two adults and a child. I remember once sitting there along with Mom and Dad, contemplating nature. Family bonding time, don't you think?

We kids were terrified that a snake was down in the pit and ready to attack us when we sat down. The place smelled, of course, and we had to pinch our noses to keep from puking. However, the flies and bees didn't seem to mind. In fact, they loved it, they were every-where. We didn't linger in the outhouse any longer than necessary.

When it rained, we played games on the porch or snuck up into the attic to explore it while Mrs. Solar was at work. She worked at a warehouse in Derby, a huge mill built in the mid-1800s, sewing garments. The farmhouse attic had a distinctive old dry musty-aged smell all to itself. We listened to songs played on thick old 78-rpm records on Solars' wind-up Victrola. "Rock of Ages" must have been the most popular tune, because that record was the most worn.[83]

The Solars and our family played Bingo at night, played cards, or watched wrestling on television. The Solars got really worked up and excited, slamming their fists on sofa arm rests, shouting loudly at the wrestlers on television, "Kill dhem bastards! *Kill dhem bastards!*" They believed the wrestling/fighting was for real and not made-up entertainment. The adults also loved to watch *Gunsmoke* and *Lawman*, two favorite Westerns at the time. Meanwhile, there was a loaded shotgun in the corner of the living room next to the TV. We kids were told *never* to touch it.

During clear nights, Dad sat outside in one of the Adirondack chairs, smoking his pipe and staring up at the stars. Millions of stars shone. We could see many of them because we were in the country with no town or city lights on the horizon to interfere with viewing them. Sometimes Dad ran into the house and told us to come out to see the Russian Sputnik satellite moving across the sky. We gazed in amazement. Other times when it got dusk, we captured fireflies, put them in Mason jars, and capped the jars. We anticipated lighting up a room after collecting enough of them.

---

83. See Appendix C, Item 1e, Memories, Dances, and Songs: Songs.

At one time when we were about 8 years old, when we were supposed to be napping, John and I decided to have a water sports contest to see who could pee the highest up the bedroom corner wall, towards the ceiling, while standing on the mattress. So what if the farmhouse was built in the early 1900s and the walls were decorated with 1920s style wallpaper that couldn't be replaced? It didn't bother us. We figured that when the wallpaper dried, no one would know. Of course, we were wrong. The telltale "ring" stain was evident. When our parents found out, all hell broke loose. Mom had to pay Mrs. Solar for the damages. What concerned us more was the beating we got and the whacks across the side of our heads. We could still see visions of the strap. John and I are still not sure who *won* the contest. I think I did. I was older. Each of us blamed the other for coming up with yet another "brilliant idea." I looked at John and shouted, "How did you get me into this mess?"

We also attended summer camp in Connecticut one year. From New York City, we were taken by bus from the East Side House to Stepney Camp in Botsford, Connecticut, a few miles from the Solars' farm just across the Housatonic River. The camp, owned by the East Side House, opened in 1910.[84] We remember Mom sewing cloth name tags into our shirts, pants, and underwear, so these items wouldn't get lost or mixed up with those of other kids.

Stepney Camp was the first and last of our camping experiences. We hated it. We truly believe to this day that this is where we learned to hate sports. We never knew how to play baseball, since we never had any interest in it. Of course at camp we had to play, and team captains selected who was going to be on their teams. Since we were "new" there and the team captains didn't know us, we were some

---

84. Survey—East Side House (11-12-07), page 2, http://www.fordham.edu/images/academics/programs/baahp/eastside.pdf [viewed February 14, 2012].

of the *last* guys to be selected.[85] When we played, members of both teams shouted at us where to run. After hitting the ball, players on the opposing team convinced us to run in the opposite, wrong direction. We were being yelled at from both sides and were confused. Boy, did this embarrass us and totally stress us out. Now we *hated* sports even more.

At one time in the cabin John was talking after the counselor told us to shut up. One of the other kids told the counselor he thought John talked. John made a wisecrack and got punched by the counselor. John was stubborn and he deserved it.

To make a long story short, John and I ran away from camp. Counselors picked us up walking along the highway on Route 34 by the Housatonic River. Solars' farm was just seven miles away. We knew where we were going, and we would have made it, too. We had a plan. We anticipated something like this might happen, so we memorized the route between the dam and the camp days earlier as we were driven to the camp, just in case we needed a quick getaway. The next day, Mrs. Solar drove to the camp and brought us back to her farm where our parents were vacationing.

Tragedy #4: Another gruesome family experience occurred in 1955 when Hurricane Diane hit New England. The train station and most of the city of Derby was under 20 or more feet of water, and we saw naked corpses floating down the Housatonic River. Our family was in the last car to be allowed out of the area by the state police before Route 34 was closed. About a hundred people were killed during this storm, and the army had to be called out to assist. We were lucky to be on our way home.

Television host Ed Sullivan had a summer home near the farm. In the early 1950s, John and I met Mr. Joe O'Neill, who, we were

---

85. We are reminded of gym in junior high and other occasions in elementary school when classmates had to choose a partner and how badly we felt when we were not chosen. It does a number on one's self-esteem, especially if it occurs frequently.

told, was one of Henry Ford's lawyers. O'Neill was already in his 90s and a friend of Mr. Solar. O'Neill lived a few miles away, on O'Neill Road, of course.

The Connecticut experience was great for all three generations of our family, spanning almost 50 years. Our family could have purchased the 40-acre farm and buildings (house, barn, chicken coops, milk house, outhouse, garage, wood shed, well, chickens, dogs, and dog houses) for $17,000 at one time. The property was sold and is now valued at well over $3 million. The area is growing, the open pastures where we kids flew our kites, picked blackberries, and played cowboys and Indians are now woods with roads and gated homes on it. It is just not the same as those "good-old-days" we once knew.

In the spring of 1962, prior to graduation, John decided to become an industrial arts teacher. After all, he was always tinkering with things and liked working with his hands. He made it this far without getting electrocuted. Secondly, he was convinced that because students went home at 3 p.m., teachers also went home at that time and that they had an easy life. (Boy, was he ever wrong!)[86] What did he know? It seemed like a good occupation to an 18-year-old.

I, on the other hand, wanted to go into engineering. We wrote to several colleges on the East Coast and in Minnesota. The State

---

86. Teachers work longer than most people realize. A 2008 research study reported that full-time teachers work, on average, 55 hours per week. ["Miscellaneous Classroom Concerns," *NEA Today*, September, 2008, 27(1), 28] (This includes teaching and all after-school, evening, and weekend work in correcting papers at home, preparing tests, designing lesson plans, attending after-school functions as well as parent meetings, etc.) If one multiplies 55 hours x 38 weeks in a regular teacher's contract, one gets 2,090 hours of work. Divide 2,090 by 40 hours per week (average workweek), one has a typical teacher *working 52.25 weeks per year*. They do this in a *compressed* nine months of time. Many teachers also take college classes or workshops at night and over the summer, as we have done. It should also not be forgotten that when teachers " . . . are compelled not to work during the three months of summer, they won't be able to collect unemployment compensation." However, other "seasonal workers" have that right. [Mattsen, John A., "Big surpluses, but not enough to pay teachers decent salary," *Minneapolis Star Tribune*, January 15, 2000, A17.]

Joe's high school yearbook
graduation photo, age 18, 1962

John's high school yearbook
graduation photo, age 18, 1962

University of New York (SUNY)-Oswego, turned John down. (He was a late bloomer—today they would hire him as a professor.) His Grade Point Average may not have been up to their standards because of some less than stellar high school grades in German, math, history, and chemistry. I was accepted into an electrical engineering program at Pratt Institute in Brooklyn, where it would have cost me $2,000 tuition to commute by subway. We decided to head towards "tumbleweed country," at least in that direction. We once read a message that said, "Go West, young man." So we did.

PART III

Bonus Section

The journey continues. The first eight chapters of this book have been about our growing up in Yorkville, from the Early Years through the Learning Years. We are happy to offer the reader *two supplementary bonuses*—(1) additional insights into our lives as we pursued and completed *Undergraduate School (1962–1967/1968)*, and (2) our internal relationships as twins: *It's a Twin Thing*.

It is now the summer of 1962; we are 18 years old and have successfully completed high school. It is time to leave Yorkville and our family, to spread our wings, seeking higher education and newer growth experiences in the Midwest, bringing established family values and past experiences with us, to further build upon.

CHAPTER 9

Undergraduate School (1962–1967/68)

"Ya Sure, You Betcha!"

Moving to Minnesota

JOHN: We accepted an invitation to attend the University of Minnesota (the U of M) in Minneapolis. I guess at 18 we were looking for independence and adventure. We thought, why shouldn't the U of M accept us? They were collecting $1,800 per year from each of us as out-of-state students—three times the normal in-state tuition. We chose Minnesota because we had relatives living here, a natural fit.

While growing up in the industrial Northeast, prior to moving to the Midwest, we thought we knew everything. Don't all 15- to 18-year-old kids, especially those having achieved the coveted high school diploma, know everything? We thought the Hudson River separated civilization (New York City) from the rest of the world and that chocolate milk came from brown cows and meat came from the butcher. Well, that's where Mom always got her meat, didn't she? I guess we still had a *few* more things to learn.

To the Farm

Early in September 1962, Otto, accompanied by his wife and infant daughter Susan, drove us in their 1959 Oldsmobile from Manhattan to Albertville, Minnesota, a three-day, 1,200-mile trip. This would begin our half-century of living in the Midwest, the land of "Ole and Lena," Gunnar Olson, Sven Torkelson, the French's, Olson's, Larson's, and Saliny's, lutefisk, and lefse. "Ya sure, you betcha!"

Along the cross-country trip our blue-lined suitcases carrying a half-dozen white shirts and other clothes were strapped to the roof of the car. We encountered periods of heavy rain on the journey and when the suitcases were opened, the shirts were no longer white, but blue-stained—almost like being tie-dyed. Aunt Lilly was kind enough to laboriously wash and iron all of them for us. Thank you, Aunt Lilly.

We spent a few days visiting Aunt Lilly and cousins Albert and David (Uncle Hugo had since passed), before Otto drove us to our next residence, Room 1-160 in Territorial Hall on Oak Street, at the U of M campus. After unloading the car in front of our dormitory window, Joe and I looked out just in time to see Otto drive away. *Terror* set in. *Reality* set in. There we were—just the two of us. We stared at each other and said, "What the hell did we just do?" At this time our stomachs turned into knots. We got what we wished for. We had premonitions about being orphaned/abandoned. Shortly thereafter, however, we settled down into our routine of taking classes and doing homework. We revisited the farm on Pelican Lake near Albertville during Thanksgiving and Christmas breaks, 35 miles to the northwest, courtesy of Greyhound Bus Lines.

You haven't lived until you've had one of Aunt Lilly's hearty farm breakfasts, especially after returning from 6 a.m. church services on those miserably cold, dark wintry mornings. The sounds and smell of hot bacon and eggs rapidly bubbling in fat in the high heat of the cast-iron skillet and the smells of home-made bread and hot coffee vigorously percolating in the blue enamel pot on the old wood stove made for many perfect sub-freezing mornings. As we ate, Aunt Lilly and Joe and I listened to "Boone and Erickson" tell their stories on WCCO radio. The sound of her old floor-model radio with vacuum tubes and 12-inch speaker was comforting and reassuring, while the wind howled outside, rattling the frosted single-pane windows of the old farmhouse.

Early masses at St. Michael Catholic Church, in a larger neighboring town, were difficult to get up for, especially in wintertime. We froze our buns off and slid back and forth on clear vinyl-covered car seats when Aunt Lilly negotiated left and right 90-degree turns on twisty, bumpy, gravel country roads. And she had a heavy foot, too! No seat belts were installed in cars yet. Conversely, in the summer, one's rear end burned from sitting and sliding on the hot baked plastic, which seemed close to melting. That was our penance. But we got religion, anyway.

Dad wouldn't allow us to get a car until we first proved ourselves academically, which was reasonable and which we did. He bought us a used 1960 copper-toned Chevy Impala when we were sophomores. We read the *Minnesota Driver's Manual*. I had a little driving experience on the country roads. Most of Joe's driving experience was from the farm to the driver examination center in Buffalo, 10 miles away. Joe got his license. I didn't. I failed the written test. He's good at bookwork, although the examiner said that I knew how to handle the car better than Joe. I had enough practice driving in the farm fields and on gravel roads. I felt comfortable handling a car. So, the following summer, for a fee, I completed an AAA behind-the-wheel driver education class on 86th Street in the middle of New York City. When I got into the Valiant automobile for my test drive, I remarked, "I'm not driving this car!" When asked why, I told the driver education instructor, "Look, there's too much play in the steering wheel." He told me, "That's not play, that's *power steering!*" The cars that Joe and I learned to drive on the farm did not have power steering, so this was a new phenomenon to us. What a country. So, I failed my driving test in rural Buffalo, Minnesota, but passed it on Avenue "B," on the lower East Side of Manhattan, surrounded by trucks, taxi cabs, and police cars in rush hour traffic. It must have been the adrenaline rush that got me through it.

Joe, 1960 Chevy, Minnesota, circa 1964

Our cousin Albert's in-laws, the Dehmers, had a farm in the town of St. Michael. Their ancestors settled there in 1857, and the Homestead Act of 1862 deeded them ownership of the land. Abraham Lincoln originally signed the deed, which at one time we held in our hands. Decades later a town began to emerge and grew around the farm. As the population grew, people began complaining about the hog smell coming from the farm. The townspeople wanted the farm family to move the farm. Well, hello! Who was there first?

University of Minnesota

Town and Culture

As freshmen, we lived and studied on the Minneapolis campus. We were realistically in the city—similar to being back home. Therefore, moving from New York City was a little easier for us to endure. Attending a small-town college in the country might have been too much of a cultural shock.

Minneapolis is referred to as the "Mill City," and flour mills, grain silos, and railroad tracks surrounded the Minneapolis campus. That fall, as 18-year-old freshmen, Joe and I walked along the tracks one day after a good rain, puffing on our pipes, contemplating life and our future. The high humidity brought out the stench of the malt. It smelled like you were inside a box of wet oatmeal. Out of the blue, as we walked around the university, Joe blurted out that one day we would both have doctors' degrees. I dismissed it. I still don't understand why this thought ever came into his head. But Joe always seemed to have a peculiar knack for predicting future events. Twenty-seven years later, Joe's forecast materialized. Talk about psychic experiences!

Classes and Activities

As a freshman, I had to complete a non-credit class and pay tuition for it. It was called "Composition X," and it was equivalent to a high school-level English class. I passed the course with flying colors. The instructor said my writing was simple, focused, and easy to read.

We wanted to join the ROTC Air Force on campus but were turned down due to nearsightedness. So we sought out the Navy— same results. After this second try we gave up. Then the Army heard about us and quickly signed us up. We enrolled that fall and winter because the one-credit class seemed interesting and it fit easily into our schedule. One of the perks was receiving a long, heavy, warm winter trench-style army coat. The coat came down well past our knees—we looked like Gestapo. This was just the wardrobe we needed to survive those cold Minnesota winters we had heard about. But when the military professor came into our classroom and shot a blank from a M-14 rifle, the noise echoed across the room and scared the hell out of us. We made a beeline to the Registrar's Office, dropping ROTC a few weeks after the winter quarter began. We suddenly remembered we don't like real guns. But we had to give up the coats.

That hurt, but it was okay since spring was just around the corner and our first Minnesota winter would soon be history.

We were not keen on taking required P.E. classes. When Joe signed up for a dancing class, the other students, all girls, asked him if he had his uniform. Joe said, "What uniform?" The girls pointed to their black leotards as a requirement for their "Body Vocabulary" class. When Joe saw the leotards, he said, "No way, I'm outa here!" I, however, settled for bowling, golf, and square dancing for my three credits of physical education classes.

At 8 a.m. on Mondays, Wednesdays, and Fridays, we, along with 2,300 other freshmen, sat in Northrup Auditorium for our Psychology 101 class. Graduate assistants, referred by some people as "grad-asses," took daily attendance. If your seat was vacant, you were marked absent. Had a cadaver, mannequin, or blow-up doll been placed in your seat, you probably would have been counted as present.

In an introduction to engineering class that Joe took, the professor told the students, "Look left, then look right. One of you will not be here next year." Joe thought, "What a shame, these folks appear to be nice people." However, it was *Joe* who would be gone from the program.

I flunked two college classes—one in sociology at the U of M and one in social science, later at Saint Cloud State College (SCSC). I passed social science the second time around.

We completed a career interest assessment tool that helped us focus on vocational areas of interest. Test results indicated that I would be good working as a farmer, printer, undertaker, or teacher. Joe's results were printer or teacher. I knew I liked to work with people, but not dead people, so I became an industrial arts teacher, specializing in printing and graphic arts. Joe would eventually do the same. Two out of four isn't bad—how's that for a career choice?

Dormitory Life

Dormitory life was interesting. This was the first time in our 18 years that we had a bedroom with a door, and we could even lock it. What privacy. What power. We never had this growing up in our apartments, where curtains separated the three bedrooms and the only closed doors with locks on them were the doors to the bathroom and hallway (and an emergency escape door, never used).

John with ROTC trench coat, University of Minnesota Territorial Hall, dorm Room-1-160, 1962

If you needed academic help, somebody in the dorm could help you. We all helped each other. A cafeteria was available on campus to save time not having to shop for groceries, prepare meals, or wash dishes. In fact, when we went through the food line we were allowed to take more than one box of cereal each morning. I did this and in a few months I had 60 individual serving boxes of various cereals stored in my dresser. I then mailed these in a large box as a "care package" to our parents in New York City. Dad was impressed.

At one time, while preparing for the sociology exam, I thought I would study the smart way, staying up all night, while popping over-the-counter pills to stay awake. It was quieter in the dormitory at night—more conducive for concentrating on class notes. By the dawn of the early light, I was so "punchy," and "zombie-like" from not sleeping, that I flunked the test. "Vhat vas I dhink-ink?" That should teach me.

At another time, one morning before going to an early class, I was still half asleep when I went to brush my teeth. Instead of grabbing the red and white tube of toothpaste, I grabbed the red and white tube of hair cream. I was the only kid on the block with the greasy kid stuff on my teeth.

On November 22, 1963, coming back from class to our dormitory, as we walked down the hall we noticed groups of students clustered around the television watching intently. There was a motorcycle policeman parked in front of the open window of our first floor room. We heard over his police radio that President Kennedy had just been assassinated in Dallas, Texas.

We visited the farm whenever our studies allowed us some free time. We remember spending Christmas in below-zero weather, helping our cousins shovel out the barn, and helping feed the cows and do other chores. We enjoyed it. We felt productive. It was a refreshing break from our studies. While our cousins milked cows, Joe and I carried milk to the cooler, then sat on the straw floor. As cows took care of their bodily functions, steam rose from what was deposited. The heat from the animals kept the inside of the barn warm, and we, and the cows, were contented.

Decades later the barn accidentally burned down. The animals were able to break loose, exiting the barn. The blaze was so bright folks to the south thought that the nuclear plant in Monticello, five miles to the north, was having a meltdown.

We spent September 1962 to June 1963 in Minnesota and did not go home for the three-week long Christmas break. Instead we stayed at the farm and went hunting for muskrat, mink, and foxes with our cousins. After trapping, killing, and skinning them, our cousins sold the animal pelts in town. Our ROTC trench coats were a blessing, keeping us warm all winter.

John feeding cows in the barn, 1962

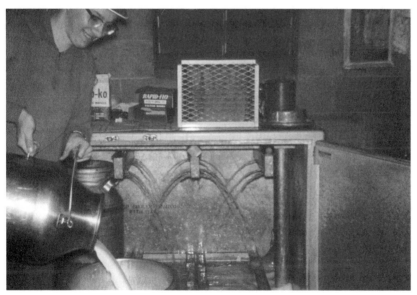

John pouring milk at the farm, 1962

Joe (ROTC coat) and cousin Al on farm,
hunting mink with dog Fritzie, 1962

I began my studies in industrial education at the University of
Minnesota in September 1962 through December 1963. Joe studied
engineering there and was having some difficulty with it—especially
with his weekly 12-page physics lab assignments. In the fall of 1963[87]
he dropped out of the program, although he accumulated a number
of math and physics credits. To pass time and earn a few dollars, he
peeled potatoes for two hours a day in food services and got a job
as a supervisor for after-school evening activities in one of the Minneapolis public schools. The writing was on the wall. After one and
one-third years—four quarters—we left the University of Minnesota.
It was time to move on and consider a smaller, state college.

Around midnight on New Year's Eve in 1963, we were at the farm
smoking cigars, drinking beer, and washing eggs. It was -20 degrees
outside. The single-pane kitchen windows were frosted up and

87. When we attended the U of M and later St. Cloud State College (SCSC), we
were on the quarter system (three quarters or 45 quarter credits were equal to two
semesters or 30 semester credits, a typical September to June academic year).

John washing eggs, drinking beer, smoking cigar,
on the farm, December 31, 1963

rattled in the wind. Our goal was to leave the U of M and enroll in
a state college. We didn't want to go back to New York in defeat. So,
we decided to visit the campuses of Mankato State College (MSC)
and St. Cloud State College (SCSC).

The next day we drove to Mankato to look at the campus.
Mankato was 85 miles southwest of Minneapolis, on Highway 169.
We took one look at the lower portion and the newer upper portion
(hills) surrounding the split campus, and said, "No way." We pictured ourselves going to class and sliding down the steep hills on ice
and breaking our legs or necks.

We immediately headed to St. Cloud, 70 miles northwest of
Minneapolis, to see if the campus was flat, in which case we would
enroll. We went, it was, we did. What a way to choose a college.
Prior to our visit we really didn't know what "St. Cloud" was.
When we first encountered the name, we thought it was an Indian
reservation.

St. Cloud State College

Town and Culture

At St. Cloud, textbooks cost $3 to $5. Tuition was $6.30 per quarter-credit hour—not the exorbitant $18 per quarter-credit we had been charged as non-resident students at the university. (School officials told each of us to go downtown, obtain a voter's registration card, and change our status from non-resident to resident, thus greatly reducing our tuition. We did so and were thankful for this information.)

The unique slogan on the radio for getting a taxicab in St. Cloud was, "Call XYZ-5050 [fifty-fifty] and we'll be there in a jiffy." Other new phrases/words we learned was, "Ish," "Oh, shut up," and "hot dish." We were definitely immersed in a Midwest-style culture, and we loved it. It was different living here. You betcha!

During the early 1960s in St. Cloud, gasoline was 21¢ per gallon. Then there was a gas war, which brought the price down to 17¢ per gallon. We had some interesting experiences at St. Cloud and met friends from New Jersey, Chicago, and Africa.

Classes and Activities

After visiting the farm one weekend during the winter, we were in a classroom when the professor noticed pieces of "dirt" on the clean floor. The dirt was dried cow manure that came off of our galoshes—the result of shoveling manure in the barn. We noted that we didn't get any brownie points with this professor. Those "farmers" from New York should know better.

At one time, Fred Lanahan, a friend from New Jersey, asked if he could review Joe's notes from a class they took together, since Fred had skipped out on a number of class meetings. Joe obliged. Fred received three more points than Joe on the test, and as a result, Fred got a "B" for the test, while Joe received a "C." Joe wasn't jumping for joy about this.

The two college classes that Joe ever flunked were at SCSC while an undergraduate student. He was a sophomore taking a junior/senior level personnel administration class. He hated the class and shouldn't have been in it, because it was an upper-level class—his fault. He and his friends partied the night before. The next day Joe knew he was in trouble when he lifted his head off his pillow. He should have stayed in bed. Being dumb, he went to class. About ten minutes into listening to the professor lecture, Joe started to simultaneously pass out and throw up. All he heard as he slid down his chair was the professor saying, "Oh, God, get him out of here. Class dismissed." A couple of seniors helped him out of the room to the men's room. Another embarrassment. Class over for sure. The other class he flunked was a metals class, a class in his major area of study. He took it over and passed it the second time around.

In 1964, Vice Presidential Candidate William E. Miller, a New York state representative, who was running for office with Presidential Candidate Barry Goldwater, flew into St. Cloud to give a speech at St. John's University in neighboring Collegeville. Fred, Joe, and I skipped classes and drove to the St. Cloud Airport. Somehow, we managed to get into the candidate's motorcade, all the way to St. John's—about 10 miles west. The local police set up roadblocks and were waving us on in our six-cylinder 1960 Chevy. I had the accelerator pedal "to-the-metal" and could hardly keep up with the police escort. Two huge busses were behind us carrying national and international press. When we got to where Miller was speaking, the three of us were able to stand several feet *behind* him, on the balcony, and wave to the crowd. Some security.

Joe and I and our friends enjoyed working for our Industrial Arts Honorary Fraternity, selling hot dogs at homecoming and sporting events for 25¢ and coffee for a nickel. To be initiated into the fraternity, our group went to an outing up north to Garrison, Minnesota, on Mille Lacs Lake, where we were involved doing some crazy and dangerous activities. We had to drive several miles into town and

Rep. William Miller, running for VP with Goldwater,
Collegeville, Minnesota, 1964

bring back an ice cream cone before it melted in the hot summer
heat. Our cars were not air conditioned at that time. A friend *sped*
us back to camp in his '59 Chevy. Then we had to move objects off
blocks of ice without using our hands or elbows—only our bare
butts. Talk about frostbite. The senior students and professors all
had a laugh—at our expense.

Tragedy #5: I was giving a presentation in one of my industrial arts
classes. My professor challenged part of my report. Other students
supported me. Thoughts of possibly quitting the program occurred
to me. The next day this professor saw me walking into the building
and ran over to apologize for being so rough with me. I accepted
his apology. He seemed to have a lot on his mind; this seemed to
continue over the years that I got to know him. A few years later, he
was at home on the telephone. Suddenly the phone dropped—the
conversation was prematurely cut short. His son, who had a history
of mental illness, had stabbed him to death. It was a total shock to

John, St. Cloud State College, dorm
with HeathKit radio behind clock; Remington manual typewriter, 1963

everyone on campus as well as citizens of St. Cloud.

Dormitory Life

Many of the out-of-state and out-of-the-country[88] students were
forced to challenge the administration. During major holidays,
the campus closed down, and out-of-state students were asked to
move into downtown hotels for one to three weeks—at their own
expense—or go home. We couldn't afford to do so. Seven of us out-
of-towners got together, organized, and protested. The president of
the college was attending a Mantovani concert off campus with his
wife and was interrupted with the news of our protests. He made a
decision and college officials finally backed off and kept Shoemaker
Hall open, forcing our residence hall director to stay and super-
vise us. The director resented this because he wanted to be with *his*

---

88. One in our group was from Africa—the Belgian Congo. There was an actual
television commercial for something called Missionary Soup. He went absolutely crazy
whenever this commercial played. From his point of view, he thought it was an absurd
commercial. He chanted loudly, "I want missionary soup, I want missionary soup!"

family during the holidays. Well, he *was* with his family—us. What was *he* thinking?

There were times when we needed to take a break from our studies and grab a bite to eat. On many nights we drove to Simonson's Truck Stop on Highway 10. They had a small restaurant connected to a gas station. For $1.15 we got two eggs, toast, and coffee. One night the Lettermen, a folk singers' group, came in and ate while we were there. They had just finished performing on campus.

Politics

Joe ran for and got elected president of the Shoemaker Hall Men's Residence Association (Shoe Hall), comprised of 400 men in two wings of the building and 200 women in a separate third wing. SHMRA was the governing body for these 600 students. The dorm's treasury had $3,600 in it, more than the entire student senate on campus. To help stimulate the economy, his philosophy was, "Spend!" (Doesn't he seem like an up-and-coming politician?) He wanted the dormitory treasury to buy him a new car—new cars were selling for about $2,000 then—and have John K., his vice president, drive him around campus. The executive council said "No," which disillusioned Joe. Checks and balances, you know. Instead, the council approved the purchase of a set of encyclopedias for the dorm and put money into a mobile float made up of chicken wire and colored tissue paper for the homecoming parade. When there was $50 left in the dorm treasury the following April, Joe resigned. But he had gotten "bitten" with the taste of power, which to this day has never left him, remarking and truly believing, "It's good to be king!"

One of the platforms Joe ran on, jokingly, was to get *younger* maids (dormitory cleaning ladies). We referred to them as "The Linen Sisters," because they brought new linen to our rooms and cleaned the bathrooms each week.

Sometimes, when one of the maids entered your room with her master key, she would knock and enter, not always waiting for an answer. On at least one occasion, one of the cleaning ladies entered a room without knocking, surprising a stark-naked male who was about to head to the shower. She blurted out, "Why, why, you have no clothes on." The student responded, "Correct, and in one minute, you're not going to have any clothes on, either." She screamed and ran out of the room.

In all seriousness, "The Linen Sisters" were really concerned that they could lose their jobs to "younger maids," if Joe achieved political power. Of course, he had no power to change their employment contracts and never had any intention to do so. It was merely an attention-grabbing gimmick. He was just mimicking what the big boys (politicians) did, or so he thought.

Salesman

Joe developed a lucrative business renting and re-renting the same used textbooks to students for $3 or $4. He had students lined up outside his office (dorm room) each quarter, because he made them an offer they couldn't refuse. However, there were times when stress came with the territory—the stress of learning that one of his renters had attempted suicide or was leaving college. How would he get his books back if this happened, he wondered?

Friends

We met some long-lasting friends in college. They were Gary Anderson and Frank Miller (both English majors), Fred Lanahan (social studies major), Duane Mode (art major), and Bill Lyke (industrial arts major), to name a few.

Gary was an intellectual who, after graduating from college, worked for the Wisconsin state department. He wrote a curriculum guide on alcohol and drug education. We found out that he grew up just a block and a half from where we now live in Crystal, Minnesota.

Joe and I helped Frank publish his collection of poetry, *Shirt*. Frank was a friendly guy, but definitely "deviated from the norm."

While teaching English in a public school in Princeton, Minnesota, Frank mesmerized the students. He told them if they were good, he would give them a special gift at the end of class. He had the students close their eyes and went to each desk and gave them a seed, saying, "Your assignment is to take this home, plant it, and *listen* to it grow." The custodians were furious with Frank, after he dragged a birch tree into the classroom in the fall when he recited poetry about birches. The leaves were scattered all over the hallway. Frank was truly a very talented, but eccentric, man.

Frank had a habit of crashing wedding receptions. Why not? He got to eat and drink some of the finest food and libations as well as being entertained. The wedding guests of the bride thought Frank was associated with people from the groom's side and vice-versa. Who knew? Who further cared or paid attention as the evening progressed and libations were liberally consumed?

Years later Frank was on welfare living in his Minneapolis high-rise apartment. When we visited him, as he was thawing out his freezer. He was delighted to find a bag of marijuana that he had forgotten about. In college he hid his pint of booze in the bottom of a tissue box so the resident assistants wouldn't find it upon unannounced searches. Unfortunately, Frank died in his mid 40s from an overdose of alcohol and drugs. He left behind a Faberge egg for his lady friend.

When Fred was completing his master's degree at Mankato State College, on occasion Joe and I drove to meet him there on weekends. As graduation time approached, Fred planned to visit Australia, so he put his motorcycle up for sale. A man came along for a "test ride." He drove off into the sunset with it, never to be seen again.

One summer Fred stayed at an old dilapidated hotel in town. The rent was cheap for a graduate student. While the three of us were standing in the lobby next to the stairs, a body came suddenly crashing downwards, through the open stairwell, missing us by about four feet. The man was inebriated and fell over a banister from several floors above. Unfortunately he didn't survive. Had he landed on any of us, the reader might not be reading this book.

Years after Joe and I began teaching, we flew first class from Minneapolis to Fargo, North Dakota, where Duane would meet us. First class had the only two seats available on this particular last-minute flight. At the time Duane was teaching on the White Earth Indian Reservation, in Mahnomen, Minnesota. Joe and I brought fondue pots, forks, and knives with us in paper shopping bags for the weekend to help Duane throw a fondue party in the basement residence that he rented, celebrating the achievements of some of his students. Because of the sharp forks, our housewares had to be stowed in the cockpit for the flight.

During one of our school breaks, Duane came to New York City with us. He and our mother went shopping and they had to cross busy First Avenue. To be safe, Mom said to him in her broken English, "Look, Dhvane. Foist vhee look rhight, un den vhee look left, un den vhee rhunn-like-hell." Mom wasn't taking any chances. She looked in *both* directions, even though First Avenue is a one-way venue. She really didn't have to look "rhight." Better "rhight" than "shorry." Mom *was* a survivor, too.

During some of the blustery cold winter nights, at around 11 p.m., Joe and I would wake up Bill to get his car started so the three of us could drive nine blocks to a local bar for a 15¢ pony beer, a couple of hard boiled eggs, and salt-encrusted beer nuts. When the car finally started, and sometimes it wouldn't, it would "shudder" and shake from being parked outside in temperatures of -25 to -33 degrees Fahrenheit. Bill later taught photography at a high school in Puyallup, Washington. He thoroughly enjoyed teaching this subject and was an excellent teacher. Unfortunately, Bill passed away from cancer after working with job-related chemicals for many years.

Student Teaching

Joe and I student-taught at the same time but in different suburban Minneapolis neighboring school districts that were 12 miles apart. We rented a room together from the Tubmann family in Blaine, Minnesota. Student teaching totally drained all our energy (teaching, writing curriculum, preparing lessons, grading projects and tests, setting up displays, attending after-school and evening conferences, etc.). We came home from teaching one fall day, exhausted, and laid down to rest. It was about 4:30 p.m. It got dark at 5 p.m. After resting for a few hours, I suddenly got up, looked at the clock, and woke up Joe. We ran in to the bathroom to brush our teeth, shave, and get ready to head off to school. Only then did we realize it was *not* 7 a.m. the next morning, but 7 p.m. that same evening. Now we could get a good night's sleep. Thank God for weekends to work on our lesson plans, grading papers and tests, and try to wind down just a little.

I remember spending 11 hours one weekend, carefully and meticulously grading mechanical drafting assignments for ninth graders, only to give them back to the students and watch a few of them tear the sheets up, tossing their assignments into the wastebasket. It was very disheartening to see this.

As part of our student teaching I traveled to Minneapolis to visit other schools. While observing in the music room, I noted the teacher was moving feverishly around, helping one student after another with his/her assignment. When I asked the teacher how she did it, she quickly blurted out, "Tranquilizers, tranquilizers!" Then I started to think, is this what I have to look forward to as a teacher?

When Joe began to student teach, one of the principals of his junior high school brought him down to the wood lab and introduced him to industrial arts teacher Wilfred Henko. At first, Wilfred refused to shake hands with Joe. He was not expecting to have a student teacher and he had little respect or regard for the administrator. What a way to start student teaching, Joe thought. *He* was at risk. Anyway, Wilfred and Joe soon became friends and had a successful and professional mentor/mentee relationship.

There was a nurse in the building who, every Wednesday, trotted up and down the halls exclaiming, "It's hump day. It's hump day." This meant "it's the middle of the week and soon the weekend will be upon us." At first, Joe didn't understand its meaning, never having heard the phrase. He thought there might be some type of regularly scheduled "special activities" planned for the staff after school.

Tragedy #6: In January 1967, another tragedy occurred. While we were students at St. Cloud, our cousin Anne and her husband Ed Rieder were killed in an automobile accident. She was a nurse and he was an engineer. They lived in Silver Bay, Minnesota, where he worked at the taconite plant on Lake Superior. In fact, they were "pioneers" who helped create the town of Silver Bay in the early 1950s. At first they couldn't have children so they adopted two girls and a boy. Later, they were able to have a natural born child of their own.

One day, they, their 3-year-old toddler, and their dog Gypsie were returning to Silver Bay in their station wagon, carrying an 8-inch stack of plywood and other building supplies purchased in Duluth. The other three children were at home. While driving on Highway 61 on the North Shore, just outside of Duluth, a 19-year-old driver hit them head-on, allegedly on purpose so that his passenger, a pregnant teenage girlfriend, would lose her baby.[89] The force split the sheets of plywood down the middle. The girlfriend, her unborn baby, our cousin, and her husband died at the scene.[90] The toddler was in the hospital for many months. The teenage driver lived for one year and one day, before dying of complications attributed to the accident. This tragedy was a horrendous and traumatic experience for all concerned, and it was totally unnecessary!

---

89. Cars at that time were not equipped with seat belts or air bags, and I am not sure if the car's windshield was made of safety glass.

90. Rieder Memorial Drive, just north of Silver Bay on route 61, was established to honor them.

John, St. Cloud State College graduate, 1967 (Yearbook photo)

Shortly thereafter, Ed's brother Richard and his wife Verna took
the four children into their home in St. Cloud, to live with their five
other children. They had to sell the house in Silver Bay, sell their
smaller house in St. Cloud, and buy a third larger house for their
new and enlarged family of 11.

Ed and Richard had another brother, a priest in Huntington,
Indiana, named Father Ron. He wrote:

> Going to see that young man in the hospital and forgiving him
> was a major event in my life. I hated that kid. But my mother
> convinced me, her priest son, to forgive the young man. She
> told me that God's job was to do the judging; our job was to
> do the forgiving. After I forgave him, I felt such a peace and joy

Joe, St. Cloud State College graduate, 1968 (Yearbook photo)

that words cannot describe it. I'm afraid that I would have otherwise lived the remainder of life in hatred and regret. I thank God every day for the grace of this forgiveness. I still remember the young man's name and I know how good he felt after I forgave him.

A few months later, I graduated. It was time for me to get a job, begin to earn some money, and pay off those college loans. Joe continued with his studies at St. Cloud for one more year. It took him longer to graduate because he kept changing his major and he had a double major: comprehensive industrial education *and* mathematics. After that, we were both living together and working full-time as classroom teachers in the suburbs of Minneapolis, Minnesota.

When we graduated from St. Cloud State College, I received my Associate in Applied Science degree (A.A.S.) in engineering technology (1965), and a Bachelor of Science degree (B.S.) in industrial arts education (March 1967). Joe completed his B.S. degree in industrial arts education (March 1968) and a B.S. degree in mathematics (1981) with a minor in physics.

Immediately after graduating, I secured a teaching position on Long Island, New York. My plan was to return to Minnesota when Joe graduated and live and teach with him. Although we will always be native New Yorkers, we now consider Minnesota to be our home. In September 2012 we will have lived in the Midwest for 50 years. Although Minnesotans, we were told we still retain much of our New York accent. Soitenly! You betcha!

Chapter 10

Twinning

It's a Twin Thing

Philosophy We Live By

JOE: Ma and Pa "learnt us well!" Work hard, study, save for a rainy
day, and spend your money wisely. If you don't have the money
then you can't afford to buy something you want, so live within your
means. Don't make fun of others because they are different from you.
If you wish ill on someone, you are wishing ill on yourself. Always
tell the truth. And always be appreciative and say "Thank you" when
someone gives you something or does something nice for you.

Life has been good to us, not by accident or through "osmosis,"
but by good rearing, discipline when needed, setting goals, and
working towards achieving them. This is why we are "high on life."
The hard work came first, now we get to play. So, life is like a game
to us and we learned to play it. In reference to a popular song, Mom
always said, "Vhre only dan-cingk on dis oith for a short thime."
Our friend Tania says, "Expect nothing from others and you won't
be disappointed." This all seems to make sense. Surround yourself
with people who are better than yourself and people who do good
things. Those with positive attitudes and outlooks will help you
grow. Conversely, stay away from folks with negative attitudes—
they will "tear you down." Someone once said, "Show me your
friends and I will show you who you are."

Entrepreneurial Spirit

We are interested in various business activities.

- Money does not buy happiness—although in some cases it may help one to "suffer in comfort."
- We are value-oriented, like Warren Buffett, although we don't have the same patience he has. We always check for the best quality product in relationship to its price before purchasing an item. Price doesn't always win.
- The best time to buy something is when you don't have to. Being forced to make a purchase at an inopportune time can be costly.
- In your journey through life, do what you love; money will follow.
- Every now and then John tells me, "Coupon Joe," to clean out my stuffed wallet—which is not stuffed with money, but with out-of-date coupons. I save everything. It drives John crazy.
- I have a method of not losing much money at infrequent visits to the casino. Every time I win, I put half of my winnings in my pocket and play with the other half. When all the money is played out of my holding cup, I stop and exchange coins left in my pocket for bills. This way I walk away less of a loser and more of a winner and still have fun. Usually I break about even.
- Think outside of the box. That's where many hidden solutions to problems can be found. This reminds us of a true story of a man up on the roof of a three-story house doing repairs. The roof had a sharp enough pitch that he began to slide down. He knew he would be severely injured or killed if he fell off, so he made a quick decision to staple his left hand a few times with the power nail gun into the roof. The nails held him until rescue arrived. Ouch!

Work Ethics and Morals

Some say, "Hard work may not kill you, but why push your luck?" Here are some thoughts to ponder:

- Be truthful in your dealings with people. If you tell the truth, you never have to remember what you said.

- Your talent is your gift to God.
- Truth is your contract (covenant) with God.
- We generally can't say "No" to people—we have Mom's genes in us. This can add stress to our lives.
- Be optimistic. An optimistic person is generally a happier one. You will have more friends. Who wants to be around a pessimist anyway?
- Work just as hard on your last day of work as you did the first day.
- We had friends who referred to their fathers and mothers as, "My old man" or "My old lady." John and I never used such terms, which we deem disrespectful.
- You cannot buy trust, you have to earn it.
- Balance your life with spirituality.
- Before you die, all you have left to give family/society is your gift of life, your accomplishments to your fellow man and your community—your legacy.
- We believe in order to succeed in school (or work), always give the teacher (or employer) whatever they ask for, but don't stop there—give them more. You will stand out, make an impression, and they will remember you.

Give Back to Society

When people pass on, their true worth is not measured by their poverty or wealth or how much "stuff" they accumulated. True worth is measured by how much *better* they left society, because of what they did with their lives, how they raised their children and what type of people *they* turned out to be, and who was helped along the way. Will society be better off because of you and the way you lived your life? This, we think, should be one's moral goal and compass. Volunteer your time and pledge donations. Others have done this for you, many times unbeknown to you, in so many ways. You have been the recipient of these gifts.

How We See Each Other

John's Perceptions of Joe's Traits

- Joe is #1, I'm the other number.
- Joe is smarter than me—always has been.
- Joe is great at writing and "embellishing" words.
- He is detail-oriented, like me.
- He is enthusiastic about planning trips and itinerary and getting the *best* value.
- He is great at numbers and number crunching—after all, he's a math teacher.
- Joe likes to take care of internal affairs like cooking and shopping and thinking about me doing outside chores.
- Joe cares about others—he is our walking "social calendar."
- He is domineering at times. I'm not surprised because he had a 15-minute head start on life over me and keeps reminding me to "respect my elders"—him.
- He is a more attentive driver than I am.
- Joe does all his writing and editing on the keyboard. His handwriting is terrible.

Joe's Perceptions of John's Traits

- John likes to take care of external affairs, like snow blowing, painting and fixing things, watering, cutting, fertilizing and weeding the lawn, and taking the cars in for maintenance. He's good at that. If John can't fix something, no one can.
- We are perfectionists. John's Type "A" personality means that he is like a bull in a china shop. He's the only one I know who could get the salad spinner up to a very high speed, almost to the point of levitation. However, perfectionists live in a type of hell—they are rarely satisfied and generally impatient.
- He drives me crazy when he (1) drives with the radio station

set on "scan" or (2) watches television by constantly changing channels with the remote control, since he doesn't want to miss anything. Therefore it helps to have *two* remotes and two or more televisions with dueling, competitive clickers.

- John does his writing and editing by hand since he can concentrate better when not keyboarding.
- We both love to do research, collect experiences, and travel.

Pros and Cons of Being a Twin

Pros

- To fully understand a twin (or multiple), you have to be one.
- We are very protective of each other.
- We have similar interests.
- You can only make a first impression once. Twins make it *twice*. Multiples *three* or more times.
- We can double our wardrobe for half the price, by wearing each other's clothes.
- You have constant companions of the same age in the early years—you are never alone. In our case, we *still* are our best companions and we live together.
- When walking with your twin, you get a lot of attention from strangers, many of whom constantly ask, "Are you a twin?" We still get asked that question more times than we care to remember, and strangers always seem delighted when we answer "Yes."
- People remember you more easily—you are always "one of the twins." To distinguish ourselves, I have a mustache; Joe doesn't. So remember, John "ON," Joe "NO."
- We can be in two different places at the same time.
- We are each other's best friends (when we aren't arguing about something).

John and Joe, Twins Days Festival, Twinsburg, Ohio,
August 7, 2009 (John Robinson, photographer)

- Sometimes I kid Joe by saying if he dies first, I will have him cremated and sell his two titanium serial-numbered hips on *eBay* to the *lowest* bidder.
- We think alike. One can start a sentence and the other can finish it.
- We can drive our students crazy by confusing them; we can fool a lot of people.
- Since we are usually invited to the same functions, we never have to go to a party of strangers and feel alone.
- Twin telepathy. We are generally on the same "frequency" and can have the same feelings or thoughts simultaneously. This can be good.
- Some twins have psychic ability to predict if something good or bad is going to happen. What percentage of twins or multiples have psychic abilities or experiences? Is this good or bad?

- As a child, if I did something bad, Joe got blamed or spanked. This also can be good. I didn't mind.
- We could help each other with homework and survive in the educational arena.
- Twins have synergy (1 + 1 = 3). (This must be the new math.)

Cons

- Not all twins are alike, even those that look alike.
- We don't always get along and sometimes get into heated arguments.
- As a youngster, if one of us did something bad, the other got blamed and spanked. The one that got punished *did* mind.
- Getting mixed up (names, eyeglasses, medications, business accounts).
- Some twins share the same identity, especially in the early years, which may hinder or delay their development as unique individuals.
- Some twins have dreams that predict the future, a future they may not always want to know. *It's a twin thing!*[91,92]

---

91. The Twins Days Festival is held annually the first full weekend in August in the Cleveland suburb of Twinsburg, Ohio. It is the largest gathering of twins and other multiples in the world and has been held continuously since 1976. In 1995, 2,798 sets of twins/multiples attended. In 2009 when we attended, 1,902 sets participated.
92. See Appendix C, Item 1f, Twins, and Item 2, Twins Days Festival.

Afterword

Thank you for taking a journey with us back in time, to the first 18-plus years of our lives growing up on an island in a village called Yorkville. We hope you found reading *Yorkville Twins* interesting and enriching, rediscovered some of your own childhood memories, and also gained insight into the immigrant experience and what it is to be an American—insight about how we twins created our future and managed our lives together at a very different time and place. We hope we have given the reader a better understanding of the history, culture, and social mores of life in our ethnic neighborhood well over a half-century ago. As teachers, we consider the world to be our classroom (demonstrated through reading of this book) and because our memoir is published, we hopefully will continue to teach through it long after we are gone. We tried to educate as well as entertain you, using humor. We shared our successes, disappointments, tragic events, and accomplishments. In addition, we hope you learned useful information or perspectives that you might use and benefit from in *your* life. We hope we jogged your memory and brought back many fond remembrances of your early years growing up, a time gone by, never to be repeated. Good memories are a wonderful thing—like a camera they capture and record the past, soothe and delight the soul.

For us first-generation Americans, living in Manhattan at the time was our age of innocence, naiveté, and above all, discovery. With all its problems, you couldn't find a more challenging, more dynamic, more interesting, or crazier place in the world to live and grow up in than Yorkville. It was an unforgettable experience and a journey of survival. We didn't succeed alone; we had help along the way. We are richly and truly blessed.

P.S.: In hindsight, we cannot help but wonder how our lives might have been different had we not held jobs after school during our formative learning years, but used that time instead to study longer and harder. We learned much during that time in our entrepreneurial pursuits, grew in many ways, and even earned some needed money. However, could we have gone to and graduated from one of the more prestigious Stuyvesant, Bronx Science, or Brooklyn Tech High Schools? What future opportunities would we have had had we made those changes? What other professions could we have gone into? Where would we be now and what else could we have accomplished with our lives? Would we still have moved to the Midwest or elsewhere or stayed in New York? How would our lives be different today? In what ways would they have remained the same? Would John and I share the same profession? Would we still be living together?

For those readers interested in reading two great books with period photographs about growing up ethnic in New York City *before* WWI, decades before we lived there, read Marie Jastrow's books, *A Time to Remember* and *Looking Back*. Another interesting read is Olga Leone's memoir, *74th and York*.[93]

Thank you for taking your journey with the Yorkville twins.

"Bůh zehnej Americe!"
"Gott beschütze Amerika!"
"God bless America!"[94]

"Nashledanou" **and** *"Auf wiedersehen"*

---

93. See Appendix C, Item 3a, Yorkville.
94. See Appendix C, Item 1e, Memories, Dances and Songs: Songs.

Mom and Dad enjoying a meal
at 420 East 81st Street, 1979

Joe and John Gindele in the Carpathian Mountains of Transylvania (near the
Ukraine in northwest Romania) on their way to Dracula's castle and home.
(Thomas Lindemann, photographer, 10/2007)

Disclaimer

The events in this book are true, more or less. Numerous identities and details were changed in order not to offend or embarrass anyone. In describing events of the era, we generally used the vernacular of the day to give the reader a truer feeling or "flavor" of the language of people and the mores and events of the period. We say it as we experienced it and hope the reader is not offended.

The authors and publisher have attempted to ensure material found in this book is as accurate and up to date as possible. We apologize for any errors or inaccuracies found. Any remarks slighting people, products, or companies are unintentional.

Some terms and phrases referenced in the text (including in the appendices) may be registered trademarks, service marks, or other product names or titles owned by others. These terms and phrases are used in an editorial fashion for reference only, and no endorsement of the referenced individuals, goods, or services is implied.

Appendices

Appendix A: Relatives, Friends, and Neighbors

Appendix B: Radio and TV Shows, Movies, Actors, and Actresses
That Our Family Enjoyed

Appendix C: Annotated Resources
1. Internet Search Terms and Websites
2. Organizations
3. References

Appendix A

Relatives, Friends, and Neighbors

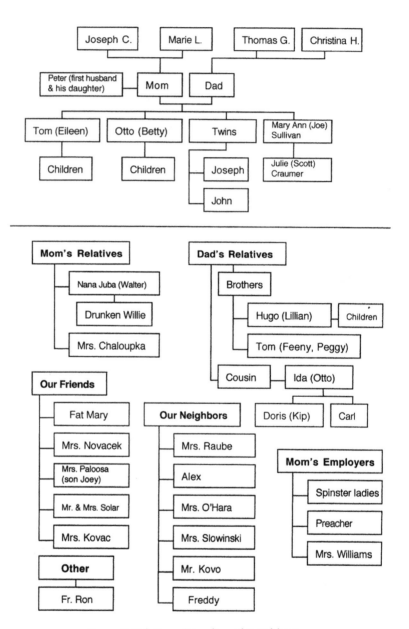

Figure 6: Relatives, Friends, and Neighbors

APPENDIX B

Radio and TV Shows, Movies, Actors, and Actresses That Our Family Enjoyed

(Readers are encouraged to think about
their favorite programs and entertainers.)

Radio Shows

The Abbott and Costello Show, The Adventures of Ozzie and Harriet, The Aldrich Family, Amos 'n' Andy, Bing Crosby, Dick Tracy, Edgar Bergen-Charlie McCarthy, Fibber McGee and Molly, Gangbusters, The George Burns and Gracie Allen Show, The Goldbergs, Grand Ole Opry, The Great Gildersleeve, Gunsmoke, Inner Sanctum Mysteries, Jack Armstrong, The Lone Ranger, The Shadow, Sherlock Holmes, Strike it Rich (Heart Line), Superman, and *The Whistler.*

Television Shows

Adventures: *The Adventures of Rin Tin Tin, The Bowery Boys, Captain Video and His Video Rangers, Davy Crockett-Indian Fighter, Flash Gordon, The Invisible Man, Our Gang, Ramar of the Jungle, Robin Hood, Sea Hunt, Sergeant Preston of the Yukon, Sheena Queen of the Jungle,* and *Superman.*

Comedy: *The Abbott and Costello Show, The Bob Hope Show, The Colgate Comedy Hour, Dean Martin and Jerry Lewis, The Donald O'Conner Show, The George Burns and Gracie Allen Show, George Gobel, The Jack Benny Show, The Jackie Gleason Show, Jonathan Winters, Laurel and Hardy, Mae West, Martha Raye, The Marx Brothers, The Milton Berle Show, The Phil Silvers Show, The Red Buttons Show, The Red Skelton Show, The Steve Allen Show, The Thin Man, The Three Stooges Show, W. C. Fields,* and *Your Show of Shows (Sid Caesar and Imogene Coca).*

Drama: *Alfred Hitchcock Presents, Ben Casey, Boston Blackie, Charlie Chan, Dr. Kildare, Dracula, Dragnet, Fireside Theater, The Ford Television Theater, Frankenstein, General Electric Theater, General Hospital, Goodyear Television Playhouse, Guiding Light, Hallmark Hall of Fame, Highway Patrol, I Led Three Lives, I Spy, Kraft Television Theater, The Loretta Young Show, M Squad, Manhunt, Martin Kane Private Eye, Matinee Theater, Medic, Naked City, Perry Mason, Philco Television Playhouse, Playhouse 90, Ralph Belamy, Rescue 8, Route 66, Sheriff of Cochise, Sherlock Holmes, Texaco Star Theater, The Twilight Zone, U.S. Marshall, United States Steel Hour, The Untouchables, Victory at Sea* and *You Are There.*

Family Shows: *77 Sunset Strip, The Adventures of Ozzie and Harriet, The Aldrich Family, The Amos 'n' Andy Show, The Andy Griffith Show, Art Linkletter, Arthur Godfrey's Talent Scouts, Beulah, Bing Crosby, Blondie, The Bob Cummings Show, Candid Camera, Car 54-Where Are You?, December Bride, Dennis the Menace, The Dick Van Dyke Show, Dinah Shore, The Donna Reed Show, Father Knows Best, Frank Sinatra, The Gale Storm Show, The Gary Moore Show, Gisele MacKenzie, The Goldbergs, Hawaiian Eye, Hazel, The Honey-mooners, I Love Lucy, I Married Joan, Jimmy Durante, Jon Gnagy (Learn to Draw), Kate Smith, The Kraft Music Hall, The Lawrence Welk Show, Leave it to Beaver, Liberace, The Life of Riley, Life with Father, Make Room for Daddy (The Danny Thomas Show), Mama, The Many Loves of Dobie Gillis, The Millionaire, Mister Ed, Mister Peepers, The Munsters, My Friend Irma, My Little Margie, My Three Sons, Our Gang (Little Rascals), Our Miss Brooks, The Patty Duke Show, Perry Como, Shower of Stars, Ted Mack & The Original Amateur Hour, The Tennessee Ernie Ford Show, This is Your Life, Toast of the Town (The Ed Sullivan Show), The Today Show, The Tonight Show with Jack Paar, Topper, You Asked for It, Walt Disney, Wide Wide World,* and *Your Hit Parade.*

Game Shows: *$64,000 Question, Beat the Clock, Break the Bank, Concentration, I've Got a Secret, Name That Tune, The Price is Right, Queen for a Day, Strike It Rich, Stump the Stars, To Tell the Truth, Truth or Consequences, Twenty-One, What's My Line?, Wheel of Fortune, Who Do You Trust?,* and *You Bet Your Life (Groucho Marks).*

News Programs: *The Big Picture, Edward R. Morrow, Face the Nation, The Huntley-Brinkley Report, Meet the Press,* and *Mike Wallace.*

Westerns: *The Adventures of Jim Bowie, Andy Divine, Annie Oakley, Bat Masterson, Bonanza, Broken Arrow, The Californians, Cheyenne, The Cisco Kid, Colt .45, Death Valley Days, Fury, The Gene Autry Show, Gunsmoke, Have Gun-Will Travel, Hopalong Cassidy, Johnny Ringo, Laramie, Lawman, The Lone Ranger, Maverick, My Friend Flicka, The Outlaws, Pony Express, Rawhide, The Real McCoys, The Rebel, The Restless Gun, The Rifleman, The Rough Riders, The Roy Rogers Show (and Dale Evans), Sky King, Tales of West Fargo, The Texan, The Virginian, Wagon Train, Walter Brennan, Wanted: Dead or Alive, Wild Bill Hickok, Wyatt Earp,* and *Zorro.*

Young People's Shows:
Older: *Dick Clark's American Bandstand,* and *Disneyland.*
Kids: *Big Top, Bozo the Clown, Captain Kangaroo, Casey Jones, Dick Tracy, Ding-Dong School, Howdy Doody, Kukla, Fran and Ollie, Lassie, The Mickey Mouse Club, The Paul Winchell & Jerry Mahoney Show, The Pinky Lee Show, Romper Room,* and *The Shari Lewis Show (& Lamb Chop).*
Cartoons: *Betty Boop, Donald Duck, Felix the Cat, The Flintstones, The Huckleberry Hound Show, Looney Tunes, The Mickey Mouse Club, The Mighty Mouse Playhouse,* and *The Rocky and Bullwinkle Show.*

Appendix C

Annotated Resources

(Please read *Disclaimer* on Page 250 before proceeding.)

1. INTERNET SEARCH TERMS AND WEBSITES
(Where indicated, use quotation marks for Search Terms. Some websites take a little longer to open, so please be patient.)

a. New York City

Search terms:
- Blackout [November 9, 1965] (Power failure in the Northeast)
- Emma Lazarus's sonnet, "The New Colossus"
- New York City images
- New York City pictures
- Welcome to New York City, city guide (Original DVD 60 min.) (Contemporary New York: 22 sites visited.)

Websites:
- Forgotten New York City (Neighborhoods and street scenes) http://www.forgotten-ny.com/index.html
- New York City maps of subways, streets, etc. http://www.gonyc.about.com/od/maps/lbl/centralpark.htm
- NYC: Official Website. From 1939 to 1941 and 40 years later, city workers photographed each building in all boroughs for the purpose of taxing real estate property. These photographs can be purchased by scrolling to the lower right side of the page: http://www.nyc.gov

Tenement Living Conditions
Search terms:
- Child bathing in sink [George Eastman House] (in a tenement building)

- The History Box: Tenement Life: Visual Tour (Photos of early tenement living conditions in New York City)
- Kitchen in cold-water flat in Perry Street, Greenwich Village [George Eastman House] (Kitchen in tenement building)
- New York 1940—Bowery [George Eastman House] (Driving under the El)
- New York City, Tenement Life
- N.Y. tenement family gets fresh air on a hot day [George Eastman House] (Surviving the heat)
- Street play in the early days—New York [George Eastman House] (We built these scooters.)
- Tenement Life 1860–1910 [YouTube] (Photos with music and movie of poor living conditions)
- Tenement Museum—New York City (Explore a tenement building in NYC.)

Websites:
- Tenement clotheslines:
    http://www.loc.gov/pictures/resource/cph.3c07329/

Trains/Transportation
Search terms:
- 3rd Avenue El
- 3rd Avenue El: 89th Street (1954 Photo by Joe Frank)
- 3rd Avenue El—early 1950s [YouTube] (Excellent scenes on, in, and around the El)
- 3rd Avenue Elevated in New York City [YouTube] (Wabash Cannonball tune)
- The End of the Third Avenue El [You Tube] (Last journey of the El prior to being demolished, 1955)
- Andreas Feininger: The Bowery under the shadows of the Third Avenue El (1940)
- Images for historic subway photos

- IRT East Side Line: 77th Street—NYC subway resources (Photos and mosaic art work)
- IRT East Side Line: 86th Street—NYC subway resources (Photos and mosaic art work)
- IRT Manhattan Wood El Cars (Photos of old subway and El trains in New York City)
- New York City subway history, photos
- New York City subway photos
- A ride on the 3rd Ave El—1950s New York City [YouTube]
- Third Avenue El
- "The Vanishing El" [YouTube]

Websites:
- All about the NYC subway system with historical photos
  http://www.nycsubway.org
- Picture of 77th Street & Lexington Avenue neighborhood IRT subway station mosaic (built in 1918). Photo by Roberto C. Tobar.
  http://www.nycsubway.org/perl/show?92965
- Picture of 86th Street & Lexington Avenue neighborhood IRT subway station mosaic (built in 1918). Photo by Roberto C. Tobar.
  http://www.nycsubway.org/perl/show?97332
- Picture of subway train approaching 89th Street on the 3rd Ave El (1954). Photo by Joseph Frank.
  http://www.nycsubway.org/perl/show?26048

b. Manhattan

Search terms:
- Commerce High School, New York, New York (Classmates & alumni)
- High School of Commerce (King's views of New York) (Photo of our school)

- "The High School of Commerce, New York City" (The School Review, Sept. 1903)
- Images for Central Park, New York City (photos throughout the seasons)
- Manhattan Board (bulletin board for former residents)
- Manhattan, New York
- Manhattan, New York photos
- Manhattan Zip Code Map
- Zip Code Map, Manhattan, New York City, NY—Citidex (Manhattan zip codes)

Websites:
- Major Manhattan neighborhoods: (Credit to USATourist.com)
  http://www.usatourist.com/english/places/newyork/neighborhoods.html
- Manhattan in motion: Mindrelic. See the city in time-lapse photography.
  http://vimeo.com/24492485
- Manhattan map: Central Park
  http://gonyc.about.com/od/maps/l/blcentralpark.htm
- Manhattan Zip Codes (New York County): Double-click on Manhattan island to expand the map showing distinctive ZIP code boundaries (a) 10065 covering 60th to 69th Street; (b) 10021 covering 69th to 76th Street; (c) 10075 covering 76th to 80th Street; (d) 10028 covering 80th to 86th Street; (e) 10128 covering 86th to 96th Street, all of which make up the Upper East Side. Select any of the six toolbar choices presented.
  http://www.zipmap.net/New_York/New_York_County.htm

c. Upper East Side

Search terms:
- East Side House Settlement—*Wikipedia*
- East Side Settlement House

- Manhattan's Upper East Side pictures (Collage of pictures)
- Our Town—East Side Manhattan news
- Settlement House
- Upper East Side
- Zip Codes for Upper East Side, New York City [10021; 10022; 10028; 10065; 10075; 10128]

Websites:
- Manhattan Neighborhood map: Upper East Side.
  http://www.gonyc.about.com/od/manhattan/l/bl_uppereast.
  htm
- Upper East Side landmarks, demographics, cultural and educational institutions, movies, television programs, books and famous residents. Read license terms at:
  http://creativecommons.org/licenses/by-sa/3.0
  http://en.wikipedia.org/wiki/Upper_East_Side

d. Yorkville

Search terms:
- Carl Schurz Park
- "Carl Shurz Park, New York City" [YouTube] (A great video where we walked and played as kids by Gracie Mansion and the fireboat station, roller-skated, rode our bikes, played in the sand and on the swings and cooled off under the sprinklers.) (Note: [sic] No "c" in this Shurz title.)
- Gracie Mansion (Mayor's residence)
- Green Dougherty (Forum for Yorkvilleites)
- Horn & Hardart Automat
- Jan. 26th, 2011 Snow storm in Yorkville, Manhattan [YouTube] (2011)
- "John Jay Park, New York City"
- A Look at Old Yorkville, one story at a time [*Our Town*] (Yorkville stories, July 28, 2010)

- Lost City: Lost City's Guide to Yorkville [April 13, 2009] (Past and present photos of ethnic shops.)
- Lost City: Old Yorkville memory [Feb. 23, 2011]
- Lost City: Yesteryear's Yorkville [June 10, 2011] (Pictures and comments of old Yorkville)
- Memoirs of Yorkville
- My Yorkville memories (Gotham Center)
- NYC: Manhattan hoods—Yorkville [August 16, 2008] (Neighborhood photos)
- NYC: Manhattan hoods—Yorkville Skyscraper City [December 31, 2005] (More photos)
- Our Town: Upper East Side & Community (Yorkville stories by Tommy Pryor)
- Real Estate video—Yorkville, Manhattan (Great video of Yorkville)
- Yorkville: A neighborhood recalled [Dec. 7, 2006] (Read and post text, comments, pictures, reviews.)
- Yorkville, Manhattan | Facebook (About folks who lived there in the late 1950s and 60s.)
- Yorkville, Manhattan (Gotham Center)
- Yorkville Manhattan neighborhood pictures (Collage of pictures)
- Yorkville Manhattan photos (Collage of photos)
- Yorkville Message Board (forum to reconnect people)
- Yorkville Message Board | Facebook
- Yorkville: Stoops to Nuts (Centanni Broadcasting Network) with Tommy Pryor (Neighborhood Storytelling Program)
- Yorkville: Stoops to Nuts (Stories, photos devoted to neighborhood places and characters)
- Yorkville Stories

Websites:
- Apartment building directly across the street from our ground-floor apartment at 410 East 81st Street where Frank's Bar and

Grill (buildings 405, 407, 409) was located:
http://www.greendougherty.com/yorkville/yorkville_
streets_81st_crowd1.htm

- Facebook: Yorkville, East Side of Manhattan in New York City. About people who lived there in the late 1950s and 60s. (View Wall, Info, Discussions, Photos.)
http://www.facebook.com/group.php?gid=51910996750

- German American Bund (Marching parade on 86th Street):
http://www.loc.gov/pictures/resource/cph.3c17148/

- Gotham Center discussion boards search: Yorkville, Manhattan. People sharing stories about growing up/living in Yorkville.
http://www.gothamcenter.org/discussions/viewtopic.
php?id=415&p=1

- Lots of comments and photos of Yorkville by those who lived there: A New York City Community site forum for Yorkville, the Upper East Side, and East Harlem. Create a family website. Reunite with others via photos, videos, and message boards.
http://www.myfamily.com

- The Original Yorkville Board's Message Board is an open forum.
http://boards2go.com/boards/board.cgi?&user=
marty&page=1

- Yorkville, NYC and map. Streaming neighborhood photos. Click on (1) Photos and Videos, and (2) Maps and NabeSpots.
http://nabewise.com/nyc/Yorkville

- Yorkville sounding board. Click on Yorkville Project, Videos, and Dougherty's Additional Links (Get More Information) for everything you wanted to know about Yorkville. Also click on Yorkville Message Board for comments/pictures by former Yorkville folks.
http://www.greendougherty.com

Ethnic Matters

Search terms:
- Czechs in Yorkville, Manhattan [Do similar searches for other nationalities.]
- German Broadway (East 86th Street in Yorkville)
- German movement in New York City
- German traces NYC: Carl Schurz Park (View "German Traces Map" for the Germans in Yorkville, Manhattan)

Websites:
- The Yorkville/Kleindeutschland Historical Society. Its goal is to preserve the history of Yorkville's ethnic Germans.
    http://www.yorkville-kleindeutschlandhistoricalsociety.com/contactus.html

People

Search terms:
- Famous people from New York
- Notable residents of Yorkville, Manhattan
- Notable Yorkville, Manhattan residents

Websites:
- More famous Yorkville people.
    http://www.greendougherty.com/yorkville/yorkville_families_famous_people1.htm
- Search: Famous people from New York.
    http://www.worldatlas.com
- Yorkville, Manhattan: More notable residents. Read license terms at:
    http://creativecommons.org/licenses/by-sa/3.0/.
    http://en.wikipedia.org/wiki/Yorkville,_Manhattan

e. Memories, Dances, and Songs

Search terms:

Memories
- American Memory from the Library of Congress (Browse collections)
- Do you remember
- Do you remember—slang (Slang words of the past)
- Do you remember these?
- Memory Lane
- My Yorkville memories (Gotham Center Discussion Boards)
- Radio and Television programs of the1940s, 50s, and 60s (adventure, cartoons, comedy, drama, family shows, games, kid shows, westerns)

Dances
- "Beer Barrel Polka"—Myron Floren [YouTube]
- "Edelweiss" (from the *Sound of Music*) [YouTube]
- "Hungarian Czardas" [YouTube]
- "Moonlight and Roses"—Jim Reeves [YouTube]
- *"Tales from the Vienna Woods* Waltz"—Johann Strauss II *Geschichten aus dem Wienerwald* [YouTube]
- "The Blue Danube Waltz"—Vienna Philharmonic Orchestra
- "The Blue Skirt Waltz" [YouTube]
- "The Pennsylvania Polka"—Lawrence Welk [YouTube]

Songs
- "America the Beautiful" [YouTube]
- "Anytime You're Feeling Lonely"—Cindy Clark [YouTube]
- "Kate Smith Introduces 'God Bless America'" [YouTube]
- *"Lili Marleen"* in German—Marlene Dietrich [YouTube]
- *"Muss i denn"*—Marlene Dietrich [YouTube]
- "New York, New York"—Frank Sinatra [YouTube]
- "On the Sidewalks of New York"—Nat King Cole [YouTube]

- "On Top of Old Smoky"—Hank Williams [YouTube]
- "Rock of Ages"—Johnny Cash—Softly and Tenderly [YouTube]
- "*Sah ein Knab ein Röselein stehen*" [YouTube] ("*Heidenroselein*" by John Kelly & Maite Itoiz, May 5, 2007.)
- "Take Me Out to the Ball Game" Edward Meeker, September 1908 [YouTube]
- "You Are My Sunshine"—Elizabeth Mitchell [YouTube] (Nov. 24, 2008)
- "You're a Grand Old Flag" [YouTube]
- 1950s Rheingold Beer Ad [YouTube]
- German Beer Song [YouTube] [N.B., "Song," not "Songs"]
- Songs of WWII
- WWII Songs

Websites:
- 1960s slang words. http://the60sofficialsite.com/Do_You_Remember_The_60s_Slang_.html
- American Memory from the Library of Congress. Access to print, audio, video media documenting America. Browse collections by topic, date, media-type, place, or search terms. http://www.memory.loc.gov/ammem/browse/index.html
- Music and songs of yesteryear. Do you remember these? http://oldfortyfives.com/DYRT.htm
- Musical video bringing back memories of the 1940s. http://objflicks.com/decadeofthe1940s.html
- Oldies but Goodies: Internet Television Programs of Yesteryear. http://www.oldiestelevision.com
- Step Back in Time: Memory Lane [Previously Classmates.com] (Travel back in time to yesteryear via nostalgic movies, pictures, music, television and radio, old magazines, etc.). http://www.classmates.com/memorylane

f. Twins

Search terms:
- Facts and figures about twins
- Famous parents of twins
- Famous twins
- List of twins—*Wikipedia*
- Psychic twins
- Twins
- Twins' psychic experiences

Some well-known twins:
- Jena and Barbara Bush
- Leigh and Leslie Keno (*Antique Road Show*)
- Ann Landers and Abigail Van Buren
- Liberace (twin died in childbirth)
- Elvis Presley and Jesse Presley (died in childbirth)
- Drew and Jonathan Scott (*Property Brothers,* Canadian TV)
- Tyler and Cameron Winklevoss (Facebook fame)

g. Miscellaneous

Search terms:
- Housatonic River, Oxford, Ct.—Flood—04-17-07 [YouTube]
- Stevenson Dam, Oxford, Ct. [YouTube]

Websites:
- Birth events. To find out what events occurred in the year of your birth, go to:
    http://www.datesinhistory.com
- High quality royalty-free or low-cost stock images using search terms.
    http://www.dreamstime.com
- The Pledge of Allegiance, its meaning and history.
    http://www.wvsd.uscourts.gov/outreach/Pledge.htm

• Virtual Address. Type in any N.Y.C. address or your home address and see what appears (e.g., Virtual homes 410 East 81 Street, NY; 420 East 81 Street, NY).

http://www.vpike.com

2. ORGANIZATIONS

Community Board 8 of the City of New York
505 Park Avenue, Ste. 620, New York, New York 10022
(212) 758-4340; FAX: (212) 758-4616
info@cb8m.com
http://www.cb8m.com
This advisory board represents the Upper East Side and Roosevelt Island with concerns directed to city officials.

George Eastman House, International Museum of Photography and Film Collections
900 East Avenue, Rochester, NY 14607
(585) 271-3361
http://www.eastmanhouse.org
The story of photography & motion pictures. Search for a term (e.g., tenement) and make a selection.

Friends of the Upper East Side Historic Districts
966 Lexington Ave, #3E, New York, NY 10021
(212) 535-2526; FAX: (212) 535-2155
info@friends-ues.org
http://www.friends-ues.org/
Friends of the Upper East Side Historic Districts, founded in 1982, is an independent, not-for-profit membership organization dedicated to preserving the architectural legacy, livability, and sense of place of the Upper East Side.

The Gotham Center for New York City History
CUNY Graduate Center, 365 Fifth Avenue, Rm. 6103, New York, NY 10016-4309
(212) 817-8460, FAX: (212) 817-1541
gotham@gc.cuny.edu
http://www.gothamcenter.org
The Center provides links to history-related sites and neighborhood stories used to explore New York City's past. Good discussions, resources, books, forums. Use Search Terms.

Gracie Mansion
East End Avenue—88th Street, New York, New York 10128
(212) 639-9675 (in NYC call 311)
www.nyc.gov/html/om
http://www.nyc.gov/html/om/html/gracie.html
gracietours@cityhall.nyc.gov
Mayor's home in Yorkville, built in 1799. Reservations for public tours are required.

The Library of Congress
101 Independence Avenue SE, Madison Building, LM 337
Washington, D.C. 20540-4730
(202) 707-6647; 5640, FAX: (202) 707-6647
14 million images by topic, collections
Prints, photos, reproductions for sale
http://lcweb.loc.gov/rr/print
Digitized prints and photo online catalog
http://www.loc.gov/pictures
Images listed by topics
http://www.loc.gov/rr/print/list/listguid.html

Library of Congress Duplication Service
   http://www.loc.gov/duplicationservices
For photo reprints

Lower East Side Tenement Museum
91 Orchard Street, New York City, NY 10002
(212) 982-8420; (212) 431-0233; FAX: (212) 431-0402
   http://www.tenement.org
Tour a tenement apartment on the Lower East Side to learn about immigrant families who lived there in the late 1800s and early 1900s. Visit the office and Museum Shop. Tours begin at 108 Orchard Street.

Manhattan Chamber of Commerce
1375 Broadway, Third Floor, New York, New York 10018
(212) 479-7772; FAX: (212) 473-8074
   info@manhattancc.org
   http://www.manhattancc.org
Provides detailed demographic data for each Manhattan zip code. Type in a term or zip code.

Museum of the City of New York
1220 Fifth Ave. at 103rd Street , New York, New York 10029
(212) 534-1672; FAX: (212) 423-0758
   mailto:info@mcny.org
   http://www.mcny.org
Click "Collections" to view thousands of images of N.Y.C. (search by photographer, era, borough); "Shop/Books" to view their book collection.

New York Historical Society Museum and Library
170 Central Park West, New York, NY 10024-5194
(212) 873-3400; FAX: (212) 595-5707

info@nyhistory.org
http://www.nyhistory.org
New York's first museum and one of America's oldest independent research libraries with over 400 years of American history through the prism of New York. Hundreds of thousands of artworks, photos and prints, and millions of manuscripts can be viewed.

The New York Public Library
Stephen A. Schwarzman Building
Fifth Avenue and 42nd Street
New York, New York 10018-2788
(917) 275-6975; (212) 930-0641; FAX: (212) 930-0849
   http://digitalgallery.nypl.org/nypldigital/index.cfm
   http://www.nypl.org
Access to over a half-million digital images (photos, manuscripts, prints, posters, etc.) of New York. Search "tenement" images, etc.

The New York Public Library Photography & Prints Collection
Miriam & Ira D. Wallach Division of Art,
Prints and Photographs. Study Room 308
(212) 930-0837; (917) 275-6975; FAX: (212) 930-0530
   phgref@nypl.org
   http://www.nypl.org/research/chss/spe/art/photo/photo.html
Collection of over half a million photographs and prints.

Statue of Liberty-Ellis Island Foundation, Inc.
American Family Immigration History Center®
17 Battery Place, #210, New York, NY 10004-3507
(212) 561-4588
   http://www.ellisisland.org
The place where most immigrants entered to be checked, processed and either sent back to their homeland due to sickness, or allowed to enter the United States of America. Search for ships' passengers and

family history. This research center is located at Ellis Island in the museum.

Twins Days Festival, Twins Days, Inc.
9825 Ravenna Road, Twinsburg, OH 44087
(330) 425-3652; FAX: (330) 425-0849
  info@twinsdays.org
  http://www.twinsdays.org
Their two-day annual event takes place in Twinsburg, Ohio, on the first full weekend in August when thousands of twins and other multiples participate from around the world.

3. REFERENCES

a. Yorkville

Bodnar, Theodore A. "Letters: Yorkville recalled." *New York Times*, July 3, 1983.

Boland, Kevin N. *One Day as I Stood Lonely: Yorkville.* Blooming-ton, IN: Xlibris, 2010. [258 pp.] Boland grew up Irish Catholic during the 1940s and 50s in what was considered a very tough neighborhood in New York City. His memoir describes his friends and how they banded together for mutual amusement and protection. This is an easy and fun read which draws the reader onto the streets to share vivid and sometimes frighten-ing and dangerous experiences that became a formidable part of Boland's growing up. It is an historical and social account of an era gone by.

Ellis, Rosalind, "A Plan to Preserve Yorkville History," *Our Town.* Upper East Side News & Community (New York), May 4, 1980.

Jastrow, Marie. *Looking Back: The American Dream Through Immigrant Eyes: 1907–1918.* New York: W.W. Norton & Com-pany, 1986. [202 pp.] This is a memoir of the Jastrow family's early years in America from the turn of the 20th century to the end of World War I. There are many period photographs and narrative discussing their early life growing up in Yorkville. The Jastrows lived at 526 East 81st Street between York Avenue (then, Avenue "A") and East End Avenue—just one block east of where we lived. The patriarch of the family found success in America as measured by freedom and that what was highly valued was one's ability as contrasted with one's birthplace. Jastrow paints an accurate portrait of Yorkville life and harrowing living conditions during that time period.

Jastrow, Marie. *A Time to Remember: Growing up in New York City Before the Great War.* New York: W.W. Norton Company, 1979. [174 pp.] Her story is one of intra-family conflict with the patriarch's stubborn attitude to retain his traditional ways in this new land versus his spouse and children's desire to break tradition and to assimilate into the new American society. Born in 1897, Jastrow came to America at age 10 and wrote her first memoir at age 82. She describes Yorkville in detail, including life as an immigrant around 1900 (when our grandmother came to America). Her mother worked at a bakery on 81st Street and Avenue "A." In 1991, Marie died at 93 in Tucson, Arizona, 30 miles north of Green Valley where Tante Ida moved, lived and died at age 94.

Leone, Olga. *74th and York: Growing Up Czech in New York City.* Tucson, Arizona: Ghost River Images, 1998. [351 pp.] This memoir depicts Olga's early Czech upbringing and childhood experiences in Yorkville during the 1920s and 30s. It shows how old country traditions and family values provided her with life-style tools needed to make it in the new world. She describes family travels around town and in the country, visiting friends and other family members. Born in 1920, she lived in various apartment buildings (1382 and 1396) on York Avenue where

Uncle Tom and Peggy lived (at 1374 York Avenue). Olga was a writer and artist and wrote about her first 18 years growing up Czech. In 2007 She died at 87 in Connecticut, after first moving to Green Valley, Arizona. Ida's son Carl knew her, since he was a caretaker in the building where Leone lived.

Lofaso, Anthony. *Origins and History of the Village of Yorkville in the City of New York.* Bloomington, IN: Xlibris, 2010. [126 pp.] Lofaso's book traces the historical progress of Yorkville from 1776–1885 (even into the early 20th century) and describes two influences on Yorkville's development. With the arrival of mass numbers of immigrants living in overcrowded housing with poor sanitary conditions in lower Manhattan, there was a need to improve their lives. That need was met by (1) cheaper available land in the north, and (2) reliable and inexpensive transportation (streetcars, railway system and the "El"). These factors helped play a significant growth in the development of Yorkville's working class neighborhood that flourished for over seven decades. As families headed north it caused an explosive growth in the construction of tenement apartments with running water and enclosed toilets. Lofaso should have been a history professor as he clearly describes the changes taking place in regards to streets, avenues, places, and the movement of people. *Origins* includes great photos and prints from historical organizations as well as Lofaso's own collection, and describes stories of important leaders and shakers, with citations throughout its ten chapters. It is an informative and engaging read.

Survey—East Side House (11-12-07). http://www.fordham.edu/images/academics/programs/baahp/eastside.pdf [viewed February 14, 2012.]

b. Yorkville related

Marx, Harpo, and Rowland Barber. *Harpo Speaks!* Limelight ed. New York: Proscenium Publishers, 1962. [482 pp.]

McCabe, John. *Cagney.* New York: Alfred A. Knopf, 1997. [439 pp.] Born in 1899, actor James Cagney lived in Yorkville at 429 East 79th Street[95] from age 1½ to about 9. He also lived at 420 East 78th Street,[96] adjacent to 418 where our parents later lived. His family moved to an apartment at 166 East 96th Street[97] near Lexington Avenue, where he made communion and was an altar boy at St. Francis de Sales Roman Catholic Church (135 East 96th Street).[98] In 1986 his funeral mass was held there.[99] Cagney graduated from P.S. 158[100] (as did our brother Tom and cousin Carl) and from Stuyvesant High School.[101] Cagney attended the East Side Settlement House and its Stepney Camp in Connecticut,[102] as we and our siblings have done. He also swam in the East River with his friends,[103] as brother Otto and his friends had also done.

Remnick, David. *The Bridge: The Life and Rise of Barack Obama.* New York: Alfred A. Knopf, 2010. [656 pp.]

Robinson, Ray. *Iron Horse: Lou Gehrig in His Time.* New York: HarperPerennial, an imprint of HarperCollins Publishers, 1990. [300 pp.]

---

95. McCabe, John. *Cagney.* (New York: Alfred A. Knopf, 1997), 5.
96. Ibid., 27.
97. Ibid., 12.
98. Ibid., 374.
99. Ibid., 380
100. Ibid., 25.
101. Ibid., 25, 28.
102. Ibid., 28.
103. Ibid., 8.

c. New York City related

Diehl, Lorraine B. and Marianne Hardart. *The Automat: The History, Recipes, and Allure of Horn & Hardart's Masterpiece.* New York: Clarkson/Potter Publishers, 2002. [128 pp.]

Frommer, Harvey, and Myrna Katz Frommer. *It Happened in Manhattan: An Oral History of Life in the City During the Mid-Twentieth Century.* New York: Berkley Publishing Group, 2001. [336 pp.]

Gale Encyclopedia of U.S. History: Tenements. http://www.fordham.edu/images/academics/programs/baahp/eastside.pdf [viewed February 14, 2012.]

Granfield, Linda. *97 Orchard Street, New York: Stories of Immigrant Life.* Toronto, Ontario, Canada and Plattsburgh, New York: Tundra Books, 2001. [56 pp.] Describes living conditions of immigrants in a tenement apartment building during the late 1800s and their daily struggles of survival. Although the book describes life on the Lower East Side, much of it resembled living conditions on the Upper East Side as well.

Kendall, Alan. *George Gershwin: A Biography.* New York: Universe Books, 1987. [192 pp.]

Plunz, Richard. *A History of Housing in New York City.* New York: Columbia University Press, 1990. [422 pp.]

Riis, Jacob A. *How the Other Half Lives: Studies Among the Tenements of New York.* New York: Dover Publishers, 1971. [233 pp.]

Stelter, Lawrence. *By the El: Third Avenue and Its El at Mid-Century (second edition).* New York: Stelterfoto, 1995, 2007. [132 pp.] Beautiful colored photographs by Lothar Stelter supported with interesting narration of New York City's urban mass transit of the Third Avenue elevated subway line. An historical treasure trove capturing scenes, culture, and ethnic neighborhood characteristics of an era gone by over a half-century ago.

World Book Encyclopedia, 2010 ed., s.vv. "The City."

d. Related to the 40s, 50s and 60s time periods

Maus, Richard. *Lucky One: Making It Past Polio and Despair.* Northfield, MN: Anterior Publishing, 2006. [210 pp.] *Lucky One* is a compelling story about the timeless quest that every child embarks upon: the search for acceptance, connection, identity, and purpose. Moving back and forth between a supportive home and a renowned children's hospital, Richard Maus did not feel like he belonged anywhere. *Lucky One* is the story of a child's struggle to make it through pain, depression, and despair to a rewarding life and career. Maus contracted polio at four months old, was hospitalized for 938 days over 15 years and had 16 operations. As a young student he contemplated suicide and prepared to kill someone in self-defense in high school. He flunked out of two colleges, graduated from a third with majors in mathematics and physics, earned a master's degree and pilots license and was a public school teacher. The setting is rural Minnesota and Gillette State Hospital for Crippled Children in St. Paul. The timeline is the 1940s and 50s. His book received many testimonials with great reviews. *Lucky One* can be obtained directly from Richard Maus, Anterior Publishing, 204 West 7th Street. Box 8, Northfield, MN 55057. (507) 645-4633. Contact: author@luckyonebook.com; http://www.luckyonebook.com

Olson, Jim. *Boomer.* Eden Prairie, MN: Edenvale Glen Publishing, 2007. [381 pp.] *Boomer* is a story of life in the Midwest. It is a story of a generation, the Baby Boomers, the peaceful decade that nurtured them and the turbulent events that wrenched them from childhood and shaped their adulthood. It is the tale of five friends, the joys that sealed them together as children and the sorrows that separated them as adults. It is the life story of Eugene, a Midwestern Baby Boomer, who frolics through his youth, stumbles through his young adulthood, and survives his imposed conflict in Vietnam, but not without scars that separate him from his family, friends and former life. *Boomer* can be obtained directly from Jim Olson, Edenvale Glen Publishing, 15157 Patricia Ct., Eden Prairie, MN 55346. (952) 949-3470. Contact: olsonj669@aol.com

Szarke, Connie Claire. *Delicate Armor*. St. Cloud, MN: North Star Press, 2011. [294 pp.] *Delicate Armor* is a wonderfully written book about Callie Lindstrom and her close fishing relationship with her Swedish Lutheran dad, spanning from her younger years through adulthood. The setting is in small town Minnesota from the 1950s to the 1990s. Connie Szarke lays out incident after incident of other relationships (good, bad, and ugly) involving friends, crazy relatives, and town folks and constantly gives the reader new surprises at each turn of the page. Her stories are so minutely detailed that the reader will find it difficult to put the book down. *Delicate Armor* is a keeper! Available through Amazon.com, http://www.barnesandnoble.com and independent book stores. www.connieclaireszarke.com

e. Miscellaneous

Mattsen, John A. "Big surpluses, but not enough to pay teachers decent salary," *Minneapolis Star Tribune*, January 15, 2000.

"Miscellaneous Classroom Concerns," *NEA Today*, 27(1), September, 2008.

Zahler, Robert. *Faith, Family & Farming: A History of St. Michael, Minnesota*, 2009. [276 pp.] The title says it all. Dad's brother farmed here and helped get sponsors for Dad and another brother as immigrants from Germany during the 1920s. Many photographs and biographical information. A rich, historical treasure. Order from: www.saintmichaelbook.com

Glossary

Air shaft
A passageway with windows to allow fresh air and some light to enter inside rooms.

Auf wiedersehen (German)
"Good bye" or "So long."

Auslander (German)
Outsiders. People not native to the area.

Austro-Hungarian Empire
An area of land where Mom and her family and the Chaloupkas, Novaceks and Solars came from. In 1918, when WWI ended, the area where they were all born became Czechoslovakia, an independent country.

Babushka (Czech)
A triangle-shaped scarf covering the head of a woman, tied under the chin. This also describes a grandmother or old woman.

"Bez práce nejsou koláce." (Czech)
"Without work there are no *kolaches*." (Without work, one cannot obtain sweet rolls/rewards.) [Printed with permission from Penfield Books, 215 Brown Street, Iowa City, IA 52245. www.penfieldbooks. com, 1-800-728-9998.]

Black market
A system whereby goods can be traded or bartered illegally.

Block
A housing area consisting of apartments on both sides of a street between two avenues or both sides of an avenue between two streets (e.g., 81st Street between York and First Avenues).

Borough
A basic local governmental unit. New York City is composed of five boroughs, including: (1) the Bronx, (2) Brooklyn, (3) Manhattan, (4) Queens, and (5) Staten Island.

Boxed rooms
An apartment with rooms next to each other, generally in a box configuration, needing a hallway to enter various rooms, i.e., the opposite of a railroad tenement flat that is configured in a straight line with no hallway accessing all rooms.

Brownstone
A reddish-brown sandstone used as an outside covering for apartment buildings built in the later 1800s.

"Bůh zehnej Americe!" (Czech)
"God Bless America!"

Caretaker
See Superintendent.

Carl Schurz Park
A park in Yorkville, on the Upper East Side of Manhattan, overlooking the East River, with playgrounds, wading pool, dog area, lawn, boardwalk, etc. It is situated between 84th and 90th Streets, between East End Avenue and the East River. Home of Gracie Mansion.

Central Park
An 843-acre park located in the center of Manhattan. It is about two-and-a-half miles long (between 59th and 110th Streets), and one-half mile wide, between Eighth Avenue (on the West side) and Fifth Avenue (on the East side).

Communism
A governmental system under dictator-type rule, where everyone in the community (the state) is supposed to have an equal economic

share of goods and property and where the state is emphasized rather than individual liberties.

Czechoslovakia
Once part of the Austro-Hungarian Empire, Czechoslovakia became an independent country in 1918 when WWI ended. In 1993, it split into the Czech Republic and Slovakia and is considered part of Eastern Europe.

"Danke schön." (German)
"Thank you."

D.I.T.
Doctor of Industrial Technology, degree granted by the University of Northern Iowa, Cedar Falls. [One of 24 research doctorate degrees acknowledged by the National Science Foundation (NSF) representing a degree comparable in level and content to the Doctor of Philosophy (Ph.D.) degree.]

"Dobry´ den." (Czech)
"Good day."

Dummkopf (German)
Blockhead, bonehead, dunce, stupid fool.

East Side House
See Settlement House.

Ellis Island
Between 1892 and 1954, Ellis Island was the main (but not exclusive) entry point where many newly arrived immigrants to America came and were processed before being allowed into the U.S. or before being sent back home due to sickness or other reasons. It is located near the southern tip of Manhattan.

"Es macht uns sehr glücklich." (German)
"It made us very happy."

Essen (German)
Eat.

Fajfka (Czech)
A pipe used for smoking tobacco.

Front room
The living room of an apartment in which the main window faces the front of the street or avenue.

German Town
See Yorkville.

"Going down"
Going from one's apartment to play in the street.

"Gott beschütze Amerika." (German)
"God bless America."

Gracie Mansion
The official residence of the mayor of New York City. Built in 1799 and located in Carl Schurz Park at East End Avenue and 88th Street, overlooking the East River. Not all mayors choose to live here. It is used primarily for public functions and meetings.

Ground floor
The first floor of an apartment building, usually directly above the basement or cellar.

"Guten Tag!" (German)
"Good day!"

Harlem
A section of NYC in northern Manhattan located between 96th Street and 158th Streets on the West Side, between the East River and Broadway.

Headcheese
Sulz—thinly sliced deli meat used to make inexpensive sandwiches, consisting of small cut-up pig snouts, eyelids, tongues, ears, etc., held together in gelatin. A favorite European luncheon meat.

Holubky (Czech)
Stuffed cabbage rolls.

Hoska (Czech)
Bohemian braided yeast bread with light spices, raisins, almonds, and candied fruit, usually made for the holidays.

Iron Curtain
A physical and psychological barrier of censorship designed to isolate Soviet and Satellite countries from countries having greater freedoms such as freedom of speech, travel, etc. Its purpose was to control the populace.

IRT
Acronym for Interborough Rapid Transit: The Lexington Avenue subway line passing through the Upper East Side.

"*Já vím.*" (Czech)
"I know."

"*Jak se mate?*" (formal Czech)
"How are you?" (informal: *"Jak se más?"*)

Jaternice (Czech)
A sausage made of pork liver, pork snouts and/or jowls ground together with spices and cereal, many times including rice.

John Jay Park
A neighborhood park located between 76th and 78th Streets and between York Avenue and the FDR Drive (East River). Established by the city, it supported the efforts of the East Side House.

Knedliky (Czech)
Raised-bread dumplings boiled and sliced like bread or non-breaded cooked potato dumplings filled with fruit.

Koláce (Czech or Slovak)
A sweet pastry with cooked fruit, poppy seed, or cheese fillings, either on top or inside the pastry.

Landlord
Owner of the apartment building.

Little Germany
See Yorkville.

Livance (Czech)
A very thin dessert pancake folded and rolled over several times and filled with pot/cottage cheese, lemon, sugar and butter, or jelly or cooked preserves.

"Nashledanou." (Czech)
"Goodbye."

Oma (German)
Grandmother.

Opa (German)
Grandfather.

"Oy vey!" (Yiddish)
A term meaning astonishment or exasperation, like: "Oh my gosh!" or "Woe is me!"

Pivo (Czech)
Beer.

Punks
Incense.

Railroad flat

An apartment with rooms aligned in a straight path like a train of cars connected together. One has to pass through each room in order to get to the last room because there is no hallway to walk through. Generally only the front and rear rooms have major windows.

Settlement house

A privately supported community building, with a socially structured program to help immigrants settle in their new neighborhoods, providing families with social services and education. Services included hot lunches, day care, after-school activities, English classes, camps and playgrounds. It helped newly arrived immigrants adjust to life in America, reduced poverty, and kept neighborhood kids from being idle and getting into trouble.

Silk Stocking District

See Upper East Side.

Stickball

A ball game played in the streets where the ball is hit with a broom handle.

Stoop

An outside staircase leading to the entrance of an apartment building.

Strycek (Czech)

Uncle.

Superintendent

Caretakers of an apartment building who clean and maintain the building and collect rent. They are the liaison between tenants and landlord, and usually get free rent.

Tante (German)

Aunt.

Tenement
A large old residential building where many people pay rent to live in self-contained apartments with walk-ups, without an elevator, and initially with shared bathing and toilet facilities in the hall. The name is usually applied to crowded low-rental apartments with minimum living standards, in older sections of large cities. Tenements are fading away as new skyscrapers replace them.

Teta (Czech)
Aunt.

Turnverein
A German club promoting gymnastics, health, cultural programs, and citizenship. It advanced nationalism. A forerunner of the Czech Sokol movement, which had similar programs, but advanced social unity instead.

Upper East Side
A Manhattan neighborhood located between Central Park (Fifth Avenue) and the East River, and 59th to 96th Streets. It covers three neighborhoods including Lenox Hill (to the south), Yorkville, and Carnegie Hill (to the north). It is sometimes referred to as the "Silk Stocking District."

Vestibule
A small entryway between an outside door and the interior part of a building or a larger room. This typically is where mailboxes are located in older tenement buildings.

Vomacka (Czech)
A white/pink sweet and sour sauce in sour cream, flavored with paprika.

"Wie geht es Ihnen?" (formal German)
"How are you?" (informal: "Wie geht es dir?")

"Wie man sich bettet, so liegt man." (German)
"You make your bed, you sleep in it."

Yorkville

One of three ethnic neighborhoods located on the Upper East Side
of Manhattan (besides Lenox and Carnegie Hills). Yorkville was a
working class neighborhood in the mid-1900s, becoming home to
large populations of Bohemians (Czechs, Poles, Slovaks), Hungarians, Germans, Irish, Italians, and Jews. Its West-East boundaries
include Third Avenue to the East River, and 96th Street to the north.
Its southern boundaries have blurred over the years, but were once
considered to be 59th or 72nd Street. Today some consider it to be
79th or even 86th Street. It was known as Little Germany or German Town.

Acknowledgments

Many people played parts in the formulation of this book. We thank Carl and Joan B., Kevin N. Boland (Yorkville author), Julie Craumer, Otto and Betty Gindele, Anthony C. Lofaso (Yorkville author), Denis and Sylvia Reilly, and Mary Ann and Joe Sullivan for suggestions regarding each chapter. Their advice and insight regarding the social mores of the time were especially crucial with respect to the first eight chapters, since they lived in Yorkville during our formative years.

We are grateful to Richard Maus (author), Jim Olson (author), Loretta Rohwer (teacher), and Connie Claire Szarke (author), who spent long hours reviewing this memoir. Their skills and suggestions improved this publication.

We are indebted to twins John Dehmer, Carol Dotterman and Patricia Kivlehan, Dr. Samuel H. Leon, Dr. Raymond Scallen, and Gerald and Harold Wobschall. Kudos also to Julie Dehmer, Lily French, Maggie Rannow, Father Ron Rieder, John Robinson, and Lucille Urban for their input. Likewise to Roberto Tobar and Louis Ferriol for suggesting resources for this book. We are beholden to Andrew M. Miller, executive director of the Twins Days Festival, Twins Days, Inc., for his support and commentary.

We also thank the Intellectual Property Clinic at William Mitchell College of Law for their review, particularly professors Jay Erstling and Irene Eckert and students Christopher Palmisano and Daria Tinaza. We appreciate and acknowledge the editorial and artistic assistance of Nancy Ashmore (editor), Dorie McClelland (book designer), Amy Kirkpatrick (cover designer), and the Roberts Group (website design). Most important, we thank *you*, reader, for your interest in our adventures.

Testimonials

Good, really good. I laughed out loud, which I normally don't do. A treasure—history will be lost without works like this.

Yorkville Twins is a celebration of life and cherished memories captured by the story of twin brothers born to immigrant parents. It is a labor of love and provides a legacy that would make their parents proud.
—Loretta Rohwer, M.S., teacher

I loved your book. It is heart-warming and inspiring—a tribute to your dedication and commitment. The twins have had an interesting life growing up with good family, good values, and hard work.
—Raymond W. Scallen, M.D. (twin, married to a twin)

Everyone comes from a different background and has events that shape their character. To be able to share that background with a sibling—no, even better, a twin—is something only a few have. Joe and John bring you into their world in a way that mixes New York moxie with Midwest enthusiasm.
—Samuel H. Leon, M.D. (twin)

Joe and John have captured the true essence of life of an immigrant family, and it's such an enduring collection of experiences of what this country was built on. Their humorous recollections were refreshing and sparked so many memories of the stories my grandparents used to share. Their detailed descriptions within these stories allowed me to get lost in a period of this country when life was simpler. My father's side of the family is Czech and I could really relate to some of these stories.

The authors' special relationship as twins is very evident in these experiences. It is intertwined with the fabric of their stories, and is one that can only be shared by twins. This book was a thoroughly enjoyable read.

—Andrew M. Miller, executive director, Twins Days Festival/ Twins Days, Inc. (twin, married to a twin)

If you are old enough and remember *Sergeant Preston of the Yukon*, then get set for a blast from your past. Joe and John Gindele will take you through dozens of moments you only thought you'd forgotten. For the younger who never watched *Amos 'n' Andy*, enjoy a unique lesson in American history. Imagine yourself to be twelve and growing up in the world's largest city. Hold your breath.

Who are these guys? Joe and John are two of the most interesting blokes you are likely to meet. *Yorkville Twins* recounts their memories of what gave rise to that uniqueness. In it we follow the boys through playgrounds and schoolrooms and family dinners. We meet their Czech and German families and friends who immerse them in colorful childhood escapades. Being twins seems to more than double their memories of precious details of outlandish adventures.

Their stories clearly reveal answers to specific questions such as "Why have Joe and John led such interesting and successful lives?" But they also tackle much larger topics, too, such as "What is it to be an American?" At this time when aspects of immigration are bothersome to many, *Yorkville Twins* reminds us how vital and important that experience has been to the growth of our nation.

For Easterners the tales of growing up in Manhattan in the 1940s, 50s and 60s will bring warm nostalgia. For those like me who grew up in quiet Midwestern towns, they reveal surprises of how different, and yet really how similar, childhood experiences can be.

For a real hoot, spend an afternoon with Joe and John Gindele. Not possible? Then enjoy your romp with them in *Yorkville Twins*.

—Jim Olson, author of *Boomer*

Joe and John Gindele have succeeded in capturing rich moments from mid-20th century Manhattan. What's more, they have had fun writing about their memories and it shows. Gifted with exquisite recall, the authors take us readers back to Yorkville with them and we are the richer for it.

—Connie Claire Szarke, author of *Delicate Armor*

I grew up in that Manhattan neighborhood known as Yorkville around the same time as Joe and John. In fact, we lived just a few blocks apart. I was mildly acquainted with a couple of kids from their block. I didn't know Joe and John, but that was typical of the neighborhood. It was simply teeming with kids, and each block was a mini-neighborhood that you ventured into at your own risk.

Growing up in Yorkville during the 40s, 50s and 60s was an unforgettable experience. As I read *Yorkville Twins* I was suddenly transported back in time to my early years. Joe and John have done a remarkable job in describing their childhood experiences in Yorkville. The stories are so realistic that I was overwhelmed by the rush of fond memories they brought to mind. There I was, back in old Yorkville again and doing the things I used to do. I was with those crazy, wonderful kids and my family once more.

Another aspect of the book that is so interesting is the fact that Joe and John are twins and the reader gets to understand how that impacts their life. I found it particularly illuminating since my very special friend, Rose, is a twin.

Yorkville Twins is a wonderful book that I found hard to put down.

—Kevin N. Boland, author of *One Day as I Stood Lonely: Yorkville*

Joe and John are survivors. They think and work outside of the box. In doing so, they succeeded and lived the American dream with passion and competitiveness. Their book is refreshing, engaging, and informative, full of exciting relationships, hilarious and entertaining (yet also tragic and sobering—even a little naughty). It's highly energized and loaded with hundreds of insightful and inspiring anecdotes. Their fascinating journey teaches us what it was like to be a twin with psychic experiences, growing up with immigrant parents in a family of seven over a half-century ago, in the greatest city on earth. A captivating book with rich annotated resources. Hollywood should make a movie about their lives. Grab hold of your seat and hang on tightly. Here comes trouble.

> **—Richard Maus, author of *Lucky One: Making It Past Polio and Despair***

The Saga Continues

If you enjoyed reading *Yorkville Twins*, please let us know—and let your family and friends know too. We are publishing a sequel to it in the form of monographs. Monographs are focused single-topic articles that you can select and download to your computer that cover 46 additional years of our lives. Some are already written, while others are being developed. Many monographs are FREE; others have a nominal cost.

We believe the reader will find them *as a group* just as rich, with hundreds of more insightful and informative anecdotes and experiences. Check our website periodically for updates as new monographs are published. Visit www.YorkvilleTwinsBook.com and download your FREE monographs *now*.

Monograph Benefits

- Continues our saga of adventure, self-discovery and growth
- Complements, supplements, and extends *Yorkville Twins*
- FREE monographs can be downloaded now
- Obtain other monographs to enhance your journey
- Download a "live" version of "Appendix 'C'" for updated, interactive engagement

Monographs Available Now

Annotated Resources

- Appendix "C" offers "live" downloadable interactive websites, and more

Education

- "A Letter to Bryan"—(College advice for a high school student.)
- Japan Internship—(Konnichiha!)
- History of Graphic Communications—How Johan Gutenberg transformed the world, impacting *your* life.
- Doctorate—Is there a doctor in you? What does it take to complete a doctoral program?

Government

- FREE *America (My Country, 'Tis of Thee)*
- FREE *America the Beautiful*
- FREE *The Pledge of Allegiance*
- FREE Rebate Yourself
- FREE *The Star Spangled Banner* (U.S. National Anthem)
- FREE Statue of Liberty Inscription (Emma Lazarus's "The New Colossus")

Other

- FREE Book Club discussion questions
- FREE *Twins Poem*

Additional monographs (i.e., 64 years of teaching experiences—the good, the bad, and the ugly—business adventures, global travel, etc.) may be developed and added to our website.

Monograph Descriptions

- **Appendix "C" offers "live" downloadable websites, and more:** This is an interactive copy of Appendix "C" found in *Yorkville Twins*. Simply "click" on any website or email address and it will download to your computer. Copy and paste the search terms. Save time and energy and avoid typing errors—no need to retype 201 websites, email addresses or search terms. They are all here for you to access anytime—quick, easy, and convenient. Appendix "C" will be periodically updated and expanded.

- In **"A Letter to Bryan"** *we plant a seed. Learn* what high school students should know and expect about undergraduate and graduate school *before* going to college. It is our advice as teachers/college instructors for high school students and others considering college—to better understand the aspects of attending and surviving college. (In this once private letter, we gave guidance tips and personal details about college and life to our great nephew prior to beginning his undergraduate studies. Since then he has successfully completed his B.S. degree.) As a *bonus,* the student will also gain a better understanding about graduate school (we plant that seed!)—from the master's degree up through the doctorate.

- **Japan Internship—(Konnichiha!)** [part of our doctoral program]: We completed an intense educational *and* industrial internship in Japan in 1985. As a result, the reader has an opportunity to participate in this experience and compare two unique cultures—Japan vs. U.S.—and *understand* some of the major cultural differences between our societies, especially in education. Many of these differences remain true today. *Learn* why the Japanese are ahead of us in so many ways, ways that might not always be good for them. We believe the reader will find this information very interesting—a real eye-opener.

- **History of Graphic Communications—How Johan Gutenberg transformed the world, impacting *your* life.** [Sample Comprehensive Exam question—part of Joe's doctoral program.] A focus on technological developments leading up to and beyond Johan Gutenberg's incalculable contribution to society. Gutenberg transformed the world, brought man out of the dark ages, and made literacy available to the human race. A time-line is traced from the beginning of time up to desktop publishing. You, the reader, are the direct beneficiary of his efforts.

- **Doctorate—Is there a doctor in you? What does it take to complete a doctoral program?** We guide you step-by-step through the process used in achieving a doctoral degree. *Discover how we did it.* Learn about the *process* of being accepted into the program and strategies required to navigate and successfully complete such an undertaking, which can take three to four or more years of work beyond the master's degree. Join us on our personal tour as we pursued our D.I.T. degree (The Doctor of Industrial Technology is equivalent in level and content to the Ph.D. degree.) We were required to complete 63 semester credits of intense coursework, write and submitted scholarly articles to refereed journals, complete internships and numerous exams—Candidacy Exam, Comprehensive Exam (covering three to four years of coursework), successfully write and complete a dissertation (i.e., write a book doing original research proving something that has not been proven before—creating new knowledge that others can verify and build upon), and complete the Oral Exam over the defense of the dissertation, all under the supervision of our six doctoral advisors. Learn about this amazing mind-stretching journey, what costs are involved in expenses, time, energy, and emotion, and discover why only 1.2% of adults in America over age 25 hold doctorate degrees. Perhaps you, or someone you know, have been wondering what is involved in pursuing such a degree. Find out now. Maybe there *is* a doctor in you.

- **Rebate Yourself** (FREE): You or someone you know may have money waiting to be claimed from a state government (or Canadian province). Over 38 million Americans have, on average, $418 each waiting for them in state treasuries holding $16 billion in unclaimed property. Imagine you and your family, colleagues and friends are in a very large room together. One out of every eight (that's 1 in 8) of you has money due you. We found over $20,000 *that we know of* for people. No fees are involved; it is legitimate, free, quick, and easy for you to search a public database from the privacy of your home or at the library. (Check with your tax preparer, attorney, police department or librarian, and they will tell you this is legitimate.) *Discover* the possibilities and rewards. We give you advice and tips to successfully navigate this process. Tell your friends to come to our website and download this free information themselves.

- **Other:**
  FREE *America (My Country, 'Tis of Thee)* (suitable for framing)
  FREE *America the Beautiful* (suitable for framing)
  FREE Book Club discussion questions.
  FREE *The Pledge of Allegiance* (suitable for framing)
  FREE Rebate Yourself
  FREE *The Star Spangled Banner* (U.S. National Anthem) (suitable for framing)
  FREE Statue of Liberty Inscription (Emma Lazarus's "The New Colossus") (suitable for framing)
  FREE *Twins Poem* (suitable for framing)
  Other areas of interest may be developed.

Go to our website www.YorkvilleTwinsBook.com and download your FREE monographs *now*. Periodically check this website for newly published monographs.

Do you know others who may also enjoy reading our memoir

(even through a book club or fund-raising organization)? Spread the news about our book to your friends on Facebook, Twitter, LinkedIn, etc. Tell them about *Yorkville Twins* and help them rediscover *their* childhoods.

Thank you,
Joe and John Gindele

P.S. Did you enjoy reading this book? If so, make gift giving easy for yourself. Consider ordering additional copies of *Yorkville Twins* as gifts for family members, friends, teachers, co-workers, and clients/customers. They make great holiday and special occasion gifts. *(Huge quantity discounts available*—see website.) Give them the gift of nostalgia and fond memories that will linger and endure. They will thank you for it. Then watch them smile, chuckle, laugh—and remember.

**"Good memories are a wonderful thing—
like a camera, they capture and record the past,
soothe and delight the soul."**

• BOOKS MAKE PERFECT GIFTS •

To order, see Ordering Information on page 303, or copy, complete, and mail in the *Quick Order Form* on pages 304–305. Get on our mailing list *now*.

About the Authors . . .

Dr. Joseph Gindele
(Yearbook photo)

Dr. John Gindele
(Yearbook photo)

Joe and John Gindele were educated in the New York City public schools. After finishing high school, they moved to Minnesota where they both completed B.S. degrees in industrial arts education, and (Joe) mathematics at St. Cloud State College, St. Cloud, Minnesota. They spent the majority of years teaching in the same Minneapolis suburban school district. John also taught in New York (Long Island), and they both taught at the University of Northern Iowa in Cedar Falls. Their 64 years of combined public school teaching on kindergarten-university levels included industrial education, industrial technology, and mathematics, and they were Work Experience Coordinators (WECEP), audiovisual coordinators, school librarians, and media specialists.

In 1971 they received M.S. degrees in industrial education from the University of Wisconsin-Stout, in Menomonie, and in 1989 their Ed.S. degrees in information media from St. Cloud State University and *simultaneously* their doctorate degrees in industrial technology (D.I.T.) from the University of Northern Iowa. Both completed educational internships in Japan and industrial internships at 3M Company headquarters in St. Paul, Minnesota.

While they taught full time and took graduate courses at night and during the summers, their entrepreneurial spirit helped them found and operate numerous businesses, including Edu-Pac Publishing Company (1971–1994) and Computer Poster Company (1973–1974). With a printing press in their apartment at the foot of one of their twin beds, they authored, printed, and published dozens of educational materials used in secondary schools and colleges in 23 countries. While their printing press hummed in one bedroom, they rented the other bedroom to student teachers. They also had numerous articles published in refereed scholarly journals. The Gindeles' publishing involvement with a curriculum on death education brought a telephone call from Washington, D.C., when a member of the U.S. Congress requested permission to use two chapters on *Teenage Suicide* and *Living Preventively* in Congressional testimony.

The Gindeles won numerous national and international scholarships and awards during their careers. In their spare time, they enjoy doing research, writing, making soup, working together, volunteering on food lines and at church, and traveling.

Decades of globetrotting experiences and meeting people helped them to better understand other cultures, and in return their own. They are grateful to have lived the American dream—living freely in America—truly a land of opportunity.

Except for one year in college, these bachelors have always lived together. Joe and John took early retirement from teaching in 1999 and 2000, respectively. They live in Crystal, a suburb of the Twin Cities of Minneapolis/St. Paul.

Books . . .
The Perfect Gift

Ordering Information

Three easy ways to obtain additional copies of *Yorkville Twins:*

1. Visit your local bookstore.

2. U.S. mail: Send $19.95 (check or money order in U.S. funds, payable to Golden Valley Publishing, LLC) for each book to:

> YorkvilleTwinsBook.com
> 8014 Olson Memorial Highway, #243
> Golden Valley, MN 55427

Minnesota residents add 7.28% ($1.45) sales tax for each book.

Add Shipping/Handling	First Bk	Each add'l*
Media Mail (up to 15 days)	4.00	1.00
Priority Mail (up to 5 days)	6.00	2.00
* Total order mailed to *one* address		

For foreign/special order pricing, contact us at:
info@YorkvilleTwinsBook.com

3. On the Internet, go to:
www.YorkvilleTwinsBook.com

Huge discounts on orders for multiple books.
Ordering is secure and simple.

FREE offers—check our website.

Thank you!

QUICK ORDER FORM

Copy pages 304 and 305 and return. PLEASE PRINT CLEARLY.
Make additional copies for shipping multiple orders to different addresses.

YorkvilleTwinsBook.com is an imprint of **Golden Valley Publishing, LLC.**
Ph: 763-537-0540 • 8014 Olson Memorial Hwy., #243 • Golden Valley, MN 55427
info@YorkvilleTwinsBook.com • *www.YorkvilleTwinsBook.com*

Title		Qty	Total
Yorkville Twins **Book** ($19.95 each)			
Minnesota Residents add 7.28% ($1.45 per book) sales tax:			
Media Mail (up to 15 days): First Bk 4.00 / Each add'l 1.00 Priority Mail (up to 5 days): First Bk 6.00 / Each add'l 2.00	Shipping/ Handling:		
Make check payable in U.S. funds to: **Golden Valley Publishing, LLC**	**TOTAL ENCLOSED**		

Ordered by:

Name

Address

City _____ State _____ Zip _____

Telephone ( ) _____ —

*Email Address

*Join our Email Club for FREE updates without any obligation. We absolutely will not share any of your information.

Items will be shipped to above address unless indicated here. Ship to:

Name

Address

City _____ State _____ Zip _____

Telephone ( ) _____ —

*Email Address _____

Send Book Information to My Friends

Send FREE no-obligation information about your *Yorkville Twins* book to my relatives, friends, and colleagues: (Use additional paper if necessary.) Please PRINT CLEARLY.

(1) Name: _____

Address: _____

City: _____State: _____Zip: _____

Telephone: (_____)_____-_____

Email Address: _____

May we tell them you recommended we send this info? (Check one):
Yes _____ No _____

(2) Name: _____

Address: _____

City: _____State: _____Zip: _____

Telephone: (_____)_____-_____

Email Address: _____

May we tell them you recommended we send this info? (Check one):
Yes _____ No _____

(3) Name: _____

Address: _____

City: _____State: _____Zip: _____

Telephone: (_____)_____-_____

Email Address: _____

May we tell them you recommended we send this info? (Check one):
Yes _____ No _____